Quotations From
Chairman Bill

The Best of Wm. F. Buckley Jr.

Quotations From Chairman Bill

COMPILED BY DAVID FRANKE

ARLINGTON HOUSE   New Rochelle, N.Y.

Compiler's Note

In compiling *Quotations From Chairman Bill,* I had access to the complete works of William F. Buckley Jr.: his books, nearly 15 years of Buckley's *National Review,* his syndicated newspaper column, "On The Right," and his occasional articles, speeches and lectures. My cutoff date for accepting quotations was the end of June, 1969.

Readers will find that some quotations are repeated under several appropriate subject headings. They should bear in mind that the dates given for "On The Right" columns are the dates on which the columns were released to the newspapers; the copy was almost always written three or four days before the newspaper release date, and subscribing newspapers may have printed the column *after* that date too. Also, in the attributions for the quotations, I have used some abbreviations: *NR* for *National Review, NRB* for *National Review Bulletin,* and *Rumbles* for *Rumbles Left and Right.* Finally, many of the *National Review* quotations are from the scores of unsigned editorials never before reprinted, or indeed attributed to Buckley.

Grateful acknowledgment is made to G. P. Putnam's Sons for permission to quote from "On The Right" columns also reprinted in *The Jeweler's Eye,* © 1958, 1962, 1963, 1964, 1965, 1966, 1967, 1968 by William F. Buckley Jr., and for permission to quote from *Rumbles Left and Right,* © 1963 by William F. Buckley Jr.; to The Viking Press for permission to quote from *The Unmaking of a Mayor,* © 1966 by William F. Buckley Jr.; and to Arlington House for permission to quote from *UP from Liberalism,* © 1968, 1959 by William F. Buckley Jr. Most of all, I extend my grateful thanks to Bill Buckley for granting me access to the material used in compiling this volume.

—DAVID FRANKE

Quotations From

Chairman Bill

Academic Cranks

... the academic community has in it the biggest concentration of alarmists, cranks and extremists this side of the giggle house.

—On The Right, Jan. 17, 1967

Academic Freedom

... one learns ever more about the powers of the Educational Establishment, and they are, of course, formidable. The rule of thumb is: Never disagree with the educators, never give them less than everything they want, and never act other than as a postulant at their shrine. It is all neatly put by Professor James Q. Wilson of Harvard University, who wrote recently a "Guide to Reagan Country" for the academically chic *Commentary* Magazine in which he ventured a number of observations not entirely congenial to orthodox anti-Reaganism, and thought to protect himself winsomely by acknowledging: "I do not intend here to write an apology for Reagan; even if I thought like that, which I don't, I would never write it down anywhere my colleagues at Harvard might read it." No indeed: academic freedom is very broadminded, but it stops short of defending the position of Ronald Reagan. Stops short, that is, of defending the indefensible.

—*NR*, Nov. 28, 1967, *p. 1321*

Academic Liberalism

Celso Furtado, minister without portfolio in the deposed government of President Goulart in Brazil, was not unemployed for very long. Moments after being finished as chief economist for the Goulart regime, he received offers to teach at Harvard, Columbia, and Yale. At H., C., and Y., economists have been preaching the necessity for government inflation at annual rates of between 2% and 5%. The professors are enormously impressed, one gathers, by Mr. Furtado's performance as economic czar, wondering no doubt whether it is the wave of the future to do as Senhor Furtado did. Which was to bring on inflation at the rate of about 150 per cent, until he was so rudely interrupted by the people of Brazil, something that is not likely to happen to him at H., C., or Y., whose alumni are far sleepier than the Brazilian peasantry.

—NR, June 16, 1964, *p. 476*

Aeroflot Soviet Airlines

On the advertisement ... it says, under "Aeroflot Soviet Airlines":— "World's Biggest and Busiest Airline. 55–Million Passengers in 1967." I thought maybe I had missed a major development and maybe they are *flying* all their political prisoners to and from Siberia.

—On The Right, July 18, 1968

Africa

We see in the revolt of the masses in Africa the mischief of the white man's abstractions: for the West has, by it's doctrinaire approval of democracy, deprived itself of the moral base from which to talk back to the apologists of rampant nationalism. The obvious answer to a Colonel Mobutu is: Your people, sir, are not ready to rule themselves. Democracy, to be successful, must be practiced by politically mature people among whom there is a consensus on the meaning of life within their society. We resist your efforts not because we wish to freeze your people in their servile condition, but because we deny the right to which you appeal.

—Up from Liberalism, p. 155

Spiro Agnew

Let's face it, Mr. Agnew is the only spontaneous thing in town, and I like that. His instincts are gloriously unprogrammed, and I like that, too. There are those who believe that Mr. Nixon appointed Mr. Agnew as a sort of personal life-insurance. No one, they reason, will pop off President Nixon while Vice-President Agnew is around. There is a view, and I share it, that in Mr. Agnew, Nixon found a high deposit of some of the best American ore lying around: toughness, sincerity, decent-mindedness, decisiveness—much of what, after a fair amount of exposure, went into making Harry Truman a relatively happy national memory.

—On The Right, Oct. 22, 1968

Air Travel

What happened to you today for which there is no rational excuse? And what did you do about it? Have you traveled on airplanes recently? A week ago, half way between New York and Minneapolis on a jet airplane, a couple of the engines acted up. They began firing like an acetylene torch. Then they would lurch drunkenly towards a complete stall, then ZOOM, they would fire again, at what felt like 10,000 RPM. Not a word of explanation from the captain or co-pilot. After twenty minutes or so, during which the apocalyptic cycle was repeated at least five times, I finally summoned first my courage, then the stewardess, and asked: "Would you mind telling me what is the probable cause of my imminent death?" She replied airily that there was apparently something wrong with the engines, nothing serious. I asked her whether or not the passengers might express their preferences on whether to crash in Ohio or in Illinois, preferring the former as I had just finished reading an article comparing the death taxes in the two states. She smiled prettily and beamed off—not, I suspect, to relay my Last Choice to the captain.

—*NR*, Feb 12, 1963, *p. 103*

Algeria

One would certainly not want to found a church on Algerian justice.

—*NR*, Aug. 8, 1967, *p. 840*

Saul Alinsky

It is sometimes difficult to understand why Mr. Alinsky fights to remove human beings from slums, since it is so very clear that his hatred for the slums is exceeded only by his hatred for those who have moved out of them.

—*NR*, Nov. 1, 1966, *p. 1104*

Steve Allen

I put to Mr. Allen a week ago a concrete proposal, and was gratified to have an answer which he gave me permission to publish. Namely, that he would join me in approving a nuclear strike by our Strategic Air Command against the nuclear installations in Red China which have recently ground out an atomic bomb. . . . History aches for such an act of greatness.

—*NR*, Dec. 29, 1964, *p. 1143*

The Polaris nuclear submarine dispatched for duty off the China coast is rumored to be the *USS Steve Allen.*

—*NR*, Jan. 12, 1965, *p. 7*

Joseph Alsop

Mr. Alsop simply cannot forgive the rebirth of conservatism in America, having himself taken the pains on more than one occasion to pronounce it quite dead.

—*NR*, July 16, 1963, *p. 13*

Now it is important to understand about Mr. Alsop that he has been a doomsayer all his public life. Indeed he can only be compared to Robert Welch for seeing the end waiting for us just around the corner of history.

—On The Right, Jan. 27, 1968

Alumni

It is a fact that alumni are held in great disesteem by students, which is strange indeed considering that only flunking out, taking the academic veil, or dying, will rescue them from the inevitable fate of alumnihood. That contempt, of course, is shared by—indeed it originates with—the faculty and administration. ... Herman Hickman used to say, when he coached football at Yale, "I believe in keeping the alumni sullen, but not mutinous." The colleges have gone way beyond that. Alumni bodies get pushed around far more than Herman Hickman's unsuccessful team ever did, only they never fight back any more. They are rapidly earning the contempt the students hold for them.

—NR, June 6, 1956, *p. 17*

America Magazine

... the editors of *America* are increasingly taking a Welch-like position towards people who disagree with them: Anyone who disagrees is not really a good Catholic; at best, he is a heathen-symp.

—NR, March 27, 1962, *p. 192*

American Civil Liberties Union

Those who cannot distinguish between a) opposing our action in Vietnam by word, which right is protected under the First Amendment to the Constitution at least for so long as our war in Vietnam is not officially declared to be that by the Congress, and b) attempting physically to obstruct the prosecution of that action by lying down in front of railroad trains carrying troops and ammunition to the front, or by collecting money to send to the Vietcong, are eligible for high office in the New York Civil Liberties Union ...

—NR, Sept. 6, 1966, *p. 875*

American Government

Our system of government is one in which procedure is greatly important: because procedure takes into account the ways of a people, their
customs, their tradition, their way of looking at things—their way of life.
The argument . . . is not whether it is "right" or "wrong" under the aspect
of the heavens that the Regents of New York State should have prescribed a prayer for those who wished to utter it at the beginning of
classes, or whether the state of Tennessee gives adequate privileges to
urban voters: but rather, what are the *means* set down by the Constitution
for correcting these measures, if indeed they are to be corrected. The
means set down are primarily legislative, not judicial: and it is a friend
of the Constitution, and a mature student of a viable political freedom,
who has the courage to remark the growth of judicial tyranny.

—ON THE RIGHT, Sept. 17, 1964

American Politics

. . . it is always useful, when doing what one wants to do, to discover a
Constitutional imperative.

—ON THE RIGHT, Sept. 20, 1966

. . . issues aren't very often settled in America on theoretical grounds,
except now and then when the nine old men go off into trances about the
meaning of the First Amendment (Thou Shalt Not Pray in the Public
Schools). They are settled mostly by sociological and practical considerations.

—ON THE RIGHT, Feb. 13, 1969

The Reagan strategists have reasoned over a long period that Mr. Reagan
is a candidate in the nature of things—as distinguished from a self-made
candidate, so to speak. Granted it is possible to defy the nature of things

by, let us say, packing one's suitcases and going off to a monastery. But very little short of that will do. Nelson Rockefeller, during the past year or so, said publicly oh maybe eighteen hundred times that he would not run for the presidency. It is even possible that he meant what he said. But what the political scientists refer to as the relationship of forces, dominates the situation. If someone is a) the governor of New York or the governor of California, and if b) he has a national following, and if c) he is identified as the leader of an important part of the spectrum— then he is available to his party for the presidential nomination. It is one of those ineluctable things in life, and the public acceptance of it is evident in the disposition to put up with the ritual hypocrisies. Nobody makes a serious effort to criticize Rockefeller for saying he wasn't going to run, any more than they criticized Adlai Stevenson, the original ambi-guist.

—On The Right. May 25, 1968

The squares who pause to wonder why it is generally said with relish that someone is a "Lindsay Republican" and with disrelish that someone is a "Byrd Democrat" are gloriously unaware of the implications of the *Zeitgeist.*

—*The Unmaking of a Mayor*, pp. 66–67

Americans

Consider the generosity—if it is as simple as that—of the typical American. The springs of hatred are simply not deep. Richard Nixon was wrong when he told Whittaker Chambers that if the American people had known what exactly Alger Hiss had done, they'd have boiled him in oil. We *do* know what Hiss did, but we harbor no such impulse toward him. I move in the most hardheaded anti-Communist circles in America, and I have yet to hear a word of hatred directed at Julius or Ethel Rosenberg; and if they had not been electrocuted, if the public had been denied that definitive expiation, still I doubt that hatred would have materialized, any more for the Rosenbergs than for Klaus Fuchs, who roams free in England.

—*NR*, Oct. 11, 1958, *p. 245*

Anti-American Demonstrations

But demonstrations against Red China? North Vietnam? The Soviet Union? The typical European would as soon demonstrate against Caroline Kennedy.

—ON THE RIGHT, March 12, 1968

Anti-Intellectualism

There is nothing so ironic as the nihilist or relativist (or the believer in the kind of academic freedom that postulates the equality of ideas) who complains of the anti-intellectualism of American conservatives. Such is *our* respect for the human mind that we pay it the supreme honor: we credit it with having arrived at certain great conclusions. We believe that millenniums of intellection have served an objective purpose. Certain problems have been disposed of. Certain questions are closed: and with reference to that fact the conservative orders his life and, to the extent he is called upon by circumstances to do so, the life of the community.

—*Up from Liberalism*, pp. 182–183

Apollo 8

CAPE KENNEDY. I write on the assumption that Apollo 8 will complete its mission, though my spirit is dogged by the direful premonition of a poet who, moments before the lift-off, confessed to me that something would go wrong. . . . All of this is science? Don't believe it. We have reached into God's territory and if it were written that there would be no trespassing, then the poet's premonition would have been correct.

—ON THE RIGHT, Dec. 28, 1968

Art and Government

Why does the government, at the peak of American affluence, need to take on the overhead of the arts? Sixty-three million dollars is a trifling sum of money, considering what is available to our great foundations, some of which have been supporting, and will continue to support, the music, dance, and art of the nation. The enormous, invaluable art museums in New York and Boston, Cleveland and San Francisco, Washington and Dallas, were every one of them provided by private philanthropy. And America is growing richer, not poorer. Why socialize the production of art?

—ON THE RIGHT, Oct. 12, 1965

Asian Defense

The moment is at hand, and perhaps for the last time, when we can view the problem as a regional one involving the future of what is left of free Asia. The time has come to summon our allies or potential allies, notably Japan, the Philippines, Malaysia, Formosa, Thailand and Australia—and tell them exactly how far the United States is prepared to go in helping them to safeguard Asian freedom, and on what terms. We should be prepared to go very far indeed. Certainly we should be prepared to use our technical resources to effect defoliation sufficient to expose the main supply routes to the Vietcong. But in return we should insist that the nations of Asia accept their responsibilities: and take the initiative in creating and maintaining an anti-Communist Asian policy. This would mean sending Asian soldiers to fight in South Vietnam if necessary, and anywhere else where the enemy threatens to erupt; facing down leftist-neutralist opposition at home, hewing clearly to an anti-Communist line; backing the United States in the United Nations and before all the councils of the world—in effect, taking over, and fighting and directing their own fight, with the aid of our tools.

—ON THE RIGHT, Feb. 20, 1965

However important our current activities in South Vietnam, they cannot serve as a substitute for Asian activity in behalf of itself. The maintenance of freedom and order in the region is primarily an Asian not a Western enterprise, and the United States Marines must not be confused as a roving world police force, at the disposal of anyone who blows a whistle, rather than bother himself to raise his own constabulary.

—ON THE RIGHT, Jan. 1, 1966

The Assassinations

The opinion-makers have been as reluctant to draw conclusions based on Sirhan's ideological inclinations as they would have been anxious to draw such conclusions if it had proved that Sirhan was, say, a member of the John Birch Society. Thus also it was with Oswald, whose objection to President Kennedy had no ideological foundation whatever except for the obvious one, namely that Oswald was a Communist, and President Kennedy was the leader of the great anti-Communist world power. But for every line reflecting on the possible nexus between Oswald's pro-Communism and Oswald's deed, 20 have been written probing illusory by-ways leading to the CIA, or the oil interests, or the fascist subculture of Dallas, or just about anything at all, rather than the reality: an amply documented history of relentless pro-Sovietism.

—On The Right, May 24, 1969

Athletes in Politics

The affluent society tends to pay more attention to what is visually pleasing, whence the emphasis nowadays on Style. It is more fun to elect popular heroes than to make heroes out of businessmen and lawyers. And besides, trained athletes are cool under stress, and know how to drive down the middle of the road, and avoid falling off bridges.

—*Jock*, Oct., 1969

Atomic Weapons

... we view our atomic arsenal as proudly and as devotedly as any pioneer ever viewed his flintlock hanging over the mantel as his children slept, and dreamed.

—*NRB*, July 24, 1962, *p. 1*

B

Johann Sebastian Bach

I thought I had seen everything—I hoped I had—in the student world of unreason. But the all-time champion effrontery was as yet uncommitted. It was left to a 17-year-old Negro boy called Rickey Ivie whose Black Student Union has touched off disorders in a Los Angeles high school in a demonstration against "racist training." An example of that training is the inclusion in the curriculum of the music of Johann Sebastian Bach. He is described by Master Ivie as "that old, dead punk." "In the world of music," he explains, "the schools keep imposing middle class values in teaching us about Bach." ... To call the greatest genius who ever lived an "old, dead punk," the least of whose cantatas will do more to elevate the human spirit than all the black student unions born and unborn, is not so much contemptible as pitiable: conducive of that kind of separation one feels from animals, rather than from other human beings.

—On The Right, March 27, 1969

Balance of Payments

[From Chairman Bill's advice to the platform committees of the 1968 Republican and Democratic conventions:] The evidence grows that fixed exchange rates are an anachronism. It is a matter of coincidence when a nation finishes a year having exported goods exactly equal to the value of goods imported and dollars spent abroad. The existing system is ultimately based not only on our maintaining such a coincidence over a period of years, but on an unending series of such coincidences, a failure in which gives rise to a strain on our economic credibility. The answer

11

(to which, according to Professor Paul Samuelson, the majority of U.S. economists now subscribe): flexible exchange rates. The advantages are manifest: the dollar is worth whatever buyers are willing to pay for it. If the dollar diminishes in value, that exactly indicates the settled estimate of its worth. It is the means by which automatic disciplinary pressures are brought to bear on 1) internal inflation, 2) increases in the cost of production, 3) inefficiency. If flexible exchange rates are adopted, and the U.S. discontinues its purchase of gold, then profligate spending abroad breeds its own *pro tanto* punishment.

—ON THE RIGHT, May 18, 1968

James Baldwin

How long, one wonders, before the Baldwins will be ghettoized in the corners of fanaticism where they belong? The moment is overdue for someone who speaks authentically for the Negroes to tell Mr. Baldwin that his morose nihilism is a greater threat by far to prospects for the Negroes in America than anything that George Wallace ever said or did.

—ON THE RIGHT, June 17, 1965

Bay of Pigs

President Kennedy, who is a proud man and a very intelligent man, realized after 72 hours, on Thursday, that we were sinking fast, and grasped, as is so human, for a rhetorical counterweight. His doughty words about the character of the Communists having been forever stamped upon the streets of Budapest, were an orotund version of the little boy's taunts hurled at the bully but only after reaching the cover of his own back yard. The words made Kennedy feel better, indeed all of us feel better: but only for so long as we were able to detach them from the context of our wretched, miserable performance on Playa de los Cochinos, where we left, rather than offend World Opinion, seven hundred brave Cubans to die, and six million others to live in slavery. If the people of the world look upon us with contempt, it is because we have been contemptible.

—*NR*, May 6, 1961, *p. 269*

The Beatles

... I am drawn to the conclusion that a devotion to the Beatles is not psychosomatic but in some way organic, and I worry all the more. ... The Beatles are not merely awful, I would consider it sacrilegious to say anything less than that they are godawful. They are so unbelievably horrible, so appallingly unmusical, so dogmatically insensitive to the magic of the art, that they qualify as crowned heads of anti-music, even as the imposter popes went down in history as "anti-popes."*

—ON THE RIGHT, Sept. 8, 1964

The Beatles know more about carburetors than they know about Christianity, which is why they, like so many others, make such asses of themselves in pursuit of Mr. Gaga Yogi.

—ON THE RIGHT, Feb. 29, 1968

Berkeley Riots

The gentlemen taxpayers of California, who have made available splendid facilities and a faculty well qualified at least intellectually for the benefit of California's students, are entitled to be firm, speaking through their Governor, in their decision to maintain in the hands of older people the responsibility to decide such questions as the reasonable limits of political activity on campus. This time I am for City Hall.

—ON THE RIGHT, Dec. 10, 1964

Better Dead Than Red

Better Dead than Red is an inaccurate statement of the American position, listing, as it does, non-exclusive alternatives. Properly stated it is: Better to face the *chance* of being dead, than the certainty of being Red.

—*NR*, Dec. 4, 1962, *p. 424*

---

*Chairman Bill subsequently reversed himself. See "How I Came to Rock," *Saturday Evening Post*, Aug. 24, 1968.

Bible

One (1) priest, joined by one (1) nun, and one (1) rabbi, propose to rename the Old Testament, on the grounds that to propose that that which governs the Jew is "old" whereas that which governs Christians is "new" is downright invidious: thus fulfilling the words of the Lord (Rev. 21:5—New Testament, Part II): "Behold, I make all things new."

—NR, June 14, 1966, *p. 562*

John Birch Society

One continues to wonder how it is that the membership of the John Birch Society tolerates such paranoid and unpatriotic drivel. Until the members rise up and demand a leadership whose programs and analyses are based other than on the premise that practically every liberal politician, every confused professor, every civil rights demonstrator, every ideologized judge, every bungling diplomat, every avid prosecutor, everyone who wants free medicine, and civil rights legislation, and government control of the economy, is an agent of the Communist conspiracy—until then, at least, they oughtn't to go about the country complaining that the Society is consistently misrepresented. Their own views are undoubtedly misrepresented. But their views aren't the Voice of the John Birch Society.

—NR, Oct. 19, 1965, *p. 917*

Black Power

The dawning consciousness of the political way up the ladder is racing through the ghettos. Strategically it may be dangerous, since the temptation is universal to substitute political for economic means of self-aggrandizement; but tactical rewards in human pride and faith in the political system are considerable.

—On The Right, May 31, 1969

Also in Los Angeles there is Ron Karenga, the head of an organization called US . . . Mr. Karenga intersperses his socio-political badinage with here and there a Swahili word, even as the greetings are in Swahili. There was one lexicographical revelation of extraordinary interest. Mr. Karenga referred to one of his concepts as "kawaida." "That," he explained matter-of-factly, "is Swahili for 'neo-traditionalism'." Catch those Swahili reactionaries!

—On The Right, May 31, 1969

Leaders of the Negro community must learn to say No to their own. Not a single black organization disavowed the strike or the tactics of the Black Students Union of San Francisco State. Roy Wilkins and Bayard Rustin have shown a monumental courage by denouncing the firebrands —they must be encouraged in their temperance. Too many black leaders now feel towards any other black leader the way the Communists felt towards Stalin: his will was theirs. White "understanding" of this phenomenon is a form of condescension: it might even be called racist.

—On The Right, June 3, 1969

Jimmy Breslin

What I said, commenting on that morning's column by Mr. Breslin reporting that John Wayne had traveled directly from the podium of the Republican Convention to the bar at the nearest hotel, was that so would I have done if I had had Mr. Breslin following me. I thought this, at the time, to be an exercise in rhetorical moderation, inasmuch as, when looking for a bar and in the company of Mr. Breslin, one hardly needs to search out an adjacent hotel.

—On The Right, Feb. 1, 1969

William F. Buckley Jr.

My hauteur may be an overreaction. My generation grew up in an atmosphere which considered conservatism benighted, so those of us who championed conservatism naturally insisted on the ultimate sophistication of our position.

—*New York Sunday News*, Aug. 1, 1965, *p. 75*

Prudence is, as the catechism teaches, a virtue. It doesn't happen to be the virtue I am myself best at.

—*NR*, Nov. 2, 1965, *p. 978*

I feel I qualify spiritually and philosophically as a conservative, but temperamentally I am not of the breed.

—Quoted in *Time*, Nov. 3, 1967, *p. 70*

I am a Russian agent. My real name is Buhkliski, and during the months of July and August 1946—nobody has ever asked me where I was during July and August 1946, which shows what is happening to our internal security—the real William Buckley Jr., touring in Europe, was abducted; and I, who had been training at an espionage center in a Moscow suburb, began my long impersonation. My paymaster at Yale University was the Catholic chaplain. What happened to the real Buckley—he was an awfully nice fellow—I don't know, though the rumor in the Party is that he is back in the States, using the pseudonym David Frye. My orders were to penetrate the right wing and immobilize and otherwise cause damage. My successes have been extraordinary, and indeed sewn into the back of my lapel, in invisible thread, is the Order of Lenin. I singlehandedly contrived the Johnstown flood, Hurricane Esther, the Vietnam War, and the election of John Lindsay. Now I have been caught. But if I had to do it all over again, I'd do the same thing for the glory of the revolution. As Stalin used to say, to me—what a wise old one he proved to be— "you're doing fine. Only watch out for H. L. Hunt and Robert Welchky. They're the only ones we haven't been able to foolsky." How right he was.

—On The Right, Jan. 16, 1968

McGeorge Bundy

... McGeorge Bundy, head of the Ford Foundation, who quit Johnson because he was too—Nixonish (he would put it differently, but not so well).

—On The Right, Dec. 5, 1968

Bureaucracy

One must bear in mind that the expansion of federal activity is a form of eating for politicians.

—*NR*, Sept. 8, 1964, *p. 763*

James Burnham

... my First Law, here it is: that no conservative movement in this country which is intelligent and serious will proceed without the counsel of James Burnham. My Law admits of no exceptions....

—*NR*, April 9, 1960, *p. 238*

C

Caesarism

... there is abroad in the land a spirit of blind submission whose political expression is the attempt to Caesarize Dwight Eisenhower, with or without his cooperation. There seems to be a deep yearning in some quarters of America for a benevolent monarch or, *mutatis mutandis*, a reigning chairman-of-the-board. The flag and Constitution have served through the years as non-controversial standards to which Americans of all political persuasions could repair. But it seems we want a symbol with flesh and blood on it.

So be it. If that is really what the country wants, let us create such an office. But only after stripping it of political power, leaving to it an exclusively ceremonial function. It's too late in the game to start back and have to live through Magna Cartas, revolutions bloody and Bloodless, and a dozen reform acts.

Or else kill off the sentiment. General Eisenhower is the only man who can do that. And he could do it with a scratch pad and a fountain pen, in five minutes—which is as long as it took George Washington to kill off, decisively and brusquely, the movement to proclaim him king in 1779.

—NR, Nov. 26, 1955, *p. 5*

Capital Punishment

The question of capital punishment is not one on which I have myself taken a position in which I feel secure. But I do believe that the argument against capital punishment tends to be animated by the same spirit that

18

has roots in the general permissiveness of an age dominated by the determinists. They are men who end up reasoning—if that is the word for it—that any act you or I do which is wrong is an act which we do as the result of a conjunction of pressures upon us which has nothing to do with the operation of our own free will. Thus no murder is an act of wickedness: it is merely a perfectly natural response, one which any sophisticated sociologist will program for you, to a group of stimuli which propelled you, ineluctably, in this unfortunate direction.

—On The Right, Jan. 19, 1965

Capitalism

"The trouble with socialism," a European observer once remarked, "is socialism. The trouble with capitalism is capitalists."

—*NR*, July 26, 1966, *p. 719*

Pablo Casals

The great Pablo Casals came to New York last week, bent over his cello, and enthralled his audience at the United Nations Building, as he had the reporters at a press conference. It is a very sad thing to have to say, but if Señor Casals had played the cello as Jack Benny plays the violin, his audience would have been just as enthralled: because to that political lot Casals is primarily a political hero (his heroism consists in stubbornly misunderstanding the nature of the Spanish Civil War, and boycotting Franco Spain), and everyone knows that political heroes are, *ex officio*, great at whatever they do. . . . We feel about Señor Casals somewhat the way Toscanini felt about Richard Strauss: "As an artist," Toscanini told Strauss heatedly, "I take my hat off to you. As a man I put on my hat ten times!"

—*NR*, Nov. 8, 1958, *p. 299*

Senator Francis Case

Senator Francis Case of South Dakota has worked very hard at making a fool of himself and, clearly possessing the raw material, has done a good job of it. An attempt was made, he broods, to bribe him to favor the Fulbright Bill which restores to the market place the function of regulating the price of natural gas; and that attempt prompted him to vote *against* the bill rather than for it, as he had intended to vote.

... Senator Case's reaction is childish. If he reasoned correctly in deciding to vote *against* his convictions as a gesture of protest against an attempted bribe, he has pointed the way to a most effective means of influencing legislation: One simply rewards legislators who are on record as opposing legislation one desires, thus causing them to change their minds. Senator Case has not grasped the meaning of the ethical stricture against succumbing to bribery. The point is that a bribe should not affect a vote in *any* way. The alleged attempt to bribe Senator Case clearly did affect, according to his own admission, his vote.

—NR, Feb. 29, 1956, *pp. 4–5*

Castro Cuba

Cuba is a symbol of American Liberalism's failure to meet the challenges of the modern world. If such a thing as Castro Cuba were not possible, such a thing as the American right wing, as it exists today, would not be possible; as things are, the American right wing is necessary, and providential. ... The point is that no one in power seems to know exactly how to deal with Castro. No one even knows how this country is to deal, not with Castro—he is merely a particularization of the trouble—but with a much larger question. We don't know how to deal with Harvard University. If Harvard wasn't able to spot Castro for what he is earlier than it did, and show us how to cope with him, who can? And yet Harvard, so dulled are its moral and intellectual reflexes, cheered, while Castro was accumulating the power to engross the full, if futile attention of President John F. Kennedy, B.S. Harvard 1940, LL. D. 1956, even while another of her illustrious sons, Norman Mailer, B.A. 1943, was propagandizing for a Committee to Hasten the Unmolested Communization of Cuba.

—Rumbles, pp. 75–76

Fidel Castro

It is, I think, generally conceded at this point that Fidel Castro is not very bright, as so often is the case with fanatics. Most recently, he moved to perfect the Cuban Revolution by putting an end to local ownership of hotdog stands, as defiant of true socialism.

—ON THE RIGHT, Oct. 17, 1968

Catholic Church

The question has frequently been raised, What, in the name of God, is going on in the Catholic Church? It is going to take a major, first-class, divine revelation to answer that question, as fresh evidence accumulates of a quite inscrutable confusion within the Vatican, the most recent evidence of which was the appeal by the Pope, presumably written for him by an assistant demagogue, for commuting the sentences of the two gentlemen who were hanged ten days ago in Rhodesia.

—ON THE RIGHT, March 23, 1968

Presumably the Pope is alarmed at some of the results of modernization. There are many examples, some of them reaching right into the tabernacle of Catholic Christianity to mess around with what they used to call the *depositum fidei* before Latin was abolished as anti-social, or whatever.

—ON THE RIGHT, July 13, 1968

Recently I was visited by a faculty member and a dozen seniors from a Catholic high school, St. Mary's in Mount Clemens, Michigan. I found them all charming, poised, and intelligent, but a little bit out-of-breath, as though they had just finished scaling a very high mountain; and indeed I learned that the Reverend Sister, the superintendent of their school, had decreed that if they consummated their plan to visit with me, they would be deprived of their right to participate in their forthcoming commencement exercises, and stripped of their academic honors. Now the Church quite rightly cautions its sheep to avoid occasions of sin, but it

is going to take me a while to get used to the notion, post–Vatican II, that I am, by the modernists, to be treated like a brothel.

—On The Right, July 13, 1968

The crisis of the Catholic Church is much written about. *Look* Magazine celebrates it every couple of issues, and its editors have even volunteered to rewrite the Apostles' Creed, reaching a new high in reader service.

—On The Right, April 8, 1969

Catholicism and Politics

Liberals are continually denouncing their conservative brethren as defiant of Catholic social doctrine and therefore, inferentially, as Bad Catholics. The other side occasionally does the very same thing—and *National Review* was itself once guilty of it by running an article called "Can a Liberal be a Catholic?" The article itself was splendid, and the author had not given it that title: it was supplied in the shop, in a routine and imprudent effort to sensationalize. (What we should have called it is: "Can a Liberal go to Heaven?")

—*NR*, Sept. 11, 1962, *p. 173*

The rummaging of the papal documents—or, for that matter, Bible-picking—for partisan tags is undignified, divisive, and unjust, whether engaged in by the Left or the Right. The encyclical literature establishes a meaningful context for political discussion, but not if parts of that literature are torn from the whole and used talismanically to hex one's foes.

—*NR*, Sept. 11, 1962, *p. 175*

Censorship

I once encountered a very angry lady in Dallas, Texas, who announced herself as head of a vigilance committee to keep dirty books out of the local libraries, and we talked a bit. I forget just how the conversation moved, but at one point I said that to pull out all the salacious passages from modern literature would require the end of individual reading. All of us would have to have private readers, like the old eccentric who forced his prisoner to read to him the works of Charles Dickens in the novel by Evelyn Waugh. Who, asked the lady book-critic, is Evelyn Waugh? The greatest English novelist of this century, I ventured; but on ascertaining that he was not a dirty writer, she lost all interest, and went off to look for more dirty books to rail against.

—*NR*, May 3, 1966, *p. 400*

Center for the Study of Democratic Institutions

... Mr. W. H. "Ping" Ferry is the assistant keeper of the zoo presided over by Mr. Robert Hutchins at Santa Barbara, California, where gentlemen scholars gather to discuss how to encourage the hatred of American institutions.

—ON THE RIGHT, Oct. 16, 1965

Remember the Episcopal Bishop of Washington who a month ago turned over a church for Rap Brown to teach hate in? Here is a parallel. Doc Hutchins, head of the Center for the Study of Democratic Institutions, and Keeper of the Dialogue, hosted a three-day meeting of students at which among other things it was proposed a) that "the institutions of this country must be destroyed"; and b) that "the dialogue wastes a lot of

time. . . . Disruption [is] more advantageous." The latest visitors to Mr. Hutchins' tax-exempt zoo were nineteen charmers. . . . What is frightening is that a center staffed by apparently civilized people should sponsor three days of such types. As for the children, we think of Mr. Russell Kirk's suggestion that increasingly he is tempted to found a Birch John Society.

—*NRB*, Sept. 12, 1967, *p. 1*

Central Intelligence Agency

WHO ELSE? DEPARTMENT. We received the other day a letter requesting a couple of copies of the December 12 *National Review Bulletin.* The request was delayed in reaching us because it had been sent to a building *National Review* left fourteen months ago. Who sent the letter? Why, the Central Intelligence Agency, of course!

—*NRB*, Jan. 9, 1960, *p. 2*

General C. P. Cabell is the deputy director of the Central Intelligence Agency, but it must not be automatically assumed that he is unqualified to say anything interesting or relevant about world Communism.

—*NR*, Feb. 13, 1960, *p. 95*

Whittaker Chambers

And Chambers was above all a poet, with a poet's understanding of political affairs—which is both good and bad, good if you know and like and learn from the poet's vision, disastrous if you read a poet the way you would read the Kinsey Report; with a dramatist's understanding of political affairs—which is, again, both good and bad. No one could with any success extract a *Weltanschauung* from Chambers' writings, com-

plete with neat and elegant trim. No more than from Bertold Brecht, or Alexander Pope, both politically minded men of letters.

—NR, Dec. 15, 1964, *p. 1102*

Caryl Chessman

The question arises whether we'd have been better off letting Caryl Chessman kidnap and rape someone two or three times a year than we now are, having allowed him to call into question the structure of our judicial system. . . . One cannot blame a man for fighting for his life with all the weapons at his disposal; but there is no reason to cooperate with him in his effort to discredit the laws we have painstakingly contrived to protect the community. . . . One wonders, finally, whether sifting through the Chessman case are the crystals of the new spirit of our time: the notion that nothing is worth dying for, hence that nothing is worth killing for. What matters is not what Chessman did, but what we may not do to him; what matters is not what we have to defend, but that in defending it we must not die or kill; what matters is not how great are the causes of freedom and justice, but that they are not great enough to warrant the supreme sacrifice.

—NRB, March 5, 1960, *p. 1*

Church and State

We doubt very much if the average Catholic politician is as slavish a follower of *Osservatore Romano* as the average Protestant—or for that matter Catholic—politician is of the *New York Times*. Catholics are totally free to reject political asides that issue from Vatican spokesmen; and they exercise that freedom far more often than, say, Adlai Stevenson exercises *his* freedom to disagree with Walter Lippmann. Catholic journals from coast to coast in America disagree vigorously and even acidly with one another on more points of practical political consequence than divide the average caucus of the Democratic Party.

—NR, Sept. 24, 1960, *pp. 169–170*

Winston Churchill

He turned over the leadership of the world to the faltering hands of Americans who were manifestly his inferiors in the understanding of history and the management of human affairs, and contented himself to write dramatically about decisive battles won for freedom on the soil of England centuries ago, battles whose victory he celebrated vicariously, having no appetite left to fight real enemies, enemies whose health he had, God save him, nourished by that fateful shortage of vision that, in the end, left him, and the world, incapable of seeing that everything he had said and fought for applied alike to the Russian, as well as the German, virus. May he sleep more peacefully than some of those who depended on him.

—*NR*, Feb. 23, 1965, *p. 147*

Civil Disobedience

That which is anarchic within me (which is very strong) tunes in strongly on the idea of a society in which people decide for themselves what taxes to pay, what rules to obey, when to cooperate and when not to with the civil authorities. But that which is reasonable within me, which I am glad to say most often prevails, recognizes that societies so structured do not exist, and cannot exist: an insight as ancient as Socrates's, so patiently explained to Crito. The indicated consequence for studied and aggravated civil disobedience seems to me to be obvious: deportation. Ideally, of course, a citizen whose disagreements with his country are organic and apparently unreconcilable should take the initiative and seek out more compatible countries.

—*New York Times Magazine*, Nov. 26, 1967, *p. 27*

Civil Liberties and General Walker

General Walker has been released . . . Either Walker is, in the legal sense, crazy, or he is not. If he is, it is up to his attorneys to so plead. If he is not, he is nevertheless branded in the public eye as putatively crazy, thanks to the effrontery of a government psychiatrist who, without even setting eyes on the General, persuaded a judge to detain him in psychiatric custody. . . . That is a pretty dangerous weapon the government is playing with. Tomorrow it could be thee, or me (Who, ME??? Yes you, bud, now come along, and don't give us any trouble . . .). One needs to bear in mind, during the next few weeks, that it matters not at all so far as civil liberties are concerned whether General Walker is found to be crazy by the psychiatrists who are now examining him. The point is that habeas corpus must not be waived at the initiative of the government, unless there is a plausible case that the defendant is homicidally bent, and such a thing was never suggested about General Walker. It may be freely conceded that the General was making, during the days before his arrest, a series of utterly incoherent statements, but if that is a sign of putative madness, then someone should put iron bars around the UN. Just as a starter.

—*NR*, Oct. 23, 1962, *p. 302*

Civil Rights

The Nazis in occupied France had all the laws and all the machine guns on their side, and still they couldn't get the French to treat them like human beings. If there is a key to the problem of racial and tribal tensions, and [James] Baldwin has it, certainly we should make it a part of our foreign aid program for export abroad. To teach Nehru how to bring freedom to the Untouchables, to teach the Kikuyu in Kenya respect for the Zulu, and the Xhosa of South Africa respect for the Panda, and the Asiatics throughout Africa understanding of the Bantu and vice versa. . . . Is it true there is no color line in Brazil, where the races have mixed for a hundred years? Tell it to the truly black Brazilian. . . .

—*NR*, June 18, 1963, *p. 488*

All right, granted: there is no land of liberty, anywhere, and never will be, anywhere, if by liberty is understood true liberty for everyone under every circumstance. But [we] live in a land where the federal judiciary spends a large proportion of its time hearing the complaints of Negroes and trying to act on them; where the white oppressors spend hundreds of millions of dollars agitating for improvements in Negro conditions and contributing to those improvements; where both major political parties exhort the public to acts of racial harmony and generosity; where the churches are increasingly urgent in their moral strictures for racial reconciliation; where the average member of the lower class of Negroes enjoys a standard of living higher than that of the average member of the upper class of Negroes in the typical African state; where the average Negro wields more political influence, locally and nationally, than the average Negro does in any state run by Negroes; and where the average Negro enjoys more rights as a minority than any white man enjoys as a minority in most of the African states run by Negroes.

—ON THE RIGHT, May 12, 1964

It is only important for Americans to pursue the demands of their own conscience, and smile courteously, if a little absent-mindedly, at the inflamed interventions of our cousins who chatter their preoccupations over our moral deficiencies while returning vast areas of the world to the conditions from which American Negroes were rescued years ago, at the very beginning of their American ordeal.

—NR, April 6, 1965, p. 273

Civil Rights and Lyndon Johnson

Lyndon Johnson is the product of generations of people who have wrestled for the advancement of freedom. And he voted fourteen times against civil rights bills designed to end white domination in the South. Why should he expect that a vision which he discovered only four or five years ago about the proper treatment of American Negroes who are literate, who have grown up in a country devoted, in its better moments, to the ideal of a free society, should guide, beginning tomorrow, the governors of Mozambique and Angola, Rhodesia and South Africa?

—ON THE RIGHT, May 31, 1966

Cassius Clay

He became a Black Muslim, which is a pseudo-religion for unbright neurotics who feel the need to hate all white people. . . .

—ON THE RIGHT, Nov. 30, 1965

Eldridge Cleaver

Had enough? Ah, but your stomachs are not as strong as those of the more educated members of the community, like the faculty members of the University of California who have invited Mr. Cleaver to give a course for credit at the Berkeley campus. Actually they really wouldn't want him for President, they are just getting their kicks without confronting the consequences: a venture in ideological onanism. I told Mr. Cleaver that the supreme irony of it all is that such support as he has is mostly from the white folks. The blacks are too dignified, too honest, too gentle. It takes middle class educated white folks to say "Cleaver for President," even as, in 18th Century France, it was the sports in the upper class who lionized de Sade. Cleaver is half right to feel such contempt as he feels for those of us who tolerate him and his disciples.

—ON THE RIGHT, Nov. 19, 1968

Cleveland

The *New York Times Sunday Magazine*, commenting on the disappointing record of Mayor Stokes after 100 days of rule, observed last spring that Cleveland will not forever survive on the basis of the reputation of its incomparable symphony orchestra. The question is in a sense spiritual: has Cleveland given up? A guest at the Sheraton-Cleveland Hotel is bound to conclude that that is the case. We read that a projected urban renewal program contemplates the construction of a new luxury hotel in Cleveland. At the Sheraton one is bound to wonder excitedly whether it will actually have waiters in it. ... I note across from my typewriter a framed tribute to New Jersey, remarking that "Governor Richard C. Hughes was a guest in this suite June 6 to 10, 1964." If the Governor actually survived four days in this hotel, he certainly deserves the tribute. Though who knows, perhaps visiting governors carry thermos bottles with hot soup.

—On The Right, May 28, 1968

Coexistence

Mr. Eisenhower, symbol of the West, is a Christian. The idolater, Khrushchev, is the revolution's spokesman. They speak of coming to terms. Neither suggests that those terms will hold out any relief for the writhing multitude who live under Communism. The light of Bethlehem is not reflected through the West to the dark places of the world: the light does not reach them. Their hope, for Christmas, is in the spirit, where rests secure against pogroms, secret police, and Summit conferences, the knowledge of a supreme historical occasion whose meaning is ultimate deliverance. They shall inherit the earth, even if they never have a Merry Christmas.

—*NR*, Jan. 2, 1960, *p. 4*

The trick of it is that individual people change, "things" don't. The premises of Soviet Communism were the same in 1945, when Dean Acheson was making preposterous assumptions about Communism, as they are today, when Dwight Eisenhower is making preposterous assumptions about Communism. And in between the premises were the same; the same when we lost China in 1949; the same when Dwight Eisenhower was hinting at the liberation of the Soviet satellites in 1952. The metaphysics of Soviet Communism did not change during that period. What did happen during that period is that the Soviet Union acquired control over, roughly, half the world, developed the hydrogen bomb, girded the moon with a rocket, and was cheered by San Francis-

cans. But these circumstantial developments do not alter—or do they?
—the essential moral and intellectual relationships of men and ideas. We
still pray, do we not, that the Lord will thrust into hell Satan and the other
evil spirits who roam through the world seeking the destruction of souls?
Or does Camp David render that prayer obsolete?

—*NR*, April 23, 1960, *pp. 258–259*

We are, it is safe to say, embarked on a new era of good feeling. The Spirit
of the Moscow Treaty, the historians may call it, always provided it lasts
as long as the Spirit of Geneva (18 months) or the Spirit of Camp David
(10 months). And even then, it is important to bear in mind, a spirit
becomes a Spirit not when the Soviet Union temporarily calls off its war.
What the Soviet Union does, when the Spirit moves her, is very simply,
and quite entirely, to mute her rhetoric—that is literally all. The rhetoric
in this instance became muted shortly after our U-2 planes spotted Soviet
missiles in Cuba and we forced them home. The rhetorical love-play
began, and the climax was reached in Washington when the Senate
ratified the test-ban treaty, quickly followed by the sale of vast amounts
of American wheat to the Soviet Union. Needless to say, during that
period the Soviet Union did not ease its thumb at any of the pressure
points against the West, not in Laos, not in Vietnam, not in Latin America, not in Cuba, not in Berlin, not in the Middle or Far East.

—*NRB*, Oct. 29, 1963, *p. 1*

And indeed the times are changing. We are told thrice a day that the cold
war is over, that the Vietnam conflict is the last gasp in a Peloponnesian
ordeal which is happily ending in a sort of grudging amiability between
the partners, and that it is only a matter of time before Barry Goldwater
Jr. and Bettina Aptheker bed down together. . . . During "the McCarthy
days"—which is for some reason a more fashionable way to put it than
during "the Stalin days"—America found it ncessary to be more actively
concerned about the Soviet's agents. But now, tra la, we can afford to be
permissive. We shall have to wait and see. . . . Experience shows us all
over the world that Communism is a fighting faith. More so than whatever faith it is the West can be said nowadays to profess.

—*NR*, April 18, 1967, *p. 396*

William Sloane Coffin

. . . Dr. William Sloane Coffin, the young divine of Yale University who serves at least half-time as a sort of Mother Bloor to left-wing students and who, if he ever came out with a constructive anti-Communist proposal other than that we should pray for the Communists, failed to take the precaution of sending me a copy.

—ON THE RIGHT, Feb. 5, 1966

Neither Dr. Coffin nor Dr. [Benjamin] Spock is a lawyer, indeed it is unlikely that either of them would recognize the Constitution of the United States if it crept into bed with them. Neither of them was ever heard to question the constitutionality of the Selective Service Act before that act was invoked to conscript soldiers to fight in this particular war.

—ON THE RIGHT, Jan. 11, 1968

Roy Cohn

The zeal with which the U.S. Attorney in New York has gone after Roy Cohn over a period of years suggests either that Mr. Cohn is soon to be revealed as head of S.M.E.R.S.H. or that the U.S. Attorney is suffering from a devil fixation.

—ON THE RIGHT, Dec. 3, 1968

Cold War

In this century alone the United States has at one time or another occupied, or caused to be occupied, a fairly large area of the globe. All of Europe. China. Japan. Cuba, the Dominican Republic, Mexico. The Philippines, Formosa. In every instance, we have withdrawn from those areas, having meanwhile made efforts here gloriously successful, there tragically defective, to encourage material progress and free institutions.

With the single exception of Austria, there is no territory in the world that was ever occupied by the Communist powers, which was subsequently set free by them. The answer to the question, How would we feel if the Communists occupied Mexico, then, calls for the time-honored reply: *Quod licet Jovi, non licet bovi.* What Communists may not do, we may do, for the very simple but utterly conclusive reason that they are war-waging imperialistic powers, and we are not.

—NR, Dec. 28, 1965, *p. 1186*

Collectivism

Back in the thirties we were told we must collectivize the nation because the people were so poor. Now we are told we must collectivize the nation because the people are so rich. It is only required, in order to accelerate our forward motion, for the Commission on National Goals to recommend federal subsidies to any college adopting as its basic economic text Mr. Galbraith's book, *The Affluent Society.* By that time it will have become a matter of historical conjecture just what society Mr. Galbraith was alluding to when he wrote his book.

—NRB, Feb. 20, 1960, *p. 1*

College Administrations

The very first thing the president of the typical university does, upon announcing that henceforward ROTC students will receive no academic credits, is to assure his audience that the decision of the faculty was reached without any thought to the political situation, absolutely none at all. That is of course sucker-bait, and the presidents know it, but they have become so much accustomed to dissimulation, which they practice upon the alumni as if they had Ph.D.'s in the subject, that they can manage to keep straight faces while saying such crooked things.

—ON THE RIGHT, May 10, 1969

College Chaplains

The college chaplain, fulfilling the function assigned to him by the typical secular college, is, primarily, a spiritual jester. He is an embellishment: the functionary who is turned on at the beginning of public meetings to intone solemnities which no one is expected to pay very much attention to, but which are commonly accepted as conducive of the proper tone. He is available to administer para-psychiatric attention to troubled students; he may even be given a class to teach, say, "Introduction to Religion": it may, moreover, be a well-attended class, if it is for credit and if the grading reflects a proper Christian charity. All this the college chaplain will do.

What he may *not* do is feign intellectual parity with the faculty. Either in his own behalf, or in religion's behalf. That implicit relegation of religion to second-class intellectual status is immediately perceived by sensitive students. The freshman who gets to know a matter of hours after arriving at a campus the subtlest distinctions between fraternity X and fraternity Z does not need much longer to perceive the little distinctions that reflect the academic vogue. If he is intellectually ambitious, as the brighter student tends to be, he quickly realizes that the college chaplain's "field"—religion—is not really accepted as a philosophical discipline, with a body of knowledge of its own: rather, in the bitter words of Canon Bernard Iddings Bell, religion is considered "a pastime, preferred by a few to golf and canasta."

—NR, Jan. 11, 1958, *p. 41*

College Protests

An overview suggests that it should be listed among student demands that the administration should not accede to them, that being the principal source of psychological satisfaction, and the only means of keeping the students' attention from cosmic re-arrangements.

*—*On The Right, May 13, 1969

Colleges

Last spring the presidents of Chicago, Columbia, Cornell, Harvard, Princeton, Stanford and Yale promulgated a set of "Guiding Principles for Industrial Gifts." The Preamble to the Guiding Principles begins by remarking such things as that "colleges and universities have a deep obligation to society," and then hurries on to discuss "the form of corporate giving most useful to the college or university" (cash). Delicately, the presidents warn colleges and universities against permitting "their names to be used in any related advertising" of their corporation donors, but hasten to grant that "Corporations obviously deserve the goodwill that is the natural and appropriate dividend of genuine philanthropy." (The distinction for which they grope is not altogether clear. Presumably it would be all right to establish a Colgate Chair of Political Economy, but not a Colgate "It Cleans Your Breath While It Cleans Your Teeth" Chair of anything. . . .

—NR, Jan. 12, 1957, *p. 41*

Can You Finish the Sentence? Department. Memo from Sarah Gibson Blanding to the Friends of Vassar. "At this time of each year when I write to the Friends of Vassar, I have high hopes that I shall be permitted the pleasure of telling you about aspects of Vassar life other than her financial problems. Each year . . ."

(Answer: ". . . these hopes turn out to be in vain.")

—NR, March 9, 1957, *p. 241*

As a general proposition, colleges are best administered by administrators, next best by faculty, and most worst by students.

—ON THE RIGHT, Dec. 23, 1965

It is becoming fashionable in some student and faculty quarters to rail against the government's presence in said colleges in any role whatsoever. With the interesting exception that most of those same students and professors do believe that, as for instance in C.C.N.Y., the total cost of their education and their salaries should be borne by government.

—On The Right, May 19, 1966

Colonialism

Colonialism became a dirty word in part because of occasional excesses by the colonizers themselves, but mostly as the result of the theorizing of Lenin, whose most influential book was called *Imperialism: The Final Stage of Capitalism.* Lenin's thesis was that the capitalist nations became stagnant as the result of the inherent deficiencies of their system and that they would then rely on colonialism as the only means of creating a market to consume the glut that the proletariat were overproducing. That thesis captivated the minds of the intellectuals, and the canard was loosed that the only interest colonial powers could possibly have in their overseas territories was to serve themselves economically.

Years have gone by since Lenin wrote his book (1917), during which the developing science of statistics demonstrated that the principal so-called colonial powers—France, Belgium, Portugal, England, the United States—were getting less out of their territories than they pumped into them, and in fact were concentrating their overseas investments not in the territories they were allegedly bent on exploiting, but in other advanced nations. The Marxist hypothesis was exploded. But the smear stuck, and sticks even to this day, so that even the average Western conservative has got on the bandwagon. And what happens, in more cases than not, is that said nations revert to a state of nationalist primitivism, a sort of coca-colonized totalitarianism.

—On The Right, Jan. 28, 1964

. . . the United States should filibuster in the United Nations against any discussions of colonialism, until the subject of Soviet colonialism is put on the agenda.

—On The Right, Feb. 1, 1964

Columbia University—The Riots

The most inflammatory issue has had to do with the proposed construction of athletic facilities on a public park adjacent to Columbia. The park in question is a nice stretch of green, dividing the Columbia campus from Harlem, which however is about as safe to traverse as the DMZ. It is the principal outdoor training ground for apprentice muggers, thieves and rapists.

—ON THE RIGHT, April 30, 1968

Mr. Kirk, poor Mr. Kirk whose office was smashed, the walls covered with graffiti, broken whiskey bottles strewn about, poor Mr. Kirk says that calling in the police was the hardest thing he ever had to do. If that is the case, poor Mr. Kirk should be relieved of his misery, and sent out to pasture. Because Columbia needs someone who will do something a great deal harder. Suspend several hundred students for a year or more, and fire one hundred or so of the instigators. If Columbia can't do that and survive as a university, then it ought not to survive as a university, because the society it seeks to serve is mortally ill.

—ON THE RIGHT, May 4, 1968

. . . there were representatives there of Mayor Lindsay, whose comment the next morning will never perish from this earth. "Mayor Scores Columbia Sit-Ins/But Backs the Right to Dissent." That is as if, stumbling into Buchenwald with the liberating army, General Eisenhower had said, waving in the general direction of the corpses, "I do deplore all of this, but I stoutly defend German dissent from the Versailles Treaty."

—ON THE RIGHT, May 4, 1968

Commonweal

May I be struck dead if I am exaggerating, but so help me I once saw in the pages of *Commonweal* a sensible anti-Communist proposal.

—*Ave Maria*, April 7, 1962, *p. 6*

Communism

I certainly do not suggest that the existence of a Communist minority is good reason for doing away with democracy, though I would say it is sufficient reason for doing away with the Communists.

—Up from Liberalism, p. 154

By all means, the Communist nations should be encouraged to wage separation, and we must hope for the happy prospect that centrifugalization will win in the end. But we can hardly bank on it, even as Kosygin could not bank on a division between France and the United States in the event of a world war. Last week in Moscow a 28-year-old who joined a protest demonstration in Moscow asking for freedom of artistic expression was told to go express himself in a concentration camp for three years. As an artist, he is no doubt aware of the varieties of Communist experience. He is unlikely to while away his time in prison meditating on them.

—ON THE RIGHT, March 2, 1967

... note to all writers, everywhere: one cannot be a Communist and a philosopher, if you will permit an ipsedixitism.

—ON THE RIGHT, Sept. 30, 1967

Communism—How to Fight It

... it is the error of many priests, ministers and rabbis who preach that we can beat the Communists by burnishing our own souls. Be honest, moral, tolerant, encourage national unity and racial integration, be charitable towards those with whom you disagree and—you will go to Heaven, to be sure, but your passage there might well be expedited by a Soviet bullet. ... Alas, if every one of us were as angelic as Raphael, it would not follow that we would win the war against the Communists. The Communists know how to conquer good people too. What did our greed and materialism and pornography and dope traffic and all the rest of the ignominious blotches on our culture ... have to do with the loss of Czechoslovakia? Our failures have been primarily failures of 1) understanding, 2) will, and 3) imaginative statecraft.

—NR, April 10, 1962, p. 238

Communist Fronts

How does one identify a Communist front? By definition, the job is not easy. If it were instantly recognizable as such, the whole point of the thing would be lost. By definition, a front desires respectability; desires to conceal the truth it is engaged in concealing by leeching on to the prestige of people whose integrity is taken for granted. Apart from the obvious fact that the goals will be in accord with Communist objectives, the first thing to look for in political manifestos that touch on points of friction between East and West is any trace of anti-Communism. It is an extraordinary thing—and one wonders and wonders why the Communists over the years have been so steadfastly lacking in subtlety—but it is almost uniformly the case that no Communist front will criticize any word, thought, or deed of the Communists, not even in the high cause of plausibility.

—NR, July 13, 1965, pp. 578–579

Communists

Junius Scales, the North Carolina Communist who was imprisoned last year for knowingly conspiring to overthrow the Government of the United States by force and violence, and who has never cooperated with the government's anti-Communist efforts, was given a pardon by President Kennedy at Christmas time, in response to pressure from Free Scales committees manned primarily by persons who are against the very existence of the Smith Act. In sharp contrast: David Greenglass, who received a thirty-year sentence in 1951 even after turning state's evidence against the Rosenbergs, languishes in jail. Free Greenglass committees make no headway, either with Presidents, or with the liberal intelligentsia. If one of these days you find yourself about to go to jail for having tried to overthrow the Government of the United States, do yourself a service and guarantee yourself the formation of a Free You Committee, by refusing to cooperate with the government.

—NRB, Jan. 8, 1963, *pp. 1–2*

Communists: As Campus Speakers

Fight him, fight the tyrants everywhere: but do not ask them to your quarters, merely to spit upon them: and do not ask them to your quarters if you cannot spit upon them: to do the one is to ambush a human being as one might a rabid dog; to do the other is to ambush oneself, to force oneself—in disregard of those who have *died* trying to make the point— to force oneself to break faith with humanity.

—NR, Oct. 22, 1963, *p. 370*

Complaining

I profoundly believe it takes a lot of practice to become a moral slob, and that if there is anything the American people are diligently engaged in acquiring, it is that skill, that indifference to things minor which carries over to things major. We simply don't complain about little things; and so a part of our nervous system becomes inert—the part which should be tingling and on edge if we are to escape totalitarianization by those who exercise great power. ... Start with the little things. Don't become a grouch. But don't let them push you around. If absolutely necessary, refuse to fasten your seat belt.

—NR, Feb. 12, 1963, *p. 103*

Congress

The tendency in American politics during the past decades has been to break the balance of things. The Executive has drawn power out of all proportion to what it was intended it should have. The same is true of the Judiciary. Congress is reduced to a sea anchor of sorts, a kind of American House of Lords with the right to a suspensory veto, good only for slowing things down for a session or two.

—ON THE RIGHT, Nov. 14, 1964

Conservatism

... I am interested in the [Liberal] approaches to the conservative dissent. I think they fall into three general categories. They are 1) Conservatism does not exist. 2) Conservatism does exist, but it is not an intellectual problem; it is one of pathology. 3) Conservatism does exist —as a lowering political force that threatens to ring in a new Dark Age.

—Up from Liberalism, p. 89

I will not cede more power to the state. I will not willingly cede more power to anyone, not to the state, not to General Motors, not to the CIO. I will hoard my power like a miser, resisting every effort to drain it away from me. I will then use *my* power, as *I* see fit. I mean to live my life an obedient man, but obedient to God, subservient to the wisdom of my ancestors; never to the authority of political truths arrived at yesterday at the voting booth. That is a program of sorts, is it not? It is certainly program enough to keep conservatives busy, and liberals at bay. And the nation free.

—*Up from Liberalism*, p. 229

Conservatism in America is rather a force than a political movement.

—*The Unmaking of a Mayor*, p. 306

There is in the air a sense of great excitement among American conservatives who have reason to believe that their time is coming. In the past few years any number of ideas developed in the garrets of conservative scriveners and roundly dismissed as radical and irrelevant, have suddenly begun to appear in the classiest political shopwindows. Four years ago they laughed themselves silly at Barry Goldwater's proposal that they sell the T.V.A. Now the Democratic Postmaster General proposes selling off the Post Office (to a public corporation). Twenty years ago, Lord Keynes's fiscal policies were written into the economics textbooks as holy writ; and now the monetary policies of Milton Friedman are beginning to displace the obsession with fiscal policy. There are other examples, the sudden perception of the metaphysical limitations of government action, the slow understanding of the derivative limitations of poverty and urban renewal programs. But the most exciting of the lot is the emergence from the fever-swamps of the idea of private schools— in preference to public schools.

—On The Right, Jan. 13, 1968

Conservative Movement

How strange it is that all the Establishment's scholars, all the Establishment's men, have not in the last half dozen years written a half dozen paragraphs that truly probe the true meaning of the American right wing.

They settle instead for frenzied, paranoid denunciations. Indeed the Left has discovered that the threat is really internal.

—Rumbles, p. 83

It is a matter deeply disturbing to ever so many people that the conservative movement was not terminated on the day that Lyndon Johnson beat Barry Goldwater so decisively at the polls. It was very generally supposed that the electorate had once and for all spoken on the subject, and that therefore the only realistic thing a conservative could do was to fold up his tent, and hitch-hike along with history. It is of course clear by now that no such accommodation is intended by conservatives, either because they are fanatics, who will not learn from experience—or because they believe that the conservative critique of modern society continues to be relevant.

—ON THE RIGHT, Jan. 25, 1966

Conservatives

The national security is a proper concern for the libertarian because without it he stands to lose—in this case—all his freedom. The conservative, who is a libertarian but other things, too, supports the large national effort that aims at neutralizing the Communist threat, because a conservative must be prepared to face reality. . . . we never lose sight of the value of what we do have, and the reason why we have it, namely, because we have a formidable military machine which keeps the Soviet Union from doing to us what it did to the Hungarians, and the Cubans.

—New Individualist Review, Nov., 1961, *p. 9*

. . . the American Right is based on the assumption that however many things there are that we don't know, there are some things we do know; on the assumption that some questions are closed, and that our survival as a nation depends on our acting bravely on those assumptions, without whose strength we are left sounding like Eisenhower, which is to say organically unintelligible; rhetoricizing like Kennedy, which is what comes of hiring Madison Avenue to make nonaction act; or writing like Mailer, which is to write without "beginning to know what one is, or what one wants"—the criticism of Mailer made by his friend, my enemy, Gore Vidal.

—Rumbles, p. 81

Conservatives in this country—at least those who have not made their peace with the New Deal, and there is serious question whether there are others—are non-licensed nonconformists; and this is dangerous business in a liberal world, as every editor of this magazine can readily show by pointing to his scars.

—NR, Nov. 19, 1955, *p. 5*

We think ... of the scores upon scores of timorous right-wingers we happen to know who will overwhelm you with dire talk about the engulfing age of socialism; about the infinite ambitions of labor unions; about the unconscionable aggressions of the ravenous state; about the terrible dangers of Communist infiltration; about the collectivist indoctrination in American schools and colleges. And yet when the occasion presents itself to make a sacrifice in behalf of their convictions, the conversation quickly turns to the weather. And if the opportunity arises for such men to act in their official capacity as, say, trustees of a foundation, or executives of a large corporation, they will, in the majority of instances, decline to undergo any inconvenience, let alone take any risk. For them, tax exemption and security against public involvement are the very highest values. That is what sets them off from the directors of the Fund for the Republic. And that is why the Left marches on, while the Right retreats.

—NR, Jan. 18, 1956, *p. 7*

Conspiracy

What, after all, does it mean, to conspire? Usually something less, as Father John Courtney Murray has reminded Sidney Hook, than to meet your partner under the bridge with complementary parts of a bomb. "To plot, devise, contrive," "to combine in action or aims: to concur, cooperate as by intention," says the dictionary. That kind of thing goes on all the time. In the White House, for instance. Within the Department of Government at Harvard, for instance. The question whether there is an Establishment some of whose members conspire together raises merely the question whether there is, or has been, coordination of purpose between people who administer in the White House, teach at Harvard, write in *The New Yorker*, and preach at St. John the Divine. Of course there is coordination, however informal, and it is as naive to believe there is not as it is naive to support that *only* conspiratorial action is responsible for historical events.

The word conspiracy, at another level, has a highly pejorative meaning, spelled out in the definition (Oxford's): "To combine ... to do something criminal, illegal, or reprehensible." It is not necessarily reprehensible for Bishop Pike and Bishop Sherrill to agree to denounce the Radical Right during the next fortnight—why shouldn't they? (What would God think if they *didn't?*) It *is* reprehensible for Joseph L. Rauh, Jr. (ADA) and Al Friendly (Washington *Post*) and Clayton Fritchey *(Democratic Digest)* to have conspired with Paul Hughes, a secret informer, in an attempt to penetrate a congressional committee. Surely it is reprehensible if professors within a department of economics or government conspire against the promotion of a scholar because his views are different from their own (assuming the professors announce themselves as advocates of academic freedom).

—Rumbles, pp. 28–29

Conspiracy Theory of History

National Review's position is that our society behaves the way it does because the majority of its opinion-makers, for various reasons, respond to social stimuli in a particular way—spontaneously, not in compliance with a continuously imposed discipline; there is no conspiracy involved.

—NR, Aug. 1, 1956, *p. 8*

The conspiracy theory of history is the talk of the town these days, having, since the publicity given to Robert Welch, replaced the ghost story at liberal campfires. Let us avoid the conspiratorial explanation for otherwise explainable events. The time, then, surely has come for those liberals so much disturbed by that sort of thing, formally and unambiguously to reject the notion, received so solemnly by so many of them during the past few years, that the trial and conviction of Alger Hiss was the result of a vast conspiracy comprehending the House Committee on Un-American Activities, the FBI, the Justice Department, and the Courts, what?

—*NR*, June 3, 1961, *p. 337*

The Constitution

The Constitution was once an instrument by which the objective rights of individuals to use and abuse their rights was generally secured. Now it is only an interesting intellectual challenge for bigthink sociologists who wrest from its Miltonic sweep and directness byzantine little sophisms that permit them to have their way in pioneering new civil rights, new prohibitions against public prayer, new electoral metaphysics (one man-one vote). ... the Constitution is, at least temporarily, gone....

—ON THE RIGHT, Sept. 20, 1966

Context

It is the context that counts, and every man is entitled to his context.

—*NRB*, Aug. 4, 1964, *p. 1*

Corruption

Conservatives will not deny, heaven knows, the disposition of many opportunistic businessmen to clip coupons from their book of ethics, if by doing so they become legal tender. . . . There are two points on which we should concentrate attention. The first has to do with the multiplier effect which the State and only the State can give to personal corruption. Let private citizen Jones bribe private citizen Smith, and the harm done is delimited by the spheres of economic influence the two men, between them, wield. Let private citizen Smith bribe public citizen Green, and the vast leverage of the State is exerted on the venality. We may not be able at a moral level to do very much very fast to check the ruthlessly preda- tory instincts of some of our citizenry, but at the mechanical level we can always hope to reduce their leverage, and that is what the anti-statist is talking about when he speaks of the unique capacity of the State to maximize the effects of wrongdoing. It is the State's unique monopoly on force that caused Henry Mencken to say disgustedly that the State is "the natural enemy of all decent, well disposed and industrious men."

—NR, Feb. 13, 1960, *p. 98*

Corruption in Government

Newbold Morris was nationally in the news on only one occasion, when he went down to Washington at the invitation of President Truman to investigate corruption in government, and actually proceeded to do so. Such was the President's shock, to say nothing of the shock of the corruptees, that in very short order Morris's letter of marque and reprisal was withdrawn, and he was hustled quickly out of town, the whole city seeming to sigh with relief and wondering amusedly that there still ex- isted a man so charmingly naive. What Morris had done was devise a little form to be filled out by all government employees, asking only two or three questions. It went something like this: Dear Sir, How much were you worth when you started working for the government? How long have you worked for the government and for how much? How much are you now worth? Sincerely, Newbold. The employees would sooner have filled out a questionnaire from Dr. Kinsey.

—NR, April 19, 1966, *p. 351*

Crime

What is remarkable about New York other than the rise in crime is the apparent resignation of New Yorkers to it. The newspapers huff and puff, as do our lords spiritual—the ministers, journalists, and even some of the professors. But I think it is probably true to say that there are more New Yorkers actively engaged in trying to eliminate the death penalty than there are New Yorkers actively engaged in trying to devise ways to catch murderers.

—ON THE RIGHT, March 25, 1965

We need, at least until such a moment as the crime rate is reversed, a much larger police force, enjoined to lust after the apprehension of criminals even as politicians lust after the acquisition of votes. Under no circumstances must the police be encumbered by such political irons as civilian review boards—or by any other contraption whose presumptive concern is for advantageous political relationships, rather than for law and order in our streets. The protection of the individual against the criminal is the first and highest function of government. The failure of government to provide protection is nothing less than the failure of government. The city of New York should investigate the feasibility of providing some kind of indemnity to victims of certain kinds of crime.

—*NR*, July 13, 1965, *p. 587* (statement announcing his candidacy for Mayor of New York City)

. . . it is no answer to the problem of crime to assume that every criminal merely midwifes a social imperative. That every criminal has been visited by a social incubus that you and I are responsible for, which, having impregnated him, requires, by the laws of nature, the birth of a crime. James Baldwin told me the other day that he does not blame the residents of Harlem for throwing garbage out of their windows, that that is their form of protest. Would we, by the same token, be entitled to throw our garbage out the window when John Lindsay passes by?

—The Unmaking of a Mayor, p. 98

Criticism

One often hears it said that one should ignore criticism. I do not agree that it is *always* wise to ignore criticism of oneself and one's endeavors, even when the criticism is ill-natured, exhibitionistic, and predictable. For even when that is the character of the criticism, there is sometimes something to be learned from it not only about oneself and one's critics, but about the world we live in.

—NR, Aug. 1, 1956, p. 7

Walter Cronkite

On Friday May 15 Walter Cronkite telephoned Gettysburg to see if he couldn't talk Mr. Eisenhower into denouncing the Horrible Extremism of Senator Goldwater. People had tried before, but Cronkite isn't just people, he's Cronkite, known to the General as "Walter," and to J. Walter Thompson as "The Anchor Man." By the time General Eisenhower was through with Walter, he was so perturbed that he can never again be described as imperturbable: more correctly, he is imperturbable except on those occasions when he sets out to do Goldwater political harm and has to sit there and take it when Goldwater reaps instead political gain.

—NR, June 2, 1964, p. 435

Cuba

The problem is that John F. Kennedy promised Nikita Khrushchev that
if NK would withdraw his missiles, JFK would promise not to liberate
Cuba. That is the kind of deal which, if it had been made by, say, Marshall
Petain with the Nazis concerning Algeria, would have had us all cluck-
clucking about the necessity to liberate a country enslaved by oppor-
tunists. The political cogency of the argument is sharpened by our appetite to prove an identical point 10,000 miles away in Vietnam.

—ON THE RIGHT, Oct. 17, 1968

Czechoslovakia—the Soviet Invasion

. . . it was only a matter of months between the Soviet Union's dispatch
of tanks to run over the bodies of students in Budapest, and the promul-
gation of the Spirit of Camp David by a mollifying American President.
Who would dare to say, now, that history will not repeat itself? That
Soviet representatives, on the heels of the most flagrant repression of the
most modest appeal for freedom in post-war history, will not in due
course resume their chummy dialogue with Western progressives, about
peace and freedom? You watch.

—ON THE RIGHT, Aug. 27, 1968

D

Mayor Daley

If the behavior of the policemen [at the 1968 Democratic Convention] was . . . a reflection of systematic totalitarian corruption by Mayor Daley, then surely the question should have arisen, how come Mayor Daley was the favorite mayor of John Kennedy and Bobby Kennedy? Where has the press been, lo these many years, during which he has been building his Fascistic satrapy? Unconvincing. And while we are at it, was Mayor Daley's manipulation of the Illinois delegation less obvious than, say, Boss Unruh's over the California delegation? But we weren't cross at him, were we? Because Unruh was with the good guys.

—On The Right, Sept. 2, 1968

Daughters of the American Revolution

Sometimes the fumes of Eastern Seaboard Liberalism are overpowering: the smell of *Partisan Review,* to greet the dawn; the *Times* for breakfast; the heat of the *Post* at midday; the *Dissent* of the evening sun; Susskind as nightcap. . . . And then you spot it, and you laugh, and laugh, and laugh till you can't bear it: at the annual meeting of the DAR last week the vote on the Peace Corps was against—2,082 to one!

—*NR*, May 6, 1961, *p. 268*

Dedication

When one declares oneself to be a conservative, one is not, unfortunately, thereupon visited by tongues of fire that leave one omniscient. The

51

acceptance of a series of premises is just the beginning. After that, we need constantly to inform ourselves, to analyze and to think through our premises and their ramifications. We need to ponder, in the light of the evidence, the strengths and the weaknesses, the consistencies and the inconsistencies, the glory and the frailty of our position, week in and week out. Otherwise we will not hold our own in a world where *informed* dedication, not just dedication, is necessary for survival and growth.

—*NR*, Feb 8, 1956, *p. 7*

Defense Research in Colleges

What do the gentlemen want? The government to start its own colleges and universities? Would we really be better off breeding a class of govern-ment-scientists unexposed to the leavening influences of the humanities, such of them as survive in the nation's colleges and universities? Do they really believe we would then be better off? Because that is exactly what is going to happen if the militants have their way.

—On The Right, Feb. 15, 1969

Charles de Gaulle

Charles de Gaulle has consistently shown that he desires to emancipate France from reliance on American leadership. One can hardly blame him. Others who depended on our leadership—the Poles, the Cubans, the Laotians, to suggest just a few—would probably not do so again, if given an alternative. But it is one thing to develop his own nuclear force—the force *de frappe* he cherishes, by which he hopes to vest France herself with sufficient nuclear deterrent power to contain the ambitions of the Soviet Union—and something else altogether to disrupt an alliance whose common purpose has been the containment of the common enemy, everywhere in the world.

—On The Right, Nov. 5, 1964

If Gaullism had conceived itself as a force that would pour lead down the backbone of the West to stiffen the general resolution in times of stress and melancholy, then the creation of the little nuclear force, the hustling and bustling around the chancelleries of the world, would somehow emerge as heroism. Divorced from any understanding of the travail of the world, Gaullism is nothing more than Azanian rodomontade. If de Gaulle wants his own atomic force in order to communicate to the Communists the seriousness of his intentions to fight for the independence of Europe in the event the United States should fall into the hands of SANE, that is one thing. If he wants his independent atomic force the more comfortably to withdraw from involvement in the common struggle against the Communists, that is another. In the past period, de Gaulle's palsied references to the "two hegemonies," wherein he refuses to distinguish between West and East, between free and Communist nations, between what there is of civilization and what there isn't of civilization, have made his entire enterprise unintelligible to those who understand that the glory of France is the glory of the Christian West, not of a factitious agglomeration of foreign and domestic notions pasted together by a superannuated autocrat.

—ON THE RIGHT, Dec. 9, 1965

The pride and misreckonings of de Gaulle will probably have the effect of rekindling the old German nationalism which three times humbled France in the last hundred years. And, in the German politics of day after tomorrow, there will unquestionably emerge a serious group that demands possession of the atom bomb. Perhaps by that time de Gaulle will be dead of old age. Many who survive him might, on his account, die prematurely.

—ON THE RIGHT, March 17, 1966

It took me many years to grasp that the reason acute Europeans like de Gaulle distrust U.S. guarantees to defend Europe by use of the bomb if necessary is that said Europeans, in American shoes, would do no such thing. Can you imagine President de Gaulle of the United States triggering his Minutemen and Polaris missiles in defense of President Nixon's

France, knowing what then would happen to *la vieille glorie*, America? That is the reasoning behind France's *force de frappe*.

—On The Right, Feb. 11, 1969

Democracy

The commitment by the liberals to democracy has proved obsessive, even fetishistic. It is part of their larger absorption in Method, and Method is the fleshpot of those who live in metaphysical deserts. Even though democracy is a mere procedure, all the hopes of an epoch were vested in it. Intellectuals have tended to look upon democracy as an extension of the scientific method, as the scientific method applied to social problems. In an age of relativism one tends to look for flexible devices for measuring *this* morning's truth. Such a device is democracy; and indeed, democracy becomes epistemology: democracy will render reliable political truths just as surely as the marketplace sets negotiable economic values.

The democracy of universal suffrage is not a bad form of government; it is simply not necessarily nor inevitably a good form of government. Democracy must be justified by its works, not by doctrinaire affirmations of an intrinsic goodness that no mere method can legitimately lay claim to.

—*Up from Liberalism*, pp. 148–149

Democratic Convention, 1968

But even before Humphrey began to speak, the fences were being put together. The honor escort that brought Hubert Humphrey to the podium was conspicuous only for the absence of Rose Kennedy. Everybody else who represented a voting bloc larger than a couple of city squares was there. . . .

—On The Right, Sept. 3, 1968

Democratic Party

To the extent the Democrats succeed in identifying Brains and their Party, they further the anti-intellectualism they deplore.

—NR, Oct. 11, 1958, *p. 235*

Democratism

Unlike the democratic absolutists, some of us are capable of rejoicing at the number of people who do *not* exercise their technical right to vote. Too many countries in the democratic world have gone down into totalitarianism because some demagogue or other has persuaded everyone who can stagger to the polls to go there, and vote: usually to give power to himself. That was the route the Argentinians took when they voted to surrender their freedom to Perón.

—NR, July 14, 1964, *p. 574*

Thomas E. Dewey

. . . the most analytical campaign statement he made [in the 1948 presidential race], as far as we can remember, was, "Ladies and gentlemen, the future lies before us."

—NR, July 25, 1956, *p. 6*

Diplomacy

"They're just like the rest of us—except that they spend a lot more," said supermarket operator Gil Shapiro who runs the neighborhood grocery nearest to the Soviet mission in Manhattan. The Soviet families, he figures, spend about $100 a day for their private food supplies, $700 a day during the current period, such are the demands of feeding Kosygin and the entire crew. "You ask what they buy? Practically everything.

They're heavy on cornflakes." (You have to understand about the Russians, Whittaker Chambers once told a visitor: they can make bombs and intercontinental missiles, but they can't make shredded wheat). You remember when Nikita Khrushchev was here a few years ago? He liked cornflakes so much he took back four cases of it. . . . Couldn't LBJ, at Glassboro, at least have threatened the Russians, if they refuse to cooperate in the Mideast, with cutting off their New York supply of cornflakes?

—ON THE RIGHT, June 29, 1967

Diplomatic Security

It is generally supposed that we are in a position to effect security in our communications from almost anywhere, and it is true that we have code devices that are pretty reliable. But as a matter of sheer tedium, it is distracting, over the long pull, to have to run the shower or whatever every time Averell Harriman wants to exchange an opinion with Cyrus Vance. The insiders will tell you that the American Embassy in Warsaw . . . is probably the most infested building in the entire world, that American ambassadors even get estranged from their wives there, on account of the necessity for total silence, lest Radio Warsaw broadcast their after-dinner conversations.

—ON THE RIGHT, May 2, 1968

Disarmament

Armament is the result of tension. The extent to which a nation is armed reflects the extent to which it is resolved to wage war against other nations, or the extent to which it feels threatened by other nations. A nation's economy, and a nation's will to expand or to resist expansion by others are the only factors that effectively limit armament. So long as these factors are unaffected, nations will not participate in any convincing international arms strip-tease.

The Soviet Union seeks to force the free world to its knees. To do so, it will either strive for a clear superiority in arms, or it will seek to maneuver any disarmament conference to its relative advantage. As for the United States, it will continue to arm with reference to the striking power of the enemy. These are the central facts of international life today, in the light of which most talk about disarmament must be written off as fetishistic.

Our reliance on disarmament formulae as effective means of securing world peace is dangerous, for reasons too obvious to enumerate. Let it be said, simply, that we have not devised a way to protect ourselves, or anybody else, from an invader except by use of arms; and we have not succeeded in curbing the appetite or redirecting the ambitions of the enemy. Our efforts should aim at the latter objective, which, unrealized, makes undue emphasis on disarmament dangerous.

—NR, April 11, 1956, *pp. 7–8*

Discrimination

This afternoon Mayor Robert Wagner danced attendance upon Mr. Khrushchev. Did he do so because Premier Khrushchev is head of a foreign state and so entitled, ex officio, to the hospitality of New York's mayor? It isn't that simple. . . . Last year Mayor Wagner ostentatiously announced his refusal to greet Ibn Saud—on the grounds that Ibn Saud discriminates against Jews in Saudi Arabia, and no man who discriminates against Jews in Saudi Arabia is by God going to be handled courteously by Bob Wagner, mayor of New York. Now, as everybody knows, Nikita Khrushchev not only discriminates against Jews, he kills them. On the other hand, he does much the same thing to Catholics and Protestants. Could *that* be why Mr. Wagner consented to honor Khrushchev? Khrushchev murders people without regard to race, color or creed, that is, on straight FEPC lines; and therefore, whatever he is guilty of, he is not guilty of discrimination, and so he is entitled to Robert Wagner's hospitality? Is that the shape of the new rationality?

—NR, Sept. 26, 1959, *p. 351*

Kenya has just finished . . . making its Indian-descended citizens officially second-class, which of course makes it imperative to side noisily with anyone who criticizes a government which has done the same thing, only to black Africans.

—ON THE RIGHT, March 14, 1968

Senator Thomas Dodd

There remains the debate in the Senate, at which Senator Dodd will have a final opportunity to raise points in his own defense. Whatever happens there, there remains also the question of what to do about the four sneakthieves who decided, after being caught by the Senator playing musical beds, that their love of country required them to bed down with Drew Pearson. Already they are being apotheosized, e.g., by the *New York Times*, which in the fatuity of the year remarks that the sneak-thieves "deserve approbation" because after all they "acted in no hope of private gain" (neither did Lee Harvey Oswald). There is going to be a lot of bitterness in the air over this one, and I for one announce the beginning of a long period of bitterness against the phony moralizers who conspired against a brave and simple man of distinguished public record, and against the tribunal which found him guilty by bill of attainder.

—*NR*, May 16, 1967, *p. 509*

For the record, before Mr. Pearson's attacks on Senator Dodd, I had, during a period of twenty years or so that he represented in one or another capacity the voters of Connecticut, met him twice. So far as I know—Drew Pearson can check on this, since I am sure he has a more accurate record of letters I have sent to the Senator than I have—I have written him three or four times, once (I do remember this) to compliment him most warmly on something or other he did or said. In the election of 1964, when Senator Dodd ran against John Davis Lodge, I voted for Mr. Lodge. Because he is my kind of Republican. So much for my own obligations to Senator Dodd. From the beginning I considered that the move against Dodd was at best imprecise, at worst an act of self-right-eousness of the kind societies go in for particularly during periods of great debauchery, like the whore crossing herself before leaping into bed.

—On The Right, June 24, 1967

Senator Thomas Dodd vs. James Boyd

It occurs only to the unusual reader to ask himself whether it is possible that during that same period it wasn't the Senator who changed, so much as the author [James Boyd]. During that same period the author, a) effected a dalliance with a lady of loose morals, whom he put on the Senator's payroll; b) became estranged from his wife and four children; c) subsequently took up with yet another lady, the secretary of Senator Dodd to whom he is now married; and d) discovered that Drew Pearson is the *fons et origo* of American morals. Now there is an anti-Pilgrim's Progress for you. ... Mr. Dodd isn't rich enough to sue the pants off Boyd, which leaves Mr. Boyd in the unaccustomed position of keeping his pants on.

—On The Right, Jan. 18, 1968

"Doing Your Thing"

We did not meet anyone who went so far as to say, for example, that Sirhan Sirhan was merely doing his thing. ...

—On The Right, June 3, 1969

The Dollar Drain

There are two ways to stop the dollar drain. One is to spend fewer dollars abroad, the other is to earn more francs, pounds, marks at home. How is the latter to be accomplished? By lowering the price of our products. How? By increasing our productive efficiency. How? Here is the rub: by cracking down on waste and featherbedding, by encouraging automation, by eliminating minimum wages: by anti-monopoly legislation of the kind that releases the disciplinary energies of the marketplace. And that means, in a word, by cracking down on the big labor unions.

—On The Right, Feb. 11, 1965

Double Standards

Test: Who said (a) "[It] is my firm belief that Dwight Eisenhower is a dedicated, conscious agent of the Communist conspiracy . . ."? Who said

(b) "Goldwater Republicanism is the closest thing in American politics to an equivalent of Russian Stalinism"? Everyone knows the answer to (a). Who knows—or will care, particularly—that the answer to (b) is William Fulbright?

—The Unmaking of a Mayor, p. 305

The Draft

One tends to forget that conscription entails the suspension of any number of basic human rights; conscription, for example, allows the government to exact involuntary servitude, and to curtail essential civil liberties. ... We should applaud any effort to determine whether we could adequately, and at reasonable cost, man the defenses of the nation with volunteers.

—NR, Oct. 27, 1956, *p. 6*

The not so very long-term objective should be to eliminate the draft in favor of a professional army of volunteers, who would greatly increase the efficiency of the armed services, and relieve the civil population of an experience which, insofar as it is unrelated to true necessity, is debasing, and an unnecessary—and therefore inexcusable—encroachment on individual freedom.

—On The Right, April 23, 1964

There exists, we discover, a committee that will inform young draftable Americans how to beat the draft. Among the quaint suggestions being offered is that a draftee feign homosexuality. I expect some of those who would try this dodge could make pretty convincing demonstrations.

—On The Right, Oct. 30, 1965

I suspect it is true that the democratist fanaticism that prevents us from repealing the draft law, and substituting instead a regular professional army, causes the discrepancy between the number of men drafted and the number of men needed to be unnecessarily large. . . . President Johnson has himself a lot of power these days, and has himself a Defense Department boss than whom no one in history has been bossier. One wonders why the President, who likes to get things done, and the Defense Department chief, who likes to economize and to professionalize, don't get on with the business of doing away with the draft, if indeed it is unneeded, and increasing substantially the size of the professional army. We would not only have a better army, but could afford one at a lesser cost, if you take into account the enormous expense of training a recruit who will become a civilian again in a couple of years.

—ON THE RIGHT, Nov. 2, 1965

The conventional arguments are that, a) a professional force renders professional services. As things now stand, an American technician becomes highly qualified, highly useful, by let us say June, and in September his tour of duty is over. b) The extra cost of luring men into a professional military force is not likely to exceed the great cost of continually training the millions of young men whose services are used over so short a period. To which conventional argument should be added, c) the great commotion caused by a draft, and the influence of that commotion on the formulation of an effective foreign policy backed up by a mobile armed force. If the United States is going to help out next year in Brazil, the year after in the Sudan, and the year after that in Nigeria, surely we do not want to replay the tensions of the existing war? . . . The influence of American youth and their epigoni, the intellectuals, the academicians, the opinion-makers, the noise-makers, on foreign policy is considerable, and in some ways healthy. Their indisposition to go and fight in these grubby wars in grubby parts of the world is altogether understandable. But until we simply give up on the rest of the world, we have got to help out. And the way to do that is primarily by making arms available, and also small, professional forces which will absorb the shock until such moment as the locals are trained to attend to their defense.

—ON THE RIGHT, Jan. 25, 1968

It is interesting how readily the language adapts itself to this idea, providing the necessary libertarian gloss. The words of the Gallup Poll are: "A remarkably high proportion (8 in 10) of persons interviewed say they would favor requiring all young men to give one year of service to the nation. . . ." But you see one cannot "require" a "gift." Or rather if one requires, there is no gift. One wonders whether the same percentage would have said yes if Dr. Gallup had asked: "Do you believe in a year's compulsory servitude for every young American?"

—ON THE RIGHT, Feb. 13, 1969

Drugs

It is exactly accurate to pronounce drug addiction a contagious disease in every relevant sense. It is generally supposed that it is exclusively the pusher who contaminates fresh victims. Recent studies indicate that however effective the pusher, the most effective contaminator is the individual himself hooked. There appears to be a compulsion of sorts, among most drug addicts, to pass on their lunacy to others. And they develop a sharp psychological eye for likely prey. . . .

The politico-philosophical key to the problem is therefore to recognize precisely that drug addiction is a contagious disease, and that under the circumstances the state is precisely empowered to exercise, in behalf of the community, the technical right to do what it can to prevent the spread of that disease, even as if it were leprosy. The first and most important step is to remove drug addicts from contact with potential victims. The victims I have directly in mind are other potential drug addicts, although there are other classes of victims besides.

—*NR*, March 22, 1966, *p. 257*

E

East-West Trade

The Young Americans for Freedom, an organization of the politically sane in the college campuses, has been picketing IBM's offices in protest against its vigorous solicitation of business behind the Iron Curtain. Vigorous, that is, in Eastern Europe. By no means vigorous as advertised in America, because the company's officials are aware that there is public hostility to trade with the Communist bloc. You are not likely, then, to see full page ads by IBM boasting, "America's Leading Manufacturer of Computers Has Sold Its 1400 Line to Bulgaria, Poland, Czechoslovakia, and Hungary ... Our newest 360 system has been sold to Yugoslavia, and is offered for sale to the other East European States. There is no accuracy like IBM accuracy. With IBM, you can fire a missile five thousand miles away and hit the town square in Armonk, New York! Put in your order now, while America still lasts."

—ON THE RIGHT, March 30, 1968

Economic Freedom

It is a part of the conservative intuition that economic freedom is the most precious temporal freedom, for the reason that it alone gives to each one of us, in our comings and goings in our complex society, sovereignty —and over that part of existence in which by far the most choices have in fact to be made, and in which it is possible to make choices, involving oneself, without damage to other people. And for the further reason that without economic freedom, political and other freedoms are likely to be taken from us.

—Up from Liberalism, p. 207

63

Economic Liberalism and Catholicism

What the Popes have in fact condemned is a) anarchy; b) the mystique of economic individualism (the kind of thing Ayn Rand is promoting); c) the notion that the state is *in essence* hostile to freedom; and d) the notion that the economically efficient solution is *necessarily* the proper solution. These are fallacies that have never dominated the pragmatic tradition of American economic liberalism, which holds indeed that historically the state is the principal parasite of the common welfare, but that it is indeed a necessary institution; that properly managed it can and does help to effect liberty; that state interference in the free market place tends under most circumstances to militate against freedom and the common good, but that state interference must not be categorically, merely *presumptively* opposed.

That last is precisely the position of the Popes, every single one of whom, from Leo XII to John XXIII, has affirmed the so-called Principle of Subsidiarity: that no public agency should undertake to do work which can be handled by a private agency; and no higher public agency should undertake to do work which can be handled by a lower public agency. That rule, together with the principles of private property and the rule of law, so frequently stressed by the Popes, are the essence of the economic liberalism of the American Right.

—NR, March 27, 1962, *p. 192*

Economic Statesmanship

Last week, Poland capitulated before 15-year-old U.S. demands that she compensate American citizens for property seized after World War II, and was reported ready to turn over $40 million to the dispossessed Americans. One day later, the U.S. Government announced it would make available to Poland, on account of the serious drought plaguing her, an extra, unscheduled, credit: $40 million.

—NR, Feb. 27, 1960, *p. 125*

Economics

Now avant-garde economists have long since made known their distrust of the marketplace—which, we are told, lacks the kind of transcendent vision that advances civilization. Civilization advances, Justice Oliver Wendell Holmes, Jr. told us, through the expenditure of tax moneys. A view shared by some non-liberals, non-conservatives, e.g. "It goes without saying that only a planned economy can make intelligent use of all a people's strength."*

—Up from Liberalism, p. 166

... economics—which to be sure has always had an uneasy time of it asserting its autonomy as a social science—has become the pliant servant of ideology.

—Up from Liberalism, p. 169

Education

... education is largely a matter of indoctrination any way you look at it, and ... there is no reason to presume unintelligence or shallowness in an "indoctrinator." Socrates was neither unintelligent nor shallow, nor, for that matter, was Adam Smith, or Lenin. But they did not approach a classroom as a vast hippodrome, where all ideas "start even in the race," where the teacher must interfere with none, because the right idea will automatically come romping home ahead of the others. Their method lay rather in exposing the latent disabilities in all but the winning contestant. "The Socratic manner," Max Beerbohm reminded us, "is not a game at which two people can play."

—Up from Liberalism, pp. 82–83

There is a sameness, both dreadful and reassuring, in the statements one is pelted with these days on the aims of American education. ... The young college president, freshly in office, must pale at the thought of the miles and miles of clichés that stand between him and that final bac-

[Hitler's] Secret Conversations, New York, Farrar, Straus and Cudahy, 1955, p. 15.

calaureate address, twenty years hence, when he will say: essentially the same thing.

—Rumbles, p. 128

Ever since the Second World War, many of our educational institutions, even while most of our teachers have tried valiantly to keep their eyes on the meaning of education, have been used as great human enclosures, to keep children off the streets, away from home during the daylight hours, fussing away at something or other for distraction's sake; and now it is proposed to use them to keep young people away from the labor market. The principal damage is to those other students who, genuinely desiring an education, are bored and distracted by the disruptive listlessness of those of their fellow students who, because they are restless at their desks, pose disciplinary problems, slow down the classes, horse around and, generally, make a travesty out of education.

We need, to begin with, a Committee Against Discrimination in Favor of College Degrees. We need, secondly, to differentiate sharply, as for instance is done in Germany, between those students who are educable, and those who are merely trainable; and the emphasis, for the latter, should be on vocational training, beginning at about the age of 14.

—On The Right, March 19, 1964

[From Chairman Bill's advice to the platform committees of the 1968 Republican and Democratic conventions:] The new thing in education is the encouragement of privately sponsored, privately administered pedagogical techniques: e.g., "I'll teach your children to read for $75 apiece." An extension of this innovative approach to education is the gradual loosening of the superstitions that publicly administered education is the most desirable kind of education for everyone. Parents who want them should receive vouchers, exchangeable at private schools of one's choosing. The social purpose would be to permit pluralism, individuation: and the adaptation of schools to the special needs of those who have special needs.

—On The Right, May 21, 1968

College graduates favor Nixon over Humphrey 46-39, which is the best thing anybody has recently remarked about the values of a college education. On the other hand, alumni of graduate schools favor Humphrey over Nixon 41-29, which confirms the worst suspicions we harbor about over-education.

—On The Right, July 16, 1968

And then [Hubert Humphrey] said that he was all for education for everyone "anxious and willing to learn." If that were America's only educational responsibility, we could close down half our schools.

—On The Right, Sept. 3, 1968

Education: A Conservative Philosophy

Schools ought not to be neutral. Schools should *not* proceed as though the wisdom of our fathers were too tentative to serve as an educational base. The Ten Commandments do not sit about shaking, awaiting their inevitable deposition by some swashbuckling professor of ethics. Certain great truths have been apprehended. In the field of morality, all the basic truths have been apprehended; and we are going to teach these, and teach, and demonstrate, how it is that those who disregard them fall easily into the alien pitfalls of communism, or fascism, or liberalism.

There is a purpose in life. It is known what that purpose is, in part because it has been divulged, in part because man is endowed with a rational mechanism by which he can apprehend it. Educators should pass on those truths, and endow students with the knowledge of the processes by which they are recognized as such. To do this is the single greatest contribution a teaching institution can make: it is the aim of education, to which all else is subordinate and derivative. If education can endow students with the powers of ethical and rational discrimination by which to discern and give their allegiance to the great certitudes of the West, we shall have a breed of men who will discharge truly the responsibilities that face them as the result of changing conditions.

—*Rumbles*, pp. 138–139

Education: Federal Aid

In the name of national security, all kinds of extra-military, or para-military, hypocrisies and subterfuges are advanced. We think, for instance, of the humbug National Defense Education Act, liberalism's answer to Sputnik, under whose provisions, *e.g.*, Howard University, a Negro college near Washington, was granted last year $100,000 toward a new dormitory for its Cooking School. As we remarked at the time, it is difficult to relate Sputnik and this grant unless it contemplated that our astronauts will take along Negro cooks.

—NR, May 20, 1961, *p. 307*

Dwight David Eisenhower

Mr. Eisenhower is nowadays viewed, by those who take refuge from the hecticities of the New Frontier and the Great Society, as the Raggedy Ann of yesteryear, the warm puppy of the cuddly past when the White House was occupied by competent bridge-playing businessmen, rather than ideological scriveners staying up late writing new laws for us to obey.

—Up from Liberalism, p. xxix

Mr. Eisenhower has always had difficulty in describing the nature of the Eisenhower program, and it is a difficulty traceable to something more subtle than the difficulty he has in formulating a phrase. The most expensive professional verbalizers in his entourage, or in his camp, have, fundamentally, the same difficulty. So that when the Eisenhower program, in conception and practice, is described, however enthusiastically, however ingeniously, or neatly, it nevertheless refuses to reduce to an orderly system of political or philosophical beliefs, or even to a consistent set of axioms or definitions as to the nature of the problem at hand, or how to deal with it. Like the pantaloons offered for sale by the Yankee peddler memorialized by Lincoln, the program seems to be "large enough for any man, small enough for any boy."

—NR, March 21, 1956, *p. 9*

No one would be more resentful than *National Review* of any effort to drain the fun out of politics, that being, we feel, one of its major justifications. But the evidence is by now unmistakable that the campaign is this year [1956] being designed to proceed on a level of vulgarity seldom before witnessed, and someone in the White House entourage, even at the risk of suffering the especially sharp slings and arrows reserved for the party-poop, should step in, puncture the damned balloon, and remind the braintrusters that a President, not a package of cornflakes, is for sale in November. . . .

—NR, July 25, 1956, *p. 6*

Last week was the week when the Reverend Elder Lightfoot Solomon Michaux informed the President of how the saints analyze the difference between his and the previous two Administrations. In the beginning was the New Deal. Then the Fair Deal. And now, said the Reverend Elder, "the Heaven-born Deal." The President was much struck by this intelligence and repeated it to Mr. Nixon and Republican lieutenants at the airport breakfast send-off for the Vice-President, whom he instructed to go out and speak the truth to all the people. "Give 'em Heaven," he said, beaming. And Mr. Nixon beamed, and Hall beamed, and all the angels sang their praises.

—NR, Sept. 29, 1956, *p. 3*

When Mr. Acheson was chased out of public life by an unusually emphatic act of public resolution, the landslide of 1952, he departed as the symbol of a futile, epicene anti-Communism, to make way, we were assured, for a vigorous, purposive, clearheaded anti-Communism. So the people believed—but not all of them. On election eve a Yale professor who was watching the returns with me over television said wearily, after listening to Mr. Eisenhower's victory speech: "*Mark my words, before Eisenhower is through he'll make Dean Acheson look like Custer's last stand.*" I think in foreign policy that is substantially what has happened, most especially since the death of John Foster Dulles.

—NR, April 23, 1960, *p. 258*

And yet it must be said, what a miserable President he was! Said regretfully: for it is painful to use such language about so good a man. But if
St. Francis of Assisi had been made president of the Chase Manhattan
Bank, he too would have made a miserable president. Our enthusiasm for
Francis might cause us to say the Chase Bank was not worthy of him,
and the failure was really the institution's, not the saint's. Let us agree
that the world is not worthy of Dwight Eisenhower. But the world is as
it is, and Dwight Eisenhower served as one of its princes, and the world
paid him no heed. None at all. And the world is worse off, by far, than
when he came to power, sustained by the sentimental faith of millions
of people, who thought that his goodness would irradiate out to the
cynical reaches of our darkening globe, and renew in the hearts of the
great malefactors the spirit of goodness.

—*NR*, Jan. 14, 1961, *p. 8*

... when the Republicans lost Ike, they lost the presidency, and found
their Party in a state of total disrepair. Mr. Eisenhower had made the
Republican Party unintelligible.

—*NR*, May 8, 1962, *p. 314*

Dwight Eisenhower is not a man of average skills. He is, on his feet, far
more eloquent than most; his personality is infinitely more magnetic than
yours or mine; he is a super-competent administrator, and incomparably
the master of his own career. He has—and the contrary opinion notwithstanding, I believe this is as surely his gift as Marian Anderson's voice
is hers—an absolutely perfected political sense. There never was, in all
American history, a more successfully self-serving politician. Eisenhower did nothing whatever for the Republican Party; nothing to develop
a Republican philosophy of government; nothing to catalyze a meaty
American conservatism. But he was unswervingly successful himself. He
never went after anything involving himself that he did not get. ...

—*NR*, Dec. 3, 1963, *p. 487*

"He recalled recently," the reporter continues to give Ike's view, "that he felt unable to support former Senator Barry Goldwater of Arizona in the 1964 Presidential campaign as vigorously as he would have liked because of what he considered the candidate's close association with the Birch Society." Now there is a statement for you—from someone who can't stand "personal politics." The fact of the matter is that Mr. Goldwater not only never had a close association with the Birch Society, he had zero association with the Birch Society. Indeed, Senator Goldwater, as far back as in 1962, disavowed the thinking of Mr. Welch in language firmer than Mr. Eisenhower has ever used about maybe anything in his life.

—ON THE RIGHT, Jan. 2, 1968

The Eisenhower Administrations

The social history of the White House under Mr. Eisenhower will, after all, record only one exclusion and one addition during his tenure. Khrushchev was added, Senator McCarthy was ejected.

—*NR*, Sept. 26, 1959, *p. 351*

Eisenhower: And Sherman Adams

Sherman Adams, it is revealed, has designs on the egghead vote. The *New York Times* reports that he—and, of course, the President—have made plans for "working quietly in the intellectual community this election year to break the Democratic Party's long monopoly of 'eggheads'." . . . Accordingly, Mr. Adams is in search of "writers who could argue or articulate Eisenhower Republicanism." Mr. Adams and his staff are in search of magicians, alas, and we warn them against pressing the search or endeavoring to distill out of Eisenhower Republicanism a philosophy of government. . . . Let the Republican Party be the Party of *no* philosophy, of a day-to-day pragmatism, of a guaranteed-surprise-for-the-voter-every-week. That is the drum the energetic Mr. Adams should beat.

—*NR*, Aug. 18, 1956, *pp. 6–7*

The Eisenhower Era

My guess is the Communists moved with whatever caution it can be said they did between 1953 and 1960 because they hadn't the least idea what Eisenhower was talking about, and thought a little prudence might be in order.

—Rumbles, p. 172

The conscious philosophical relativism of the academy, filtering down past the scholars and the intelligentsia to the masses, becomes less a *Weltanschauung*, more an attitude of mind. It is the prevalence of this attitude of mind that made it possible for Modern Republicanism to pause, triumphant, on its way to Limbo; that attitude made it possible for Dwight Eisenhower to attain a level of personal popularity no President had known since James Madison. The liberal ideology is programmatic in a sense in which the Republicanism of Mr. Eisenhower definitely is not. But the two, in time and place, are highly compatible; for encompassed by the blandness of Modern Republicanism, the stimulation of intellectual and political resistance to the continuing liberal offensive is all but impossible—as recent elections have shown.

—Up from Liberalism, p. 125

The distinctive challenge of our time, against which Mr. Eisenhower's forty-five-billion-dollar defense budget and Mr. Arthur Larson's books were powerless, is to resist the philosophical infiltration of the West by Communism. That infiltration is the end toward which the great engines of history are busily working, the grand synthesis whose name, in one of its phases, is Coexistence, and whose meaning, for the West, is death. The only defense of the West against it is the tenderest solicitude for Western values, the fastidious cultivation of the Western position, so sorely ravaged by the imprecisions and tergiversations of the leaders of the West. Liberalism cannot teach Mr. Eisenhower to talk back effectively to Mr. Khrushchev; but conservatism can, and hence the very urgent need to make the conservative demonstration.

—Up from Liberalism, pp. 195–196

Dwight David Eisenhower: Summit Conferences

We do believe that Mr. Eisenhower generates a certain moral force. It is not strong enough, alas, to split the shackles of Hungarian prisoners. But it has its effects. We should prefer that Mr. Eisenhower, rather than spend his time reiterating the platitudes, should arrive and just sit there, and say not a single word: that way his moral force can irradiate, without getting lost in the syntactical maze that envelops all things when the President opens his mouth. Just sit: and stare at Khrushchev every time Khrushchev foams and blusters, just sit amidst the rodomontade; and his presence would be felt.

—*NR*, May 21, 1960, *p. 318*

The 1956 Elections

I happen to think that if Adlai Stevenson and Dwight Eisenhower were each given a South Sea island over which to preside as absolute monarch, life in one island would not differ significantly, in internal affairs, from life in the other; in foreign affairs, the two kingdoms would be similar, maintaining, I should guess, a most fraternal relationship, what with exchange students, intermarriage, golf tournaments and much else dedicated to inter-island understanding.

—*NR*, Nov. 3, 1956, *p. 6*

". . . the program of the Republicans, which is essentially one of measured socialism, looks wonderfully appealing to the conservative, by contrast with that of the Democrats. . . . The argument by relative merit is wonderfully persuasive. In some cases it is, I think, conclusive. If one master will enslave me ninety days a year, a second only eighty-nine, if I may choose between them and must choose one, I shall unhesitatingly, all else being equal, elect to serve under the latter; and I should find no difficulty whatever defending my choice. My reasoning becomes inadequate, and perilously so, only when, in my zeal to stress the relative merit

of the less exacting master I find myself speaking approvingly, enthusiastically about him. When that happens, there is danger to mind and
morals. The danger posed by the Republican Party of today lies bare-
breasted in its universal emblem, I Like Ike. It should read, I Prefer Ike.

—NR, Nov. 3, 1956, *p. 7*

It may be . . . that the Eisenhower victory has broken the back of the hard
conservative resistance in American politics. The narrow escapes of conservatives who were re-elected, the scattered defeats of conservatives
who didn't quite make it, the enormous strength of Eisenhower, may
bring about a collapse of organized, or even informal political resistance
to the ways of progressive moderation. Well, so much more for people
like us to do.

—NR, Nov. 17, 1956, *p. 7*

Practically everybody agreed this spring that there was precious little
difference left between the Democratic Party and the New Republican
Party. Now they say that the reason the Republican Party, as such, did
so poorly, is that it just didn't move over far enough . . . Summed up the
New York Times: Dwight Eisenhower "has marked out the path, away
from reaction and toward new progress in the field of social legislation,
away from isolation and toward full acceptance of the responsibilities of
leadership in the field of international action—along which the Republican Party *must continue to move* if it is to win in its own right the
confidence of the country." *Continue* to move. Hmm . . . Is there that
much room? Or is the *Times* saying the Democratic Party should move
too, to make room for New Republicanism? If it's part of the deal for the
Democrats to move over, to allow the Republicans to move over to where
the Democrats were, so that the Republicans can then get elected, why
all the commotion? Why not elect the Democrats to begin with? Hmm.
Don't understand . . .

—NR, Nov. 24, 1956, *p. 7*

The 1966 Elections

"What did you think of the elections?" Mrs. Clare Boothe Luce asked a friend. "It was full of anomalies." "Yes," she meditated. "And some of them were elected."

—ON THE RIGHT, Nov. 15, 1966

England

England has become a sort of pleasure spa, undistracted by the major problems of life, contented to ease into a new historical role as a little Sweden.

—*NR*, May 17, 1966, *p. 455*

It must be recalled that under English socialism, all seven of the deadly sins is unemployment.

—ON THE RIGHT, Oct. 27, 1966

In her lingering economic anemia, Britain appears to the Continent more like an elderly lady in need of companionship than a vigorous potential partner.

—*NR*, May 16, 1967, *p. 506*

People are beginning to wish that the voters had been given breathometer tests when they voted in the present government.

—ON THE RIGHT, Oct. 10, 1967

I pause to remark that Mother England must have the worst internal security system in the history of the entire world. It really is a wonder that the Soviet Union hasn't by now got hold of the crown jewels, and maybe even the Prince of Wales.

—ON THE RIGHT, Dec. 14, 1967

What emerges from it all is the infantile barbarism of the oldest parliamentary governing body in the world, England's. ... God save the Queen, she greatly needs His help so long as she is burdened by her present ministers.

—ON THE RIGHT, March 14, 1968

Billie Sol Estes

Billie Sol Estes is a finished confidence man, but the technique is at least as old as the trading described by Gogol in *Dead Souls*. The idea in the Russia of the 1830's was to buy the title to dead slaves still on the census roll on account of bureaucratic inertia, present their names to the bankers, and borrow great sums of money on them. Billie's idea (or one of them) was to present to California finance companies government-guaranteed paper representing hundreds of non-existent storage tanks signed for but not delivered to cooperating farmers.

—*NRB*, May 29, 1962, *p. 4*

Etiquette

At a crowded reception at the Kremlin in the early 1930's, Lady Astor turned to Stalin and asked, "When are you going to stop killing people?" Bishop Sheen once called up Heywood Broun, whom he had never met but whose nihilistic columns he read every day, and told him he wanted to see him. "What about?" asked Broun gruffly. "About your soul," said Bishop Sheen. Now everybody knows you shouldn't talk about gibbets to executioners, especially not when they happen also to be heads of state. And who, having read the literature of decorum, will, in conversation with sinners, bring up the subject of hell? Still, etiquette is the first value only of the society that has no values, the effete society. An occasional disregard for the niceties may bring us face to face with certain facts from which, in his obsessive search for equanimity, man labors to shield himself. Such facts as that Stalin was a murderer, and Broun a cynic ...

—*Up from Liberalism,* p. 129

European Views of American Assassinations

The Ku Klux Klan is as capable of organizing the killing of a President of the United States, the most prominent Negro in the world, and the most prominent liberal politician in the world, as Monaco is of deposing de Gaulle. It is hard for a people whose history is watered with organized and even incestuous connivings for power to imagine individualistic assassination.

—ON THE RIGHT, July 4, 1968

Extremism

Question. How can I avoid being "superpatriotic"? Answer. Be superunpatriotic. Next question?

—*NR,* Jan. 26, 1962, *p. 8*

It is said God enjoys good theater: perhaps the lights will go out half way through a CBS spectacular on the dangers of the Extreme Right.

—*NR,* May 8, 1962, *p. 316*

Isn't All the Way With LBJ an extremist statement?

—*NR,* Oct. 6, 1964, *p. 851*

Rhetorical geometry would suppose that if one acknowledges the category of an "ultra-conservative Republican," one must, for symmetry's sake, acknowledge the existence of an "ultra-liberal Republican," at least in the absence of an altogether arbitrary ordinance prescribing that as one moves left from the ultra-conservative position, one traverses moderate territory, then hits a stone wall and o'erleaps the extreme liberal territory which, geographically, one would suppose would necessarily lie between moderate Republicanism and the Democratic heartland. But the area in question appears to be absolutely unoccupied.

I say absolutely because for years I have scanned the *New York Times* in search of an "ultra-liberal Republican." Not only have I been unrewarded, I have not even discovered, in all of America, from the mountains to the prairies, to the oceans white with foam, a *single* ultra-liberal: not even in the Paleontological Institute at Harvard University.

"Ultra" (or "extreme"), although it is a word of generic applicability, is exlusively reserved a) for the unfashionable Right, and b) as a euphemism for the Communist Left ("the ultra-liberal Paul Robeson . . ."). It is the scarlet letter that perpetually identifies and ghettoizes the intolerable; and any definitive study of the rhetorical folkways of our age will quickly note this dead give-away, around whose usage the entire sweep of contemporary political currents can be charted. The Establishment's hard hold over the rhetorical categories is, in political discourse, its most important weapon.

—*NR*, March 8, 1966, *p. 201*

May we be struck dead, so help us, cross our hearts and hope to die, the *New York Times* of July 29, 1968, on page three, column two, paragraph six, used the word "ultraliberals." A reporter spotting the word dropped everything and sent out a ten-bell to the lexicographical community. But then he resumed reading and, wouldn't you know it, the *Times* contrived a context that robbed the word of all its joy. The Soviet Union, in its dealings with Czechoslovakia, is insisting on the removal from leading government positions in that country of the "ultraliberals." So that ultraliberals have now become the anti-Communists. So we can relax, after all: God's in his heaven, and the *New York Times* hasn't really recognized the existence of an ultraliberal.

—*NR*, Aug. 13, 1968, *p. 782*

"Extremism in Defense of Liberty ..."

Last week Senator Goldwater clarified his famous statement on extremism, which is all right by us although the clarification was unnecessary. Two and one-half months have meanwhile gone by since Adlai Stevenson remarked at Colby College "... even a jail sentence is no longer a dishonor but a proud achievement. Perhaps we are destined to see in this law-loving land people running for office not on their stainless records but on their prison records." In private communications, Mr. Stevenson's aide Clayton Fritchey has explained that Mr. Stevenson has *always* been a law-abiding man, that what he was talking about was "students and others who have been *illegally* arrested, *illegally* fined, and *illegally* jailed." But there are gobs of students and others who have been *legally* arrested, *legally* fined, and *legally* jailed—for breaking laws. It is all right to break such laws, Dr. Martin Luther King said, because they are unjust laws. Adlai Stevenson, having by his incautious formulation suggested that he is aligned with the anarchistic Dr. King, should speak up on the subject. Perhaps some of the influential gentlemen who put so much pressure on Senator Goldwater to clarify his remarks will do as much for Ambassador Stevenson, who after all is America's voice in an international organization that seeks to submit the entire world to the rule of law, even including Martin Luther King.

—NR, Aug. 25, 1964, p. 708

"Extremism in defense of liberty is no vice, moderation in the pursuit of justice is no virtue." "Justice too long delayed is justice denied." "There comes a time when the cup of endurance runs over, and men are no longer willing to be plunged into an abyss of injustice when they experience the blackness of corroding despair." "I have been greatly disappointed with the moderates." The first of these statements was of course Goldwater's, denounced in the *New York Times* as a "Jumble of high-sounding contradictions," and by Governor Rockefeller as "shocking." The succeeding three, which no verbal taxonomist would distinguish as from a different family, are from a single statement by Martin Luther King, uttered a few months before he was given a hero's welcome at the White House, and named Man of the Year by *Time* Magazine. *Quod licet Jovi*, the Romans used to say, *non licet bovi*—what the gods can get away with, the swine cannot. Dr. King is a god in our society; Goldwater is the pauper. Talk about second-class citizenship.

A word about the philosophical content of Mr. Goldwater's apothegm. His words are, concededly, dangerous to live by—because they do not accommodate the necessary distinctions. Notoriously, battle-cries do not. Patrick Henry did not say, "Give me liberty—always understanding that liberty consists in a complex accommodation between the individual on the one hand, and the collectivity, plus objective reality on the other —or death!" By "extremism" Goldwater clearly meant "total dedication"—not bomb-throwing by native *plastiqueurs*, or bloody defiance of oppressive laws. There are, to be sure, occasions for extremism of that kind, as we are forcefully reminded on the fourth day of every July. . . . It is the context that counts, and every man is entitled to his context. In Goldwater's case, the context leaves him with a free conscience, the conscience of a conservative.

—NRB, Aug. 4, 1964, *p. 1*

Fear

It is brinkmanship of the first order to go about the country as Mr. Humphrey is now doing accusing his opponent of "exploiting the fears of the American people." What, pray, are political contests all about, if not to permit candidates to express themselves on how best to allay the fears of the American people? If the American people, A.D. 1968, are not fearful, they are either all insouciant or solipsists.

—On The Right, Sept. 12, 1968

Fifth Amendment

It was the (dissenting) opinion of Justice John Harlan of the Supreme Court that his honorable colleagues constituting the majority played fast and loose with the Fifth Amendment by sneaking it into the police station and leaving it in absolute command of the joint.

—On The Right, June 18, 1966

Foreign Aid

This year we shall have spent over four billion dollars on the moonstruck-ery of our space people. One quarter that sum would have enabled us to buy the wheat of the Canadians and Australians [which they sold to the Soviet Union], stick it in a conspicuous granary, and donate it to the United Nations on the condition that it be made available, free of charge, to any Communist nation that will give convincing proof that it is prepared to live as a peaceful partner in our disordered world. Yea, even to Russia: if Russia will tear down the Berlin Wall, grant free elections in Cuba, withdraw its revolutionaries from South America. A monument that granary could be, to the generous—yet purposive—intentions of the United States: to make economic sacrifices in behalf of world peace and freedom.

—NR, Oct. 22, 1963, *p. 334*

There have been two forms of aid to Latin America by the United States during the past thirty years, direct financial grants . . . and investment by Americans and American companies in Latin America. The results of the former are to say the least exiguous. The results of the latter have been to furnish jobs for 20 per cent of the Latin American labor force.

—NR, April 18, 1967, *p. 392*

Foreign Policy

History will remark that in 1945, victorious and omnipotent, the United States declined to secure for Poland the rights over which a great world war had broken out; and that a mere sixteen years later—who says B, must say C—we broke into panicked flight from the responsibilities of the Monroe Doctrine, which as a fledgling republic we had hurled in the face of the omnipotent powers of the Old World one hundred and forty years ago, back when America, though not a great power, was a great nation. It is the general disintegration of a shared understanding of the meaning of the world and our place in it that made American liberalism possible, and American conservatism inevitable.

—Rumbles, pp. 80–81

. . . the West must probe deeply the foundations on which it has constructed its anti-Communist fortress. For we are losing the third world war. We are losing Asia. Let us hope that however vulnerable we are to

Communist conniving we will not be so unintelligently dogmatic as to continue to contend, even as we come up for the third time, that a few more billions will keep us afloat. Money won't do it. Nor will a hypnotic reliance on Truth. The time is here for an agonizing reappraisal. *National Review* has no facile solution. But we suspect that the answer lies in power. Asia's masses want to be on the winning side. We must act like winners, and this involves changing our entire Asian policy.

—NR, Dec. 21, 1955, *p. 7*

The United States Government is trying to rival the Ford Foundation in philanthropy. It is proposed that we more or less double our give-away program lest, to quote Mr. Chester Bowles, it be said that in the middle of the twentieth century freedom died of a balanced budget. We continue to rely on the stomach theory of Communism. Foreign aid is Bipartisanship's substitute for a foreign policy.

—NR, Jan. 4, 1956, *p. 3*

They called it, immediately after the war, the "bipartisan foreign policy," that is to say, a policy presumptively backed by both Democrats and Republicans, and held immune from normal factional analysis. The trouble with the bipartisanship of 1945–1949 is that it was pretty much bipartisan on *their* side, that is to say, on the side of what we conservatives sometimes call the appeasers; and so in due course, especially after the loss of China, many Republicans and not a few Democrats turned in their bipartisan badges, checked out their six-shooters, and started to fire away at the foreign policy of Mr. Truman and Mr. Acheson.

—Ave Maria, April 7, 1962, *p. 6*

... we didn't, don't, have the nerve to face up to the Communists when the Communists really go to work against our soft underbelly, which is surely the biggest softest underbelly in the history of great nations.

—ON THE RIGHT, Sept. 5, 1964

It is not the function of the United States to guard over the political hygiene of any government, anywhere in the world; but it is most definitely our function to interfere with the establishment of Communist governments, because Communist governments conspire against other countries' freedoms. It is a matter of purely academic concern whether a Communist government is brought in by an individual, by a clique, or by a majority of the voters.

—*NR*, Dec. 14, 1965, *p. 1145*

There is, one repeats, no rational explanation for our behavior. Surrealism is here. Increasingly one wonders whether the irrational formulations aren't the most convincing. American policy needs Newspeak to present itself understandably. I have not seen any improvement on the formulation of Mr. Morrie Ryskind a few years ago when, ruefully reviewing American foreign policy, he concluded that it is the ambition of this country to emerge as the leader of the world's uncommitted nations.

—On The Right, Dec. 18, 1965

The fact of the matter is that there is much that is wrong, benighted, and, cruel in Rhodesia and South Africa; but so is there much of the same in other nations in the world, including African nations, with which the President deals amiably. And the fact of the matter is that any President who attempts to moralize categorically on life in Rhodesia without applying his own strictures to the great imperialist dictatorships of our time, is especially to be disdained because hypocrisy is doubly contemptible when motivated by cowardice. As they would put it in the Pedernales country, pick on somebody your own size.

—On The Right, May 31, 1966

The conservatives who call for bold and radical proposals have something other in mind than the boldness (we would call it recklessness) of trusting to an etiolated Soviet Union to come dreamily to the disarmament table. They fear the general indecisiveness of the day, of which the searing symbol is what so far proves to be Mr. Nixon's empty threat to hit back in Vietnam. These conservatives would be greatly reassured if

Mr. Nixon moved in Vietnam. Not merely because American lives would be saved there. But because that is the type of America the Soviet Union will not attack.

—On The Right, March 25, 1969

Foreign Policy and Fulbright's Law

One wonders how many people who are aware of the great fuss the Senator has kicked up are aware that he propounded a theoretical position on foreign policy which is dear to the conservative heart. The key sentence: *"Insofar as a nation is content to practice its doctrines within its own frontiers, that nation, however repugnant its ideology, is one with which we have no proper quarrel."* ... As theory it is impeccable, calling into question the whole thrust of American foreign policy since that awful moment when Mr. Woodrow Wilson took it into his head to make the world safe for democracy. Senator Fulbright, the influential chairman of the Senate Foreign Relations Committee, is taking the position that we have not, and should not have had in the past, any "proper quarrel" with Trujillo, or Perón, or Salazar, or Franco, or Perez Jimenez, or Chiang Kai-shek, or Duvalier, or Voerword, who do not, and never have, threatened or conspired against the essential interests of the United States. If those people who have applauded Senator Fulbright for the other things he said, would go so far as to register their approval of the Senator's re-affirmation of this traditional doctrine, the occasion would be historic indeed. American foreign policy would henceforward be liberated from the messianic cultural imperialism which has resulted, over the years, in methodological chaos.

—On The Right, April 2, 1964

Fortune Magazine

... perhaps the most exclusive finishing school of the Republican Establishment, *Fortune* Magazine.

—On The Right, June 22, 1967

France

... a relatively small and eternally quarrelsome country in Western Europe, fountainhead of rationalist political manias, militarily impotent, historically inglorious during the past century, democratically bankrupt, Communist-infiltrated from top to bottom, torn in two by the Algerian issue, insouciant toward the fate of her own citizens in Algeria ...

—ON THE RIGHT, March 24, 1964

Free Trade

The whole business of free trade is monstrously complicated. The ideal, which we shall always fall short of, is the abolition of all barriers. Those who believe that conservatives are the natural protectionists and liberals the natural free traders should reflect on the fact that it was Adam Smith, the father of the theory of free enterprise, who was the most ardent free trader of them all; and that it was the head of a socialist government in Great Britain who most recently raised all import duties by a whopping 15%.

—ON THE RIGHT, Jan. 28, 1965

... a massive educational campaign should be initiated to demonstrate the mutual values of free trade. (And I mean the value to everyone concerned. Twenty-three billion dollars, approximately, were earned by American citizens last year from sales for foreign nations.) A profitable enterprise for a Republican Party looking for something constructive to do.

—ON THE RIGHT, Jan. 28, 1965

Last week the British Broadcasting Company denied to an American tenor, Mr. Richard Cassilly, a role in *Aida*, on the grounds that, sniff, there were plenty of qualified British tenors. That, in the land that suckled Adam Smith.

—ON THE RIGHT, Feb. 13, 1968

Freedom

The conservative rhetoric has here and there run ahead of events. Even though I myself take the gloomy view that our society is marching toward totalitarianism, I should not go so far as to say that America is not now, as societies go, free—however gravely I view the restrictions on freedom implicit in, e.g., the progressive income tax, the ban on religious teaching in public schools, the union shop, the FEPCs, the farm laws, etc. Freedom is *not* indivisible. The more freedom the better, which means that some freedom is better than none at all, and more than some is better still. The conservative must, therefore, guard against the self-discrediting generalization that our society is no longer "free," while insisting, as implacably as the liberal does every time a Communist is harassed by a disciplinary law, that not an appropriation is passed by the legislatures, but that our freedom is diminished.

—*Up from Liberalism*, pp. 211–212

Freedom of Travel

. . . it is not the business of the government to prescribe safety precautions for American newspapermen. It is one thing for the government to forbid an official representative to visit China; another to rule that a representative of the *Dallas News* may not go.

—*NR*, Sept. 8, 1956, *pp. 6–7*

Ernest Bevin, a philosopher of the Socialist Party of Great Britain, was asked in 1944 what was his definition of freedom, which definition he thereupon spontaneously gave. "Freedom," he said, "is my right to go to Paddington Station and buy a ticket to any bloody place I choose." One year later Mr. Bevin was a member of a government that denied that freedom to Englishmen, even as it is now denied to them; even as Mr. Johnson now proposes, however tangentially, to constrict it for us by means of taxes on passports, and penalties on days absent from this country.

—ON THE RIGHT, Jan. 9, 1968

Sigmund Freud

How shrewd the man who observed that Sigmund Freud did more to deprive people of their privacy than any man who ever lived. How? By popularizing a set of categories of disturbed behavior into which we tend to slot people whose syndromes we vaguely recognize, inviting ourselves to ignore the infinitely various character of individual human beings.

—NR, June 1, 1965, p. 455

Milton Friedman

I remember adumbrating a plan for the salvation of Harlem back in 1965 —before Mr. Lindsay disposed of the problem—which plan I was forced to disavow, after receiving from Mr. Friedman a *postcard*—imagine, a *postcard*!—illustrating the theoretical error in my proposal. No Bull of Excommunication or notice by John L. Lewis of disaffiliation was ever more direct or more efficacious; Harlem was instantly spared salvation.

—Speech in honor of Leonard Read, delivered Oct. 4, 1968

F--- You!

... it simply isn't possible any longer to *portray* what is going on in so many situations around the country without portraying also the verbal licentiousness of the participants. I remember in Chicago on television, the night the broadcasters gangbanged the Chicago police, and the question of provocation arose and I said that from my own hotel window I had heard the crowd all night long "chanting obscenities" directed at the police, at Mayor Daley, and at LBJ. "Chanting obscenities," I had a sinking feeling, probably meant to most well-behaved listeners that the crowd was saying "Horsefeathers to LBJ," or perhaps even "Down with LBJ," or, the most abandoned among them, "To hell with LBJ." It made a great difference that the listeners should know just exactly what word the demonstrators *were* using, because it introduces an atmosphere of rhetorical totalism the visualization of which is necessary to the understanding of certain events. ... The point remains that the word is used by The Militants precisely because it does still shock. And if they could think of a more shocking word, they would use it. Presumably, that being the law of usage, if their current favorite becomes truly current—if it begins for instance to appear regularly in, say, the columns of the *New York Times*, then, like its French counterpart, it will largely have lost its capacity to arouse attention, and The Kids will have to look for another lollipop.

—*NR*, Oct. 22, 1968, *p. 1052*

Senator William Fulbright

One wonders, sadly, whether the Chairman of the Foreign Relations Committee of the Senate of the United States knows anything at all, but I mean anything at all, about the meaning of Communism, or of the great struggle that roars in the ears of humankind, in the ears, at least, of those who have ears to hear.

—ON THE RIGHT, April 4, 1964

G

John Kenneth Galbraith

Professor Galbraith is horrified by the number of Americans who have bought cars with tail fins on them, and I am horrified by the number of Americans who take seriously the proposals of Mr. Galbraith.

—Up from Liberalism, pp. 207–208

Galbraith is generally recognized as the prime piece of floating real estate in the Kennedy Development Project.

—ON THE RIGHT, June 16, 1966

I remember three years ago arriving at a television station and meeting at the elevator Professor John Kenneth Galbraith, all six feet five of that eminent intelligence, who always gives the impression that he is on very temporary leave of absence from Olympus, where he holds classes on the maintenance of divine standards.

—ON THE RIGHT, Feb. 6, 1968

Galbraith was introduced, and a line straight as a super-highway was quickly constructed by the introducer between Aristotle, Erasmus, Locke, Adam Smith, John Maynard Keynes—and your next speaker. At which point, opening his mouth to speak, the tall, austere Scotsman, for the first time since he was four-and-one-half-years old, froze. A lovely young couple had dashed up to the proscenium, and there shed their raincoats revealing, well, revealing absolutely everything. Eve was rather quickly detained, and the raincoat put back on her shoulders. But Adam bounced up on stage and holding a pig's head in hand, danced like a leprechaun around the silent, not to say awe-struck, Professor Galbraith. Out came the fuzz from the wings (police brutality—everywhere you go, police brutality), and Galbraith finally turned to his speech, but alas, not many people were really listening and, to show how upset he was, he forgot to blame Adam and Eve on Richard Nixon.

—NR, Nov. 19, 1968, *p. 1157*

Generation Gap

Youth is very mixed up—so what else is new. Adults are very mixed up too, which is one of the reasons why the youth are as they are. Let them be. But the responsibility of the adult world is to hang on to one's sanity. Seeing "Hair" makes one just a little prouder of middle class establishmentarian standards.

—ON THE RIGHT, May 7, 1968

Ghostwriters

It could be maintained that "Challenge to the Cities" is in refreshing contrast to books by the typical modern politician, who uses a ghost. One reads the opening pages and concludes that no ghost could possibly have written such sentences as Mr. [Henry W.] Maier's without incurring permanent unemployment. By the time the reader has gone through the book, he is not likely soon again to disparage the profession of ghostwriting.

—New York Times Book Review, Oct. 2, 1966

Ralph Ginzburg

The magazine *Fact* is what a New York louse named Ginzburg does, now that the courts sentenced him to however-many years imprisonment it was for violating the minimal (and they are truly minimal nowadays) laws of decency and obscenity, in his magazine *Eros*, the final number of which featured pictures of interracial coupling. Ginzburg is appealing, of course, and meanwhile has started up a thing called *Fact*, which took some 20 great big display ads in newspapers, under the heading, "Is Barry Goldwater psychologically fit to be President of the United States?" ("1,846 psychiatrists answer this question in the next issue of *Fact* Magazine. . . .") The expense involved in buying back pages of the *New York Times* for that kind of thing cannot possibly be justified in terms of any likely increase in circulation for Ginzburg's stercoricolous journal; thus suggesting that Ginzburg is using political money and, in keeping company with some of the more unscrupulous enemies of Senator Goldwater, has finally found people fit to associate with.

—*NR*, Nov. 3, 1964, *p. 940*

God

We once received an irate letter from a vigilant church group in a small Midwestern town objecting to our use, on a television panel program, of the phrase "Thank God." The churchmen had automatically assumed that anyone who thanked God on a TV panel was blaspheming. We wrote back and said that, strange as it might seem, we had *not* used the word God either blasphemously *or* figuratively. We *meant* to thank God, and we *thanked* Him, and the devil with the complaint.

—*NR*, Sept. 1, 1956, *p. 8*

Arthur Goldberg

What on earth Messrs. Goldberg and [Jacob] Javits would find to argue about in a political contest defies the imagination: one might as well have a debate between the two Smith Brothers on the matter of cough drops.

—ON THE RIGHT, April 6, 1967

Harry Golden

. . . Harry Golden, high priest of left-wing yahooism.

—*NR*, March 27, 1962, *p. 206*

Barry Goldwater

Senator Goldwater's obstinate honesty seems to appall most people who consider it: he is not a man of our time, they seem to say to themselves —and indeed he is not.

—ON THE RIGHT, Sept. 29, 1964

"No one has ever questioned his ability or his dynamic energy. But these very qualities ... have in times of peace caused him to be considered dangerous, and a little uncomfortable to have around. Then, too, [he] has always represented the extreme viewpoint. He has never stood on middle ground—he went all out for anything he advocated." The references are to Winston Churchill, the book *Why England Slept*, the author John F. Kennedy.

—*NR*, Aug. 25, 1964, *p. 708*

Concerning Goldwater, finally, there is not a breath of personal scandal. Even Drew Pearson, who can find scandal in Snow White's relations with the Seven Dwarfs, tried it and failed. It isn't that Pearson is growing feeble. It is that in Goldwater the anti-toxin overwhelms even the most poisonous lance.

—*NR*, Oct. 20, 1964, *p. 904*

I cannot think of him without recalling the occasion when a Dublin newspaper complained that the Lord Mayor of Dublin should attempt to make himself more popular with the people, and William Yeats remarked that surely considering the undisputed eminence of the gentleman involved, it would be more relevant that the people of Dublin should make themselves more popular with the Lord Mayor.

—*NR*, Nov. 30, 1965, *pp. 1127–1128*

Barry Goldwater at Home

Goldwater is the friendliest man in the history of the world, so that when he has work to do, or is conversing with someone, he simply slides the chair back out of sight, secure. The other day he neglected to do so, assuming that the ring at the door, at seven in the morning, could only be the milkman or Western Union. It was a large lady with a large camera, who whinnied with delight on spotting the Republican Presidential candidate of 1964. Could she take a picture of him? Yes, he said politely, but would she mind terribly waiting just a minute until he put on a bathrobe?

—*NR*, Feb. 21, 1967, *p. 184*

The Goldwater Campaign

Senator Goldwater met recently with friends, one of whom reported that the Senator would seek the 1964 Presidential nomination if "a) someone shows him where the money is coming from, b) an organization can display the necessary support, and c) he obtains enough convention delegates." Fair enough, boys?

—*NR*, Jan. 15, 1963, *p. 7*

As the party's nominee, he will force calmer attention to his position than has been given it by the hysteria-ridden who have heretofore acted as though to open their eyes and look at, rather than merely to curse, Senator Goldwater's dream for a better world, is to risk being turned into stone.

—*NR*, June 16, 1964, *p. 478*

As recently as a few weeks ago, when Senator Goldwater was merely the leading Republican candidate rather than the heir presumptive, Walter

Lippmann was writing that his nomination was perhaps the price we must be prepared to pay for democracy. Now he has decided, in a column which will live in the annals of puerility, that the cost of democracy is often all too high, and that nothing less than doom itself awaits the nation and the world if Goldwater becomes President.

—NR, Sept. 10, 1963, *p. 179*

... almost literally Goldwater was forced to run by Americans who seemed, some of them, to be asking primarily for their own emancipation from the decadent East.

—NRB, Jan. 21, 1964, *p. 1*

There is a sense in which Goldwater's campaign is almost necessarily amateurish, and that reason does him and his movement considerable credit. Goldwater's candidacy is altogether uncynical; that is to say, he is seeking first and foremost the popular acceptance of a fresh series of attitudes towards the world and its problems; not, first and foremost, his nomination and election. In the summer of 1961, *Harper's* Magazine revealed that during the presidential campaign the previous year, John Kennedy and his associates paid very close attention to an opinion-evaluating machine that indicated just exactly what it was the voters would most want to hear six weeks later; and the campaign was ori ented to these results. Goldwater disdains that kind of professionalism; so that easy as it would be for any halfbrained man, let alone a success-ful politician like Goldwater, to trim his sails to the popular winds, he has no intention whatever of doing so—and is quite prepared to lose if the nation rejects his views. But there are precious few grounds for concluding that his views are ignorant, by contrast with those others the pursuit of which over a period of 20 years has yielded half the world to the enemy.

—ON THE RIGHT, Feb. 29, 1964

... how can Goldwater speak his mind, considering the determination of so many reporters to distort what he says? The Goldwater campaign seems to suggest that certain subjects are untouchable in American politics—if they are raised by a man of the Right, who, *ex natura*, excites the suspicions of the press. It is questionable whether Senator Goldwater can use the word "nuclear" in any context at all—even to say, "I hate nuclear weapons." ("Senator Goldwater said last night that he hated nuclear weapons. His audience interpreted the Senator's remarks as suggesting that under the circumstances he is especially sorry that, as President, he would probably be called upon to use them ...")

—*NRB*, June 9, 1964, *p. 1*

... the traces to the East having been broken, the Republican Party will never again be dominated by the editorial writers for the *New York Herald Tribune*. Free at last.

—*NR*, June 16, 1964, *p. 479*

This is probably Lyndon Johnson's year, and the Archangel Gabriel running on the Republican ticket probably could not win.

—ON THE RIGHT, June 16, 1964

Our European critics might do well to remind themselves that every time they have got into an inglorious mess, during the past period, an insurgent American voice has bailed them out. Wilson's was a minority voice in America, on the issue of rescuing Europe from the Kaiser. Roosevelt ran athwart the view of the overwhelming majority of his own countrymen when he stirred the country against Hitler. And now an insurgent minority in America seeks to name a Presidential candidate who will stand up to the newest, and most potent threat against Western civilization. It is no more surprising that the English should reject Goldwater, than it was that they for so long have rejected Churchill. But the majority's disapproval is no reason for steady-minded Americans to reject Goldwater, any more than there was any reason for far-seeing Englishmen to yield to the British appeasers.

—NR, June 30, 1964, *p. 526*

Goldwater appears to have won the nomination—fairly, and against unfair means to deprive him of it, i.e., against means that have sought to convince the American people that a vote for Goldwater is tantamount to a vote for War & Depression. The Platform Committee would be wise to leave the platform loose: let it go—as an army of mobile guerrillas, who are working forward, somewhat uncertainly, but with an innate sense of direction, towards the crystallization of a grand objective, which might be breathtaking in its ultimate effect, a triumph of the individual over Ideology and the Machine.

—ON THE RIGHT, July 7, 1964

... the audience cheered, and promised to stay ignorant of Goldwater, and just trust to blind hatred in November.

—NR, Aug. 25, 1964, *p. 715*

... the [Democratic] national leadership was directly involved in the little one-minute spot that is going the rounds of our television screens, featuring a pretty little girl licking an ice cream cone, with audio commentary to the effect that Senator Goldwater wants to resume nuclear tests, which would contaminate the milk, which would contaminate the ice cream, which would contaminate the pretty little girl. Poor little girl. She doesn't know, and John Bailey won't tell her, that Edward Teller announced last week that the United States has developed hydrogen bombs that are 100 per cent free of fall-out: and presumably the little girl is not to be reminded that President Truman and President Eisenhower, whom we know as "moderates," conducted nuclear tests of a very dirty kind during their Administrations, on the grounds that to do so was necessary to the maintenance of the kind of freedom that permits little girls to eat ice cream cones, and big boys to lie about the dangers of doing so.

—NR, Oct. 6, 1964, p. 853

Senator Javits, who did much to confuse the categories in the first place by designating himself a Republican while voting most of the time with Hubert Humphrey, busily engaged himself during 1963 telling people that if Goldwater was nominated, it would be the end of the Republican Party for sure, and not improbably the end of the two-party system. The Senator may very well prove correct. His was, in a sense, a self-justifying prediction of catastrophe. It is like the man who predicts that tomorrow you will be dead—because he plans to shoot you.

—On The Right, Oct. 13, 1964

The liberals are confident of victory. They have every *reason* to be confident: counter-revolution—and that, really, is what Barry Goldwater is talking about—is a sweaty, brawly business, not easy to effect in Nineveh.

—NRB, Nov. 10, 1964, p. 1

In those days American conservatives, dreaming of the glorious possibility of a Goldwater victory, envisioned the scene on the Capitol steps during the Inauguration ceremony. "Do you," says Supreme Court Justice Earl Warren, addressing President-elect Barry Goldwater, "solemnly swear to defend the Constitution of the United States?" Answers President Goldwater: "I do. You're under arrest, Warren."

—On The Right, Feb. 4, 1969

Goldwater . . . will be despised because he is the first voice in the world's political center who is suggesting, implicitly, that life has no meaning in separation from certain ideals.

—On The Right, July 25, 1964

The Goldwater Campaign: The California Primary

The only sadder spectacle than Rockefeller Headquarters was the great transmission room of CBS, where Walter Cronkite, forcing a smile, conceded the defeat of Rockefeller much as if he were conceding the defeat of the Heavenly Hosts. At his side were Theodore White and Lou Harris, authors, respectively, of *The Making of the President* and *The Unmaking of a Pollster.* They took turns weeping, and finally concluded that Rockefeller got the votes of everyone in California who is a Negro, a Jew, a Mexican, and a college graduate, while Goldwater got the votes of every millionaire. Which certainly makes California the land of opportunity!

—*NR*, June 16, 1964, *p. 478*

The Goldwater Campaign: Scranton

Governor Scranton said up at Hartford that what he stood for was a "sane nuclear policy." He is in the tradition of Dwight Eisenhower, all right, who said up in Dartmouth in 1953 that what he wanted was to "be a Big Brother" to the American people. Come to think of it, they have the same speech writer, Malcolm Moos. Come to think of it—no, the mind boggles.

—*NR*, June 30, 1964, *p. 518*

The Goldwater Defeat

It will have been said, by the time these words appear, that Goldwater conservatism is dead dead dead. It is only safe to say that it is dead if one assumes that otherwise the Senator would have been elected. The undertakers are premature, I do believe. . . .

American conservatives should not then, so far as I can see, lose heart; although some of them should, finally and forever, put aside that consoling dogma they have tucked under their pillows ever since Willkie was defeated in 1940, namely, that the Republicans have only to nominate a sure-enough conservative to guarantee a sweep, coast to coast. That little romantic wraith was forever interred by the vote last Tuesday. And henceforward conservatives will, I hope, be forever liberated from the Platonic trance that one has only to make Truth available as an alternative to Error, in order to rest secure. Truth is a demure lady, much too ladylike to knock you on the head and drag you to her cave. She is there, but the people must want her, and seek her out.

—On The Right, Nov. 7, 1964 (written before the election)

And overlying the whole business was the long and tragic shadow of the corpse of John F. Kennedy. A traumatized people cried out for a period of serenity; a good long rest period in the political sanitarium. Oswald had precipitated a bloody convulsion. Goldwater was precipitating an unbloody convulsion, but a convulsion just the same. It seemed more than the average American voter was in a mood to bear. Three Presidents in twelve months is the kind of thing they go for in the banana republics, or the Balkans; not in America.

—NR, Oct. 20, 1964, p. 902

Goldwater's deathly sanction—publicly to state an explicit dissatisfaction with the Republican Party—would collapse the GOP, probably for good and all. That is Goldwater's Big Bertha: but he will probably never fire it, both because of the aforesaid goodnature and because of his sense of devotion to the party.

—On The Right, Dec. 12, 1964

So very many conservatives were weaned on the delusion that we had only to nominate a sure-enough conservative to ensure a national land-

slide, that they cannot now look defeat in the face as indicating what in
fact it is: that the majority of the American people do not, at the present
time, desire a hard conservative as President of the United States. There
is no doubt that Lyndon Johnson is a splendid politician, and that Senator Goldwater is a far worse one (which endears him to at least this
voter). But if Senator Goldwater were as good a politician as Lyndon
Johnson is said by his most extravagant admirers to be, and if Lyndon
Johnson were as poor a politician as Senator Goldwater's most adamant
critics insist he is, I do not believe the vote in November would have been
substantially different. . . . Unless conservatives realize that massive public education must precede any hope of a Presidential victory, they will
never have a President they can call their own. This conservative backed
Senator Goldwater for the Presidency not because I ever thought he
would win the election, but because I believed, and continue to believe
I was correct in believing, that his nomination would do much to crystal-
lize the conservative position in national affairs.

—NR, Jan. 12, 1965, *p. 16*

The cocks will crow, and that is to be expected; so let them go ahead and
do so, as they will full-throatedly in the months and years ahead, about
what a disaster Barry Goldwater was to his cause, his Party, his country,
the world, the United Nations, and the Milky Way.

—ON THE RIGHT, Dec. 31, 1964

Graft and Corruption

If you were running for, say, mayor of New York, which would you
prefer, a twenty thousand dollar sinecure as adviser to the International
Ladies Garment Workers' Union Retirement Fund—or the official support of New York's Labor Council? Politicians oblige people, groups,
corporations, labor union councils, Elks, Knights of Columbus, and bar
associations. The primitive notion that they tend to oblige only those
who pay them money, is the notion that skewered poor Mr. Fortas. It
is more difficult to approach a justice of the supreme court other than by
money for the obvious reasons that he is not standing for reelection. But

there are other ways: an Abe Fortas Foundation for Underprivileged Supreme Court Justices comes readily to mind. Testimonial dinners, yearly wedding banquets for Justice Douglas: there is no end to the ingenuity of human benevolence.

—On The Right, May 22, 1969

Billy Graham

If only Mr. Kennedy had founded Christianity, one would safely make decisions at Mr. Graham's rallies, without fear of aspersion by the social scientists.

—*NR*, Feb. 21, 1967, *p. 183*

The Great Society

... the implicit popular wall against doctrinaire collectivism, which true enough had stood largely firm since the end of the New Deal, has been breached. The people, counting themselves well off, are prepared to see the budget rise a few billions, and their social security taxes increased by a few hundred dollars; and they appear uninterested in the presumptive case for anti-statism, which is the presumptive case for freedom. Trouble ahead.

—*NRB*, April 27, 1965, *p. 1*

The key phrase, for cryptographers who desire to learn the meaning of the Society that is supposed to shape our future, is the following, which you will see repeated time after time: "The Great Society is concerned not with the quantity of our goods but the quality of our lives." ... what it does mean is that the Government of the United States, under Lyndon Johnson, proposes to concern itself over the quality of American life. And this is something very new in the political theory of free nations. The quality of life has heretofore depended on the quality of the human beings who gave tone to that life, and they were its priests and its poets, not its bureaucrats.

—NR, Sept. 7, 1965, p. 760

The Greek Islands

There are very good ferry facilities to get you around the Aegean but of course there is no substitute for your own boat, which can be inexpensive but usually isn't, and the mobility you thus achieve. Many of the islands have ferry service only once or twice a week, so that the adventurer who gets off and decides after an hour or two that the old Olympian god overtoyed with *this* island, and made quite a muck of it, might find no means of getting out for s-i-x days, so that if you are such, you had better bring along *War And Peace,* the *Forsythe Saga,* and *Ulysses.* The medium-priced alternative is to tour the islands aboard one of the live-in passenger cruising ships, which make deliberate stops at most of the islands, but move on before the passenger with the lowest threshold of boredom is likely to fret. The very best way is on your own *sail* boat. . . . And then go off, and sail about these islands, poor, scrawny, white, history-laden, contented, calloused, irresistible, unforgettable.

—NR, July 2, 1968, p. 667

Greek Junta

No Constitution will ever produce a divine and eternal equilibrium between freedom and order. Papadopoulos is not likely to succeed where Plato and Aristotle failed.

*—*ON THE RIGHT, *June 25, 1968*

Dick Gregory

. . . the vote for Mr. Gregory when he ran for mayor in Chicago a year ago, with by the way the support of Martin Luther King, was approximately 3 per cent. Never mind, the point of this dispatch is of course that Mr. Gregory is more popular among genteel young white aristocrats than he is among the generality of his people, who are too wise, and perhaps too grateful, to applaud the perversion that the United States is the most racist country in the world, bar none; and too intelligent to suppose that whatever its faults, the best way to cope with them is to burn the nation down.

—ON THE RIGHT, Dec. 26, 1968

"Group Dynamics"

It was via "group dynamics" that the White House Education Conference was led by the nose to a prestipulated consensus calling for federal aid to education. We are relieved to see that the liberals have thus resolved the thorny conflict that sometimes arises between the bull-headed masses and the enlightened elite. Congratulations!

—*NR*, Dec. 21, 1955, *p. 4*

Gun Controls

What a great many people in the United States want to have guns around for is in case they should need to use them for self-protection, in the event of a complete breakdown in law and order. Those who disdain that sentiment should perhaps imagine themselves a) with a gun, and b) without a gun, living with children in a tenement building and spotting an arsonist down the hall. In such contingencies, it is natural to desire speedier means of relief than a telephone call to the American Civil Liberties Union.

—ON THE RIGHT, June 29, 1968

H

Haight-Ashbury

... the biggest broken record in America ...

—*NR*, Oct. 3, 1967, *p. 1058*

Harper's (when John Fischer was editor)

... Mr. Fischer (and in this respect he is typical of the whole class of liberal publicists) sees himself caught up, within the pages of his magazine, in exhilarating controversy involving alternatives of cosmic moment. In fact he presides, as editor of *Harper's*, over endless discussions which added together do not generate enough noise to wake a fellow exurbanite suffering from insomnia. A magazine like *National Review*, is, in short, foredoomed to horrify such a man, whose idea of a chiller is a gladiatorial contest to the death between, say, Arthur Schlesinger, Jr. and Richard Rovere on the Challenge of Our Times. And horrify him we do.

—*NR*, Aug. 1, 1956, *p. 7*

Averell Harriman

... Averell Harriman, who can accomplish less in more time than anybody in America.

—On The Right, July 22, 1965

105

Mr. Averell Harriman has received considerable if not considered publicity in recent days as our emissary to Paris where we are to discuss with the North Vietnamese the future of South Vietnam. On a number of points there is general agreement, namely that Mr. Harriman is a stout-hearted gentleman bred in the Yankee tradition, who knows how to bargain tenaciously. The legendary Harriman sleeps little, remembers everything, and comes home to Washington with the bacon. Unfortunately, as the spoil-sports say, there is the record. It is rather dismal. . . . The point is: Ave is something less than Talleyrand, so don't be too disappointed. And if you're South Vietnamese, batten down the hatches.

—On The Right, May 14, 1968

Harvard

[Student Council President Howard J.] Phillips was warned by the Student Council not to go about the country sowing the impression that the student body at Harvard is conservative. Harvard is very urbane, and can take almost anything, as everyone from Fidel Castro to Gypsy Rose Lee has, over the years, found out; but not *that*. . . . To begin with, no one in his right mind would believe the Harvard student body is "conservative," and therefore anyone who so presumes, on the exiguous basis of what Howard Phillips believes, is so invincibly innocent as to be incapable of salvation, even by so mighty an instrument of edification as a vote of censure by the Harvard Student Council.

—*NR*, June 3, 1961, *p. 348*

. . . .For further details, address Freak House, Harvard U., which by the way is suffering a population explosion.

—*NR*, Aug. 28, 1962, *p. 131*

. . . Henry Kissinger, who is the anti-Communist at Harvard . . .

—On The Right, April 13, 1968

Harvard University—the Riots

Will it—the melodrama has us at the precipice—actually *punish* the malefactors? Or will it go the usual route and produce a professor of whatever who will patiently explain in behalf of the faculty why it was —perhaps deplorable—but in certain ways understandable—taking every factor into consideration—never losing sight of the psychological strains of the day—bearing in mind the necessary consequences of the Industrial Revolution—to say nothing of the French Revolution—why it is perhaps understandable that some students should feel it necessary to sling college deans over their shoulders, march them down the stairs of the Administration Building, and fling them to the ground. After all, they did not fling them into the Charles River, which suggests the triumph of moderation. Up Harvard.

—On The Right, April 17, 1969

Heaven and Hell

I recall with pleasure a dialogue several years ago between the journalist Ralph de Toledano and his publishers. They had sent Toledano the proof sheets on his latest novel. In going over them he noticed that wherever the word Heaven or the word Hell appeared, they had not been capitalized, as the manuscript had prescribed, but appeared instead in small letters. Toledano painstakingly corrected each of them, elevating them once again to upper case; and sent back the proofs. He received a telephone call. "Ralph," said the publisher, "we have a set of style rules over here we must observe. Why do you insist on capitalizing Heaven and Hell?" "Because," replied Toledano evenly, "they're places. You know, like Scarsdale."

—*Up from Liberalism*, p. 131

Hell

. . . the only 4-letter word that nowadays shocks the courts.

—On The Right, June 30, 1964

Lillian Hellman

Lillian Hellman, the playwright who used to express herself politically by joining Mr. Stalin's little front organizations, and who declined in 1952 to say whether or not she was a Communist, jumped to her feet in protest and said that she wondered just how two people such as Mr. [George] Kennan and herself could have come from the ranks of the same generation. She defended the young students Mr. Kennan had criticized as far better people than her own generation had been, notwithstanding their foibles, adding, "Since when is youth not allowed to be asses?" To which the embarrassed company did not make the obvious comment that surely for at least as long as old ladies are allowed to be asses.

—ON THE RIGHT, Dec. 7, 1968

General Hershey

General Hershey's recent statement to the effect that draft boards should reclassify students who engage in unruly protests against the Vietnam War is to say the least unfortunate. . . . If the laws against civil disobedience are going to be tightened, or enforced, by all means let us go after the students who are guilty of civil disobedience. But to go after them by threatening instant conscription is to fall into the fascistic temptation for instant action which President Harry Truman flirted with 20 years ago when he proposed to draft into the army illegal strikers. The President's furious bill was stopped dead in Congress by a resolute conservative, Senator Robert Taft, who earned favorable notice in John F. Kennedy's *Profiles in Courage* for his cool constitutionality during that period of inflamed Democratism. Cool Republicans should note, and speak back to General Hershey.

—ON THE RIGHT, Nov. 21, 1967

Hippies

In the wake of yet another disappearance of a teen-ager into the mortal coils of the flower world in Greenwich Village, where love is exercised through rape made tolerable by drugs and abstract declarations of fellowship with the North Vietnamese, one wonders anew about the pretensions of Progress. The hippies are this season's version of the noble savages whose intimidation by society so grieved Jean-Jacques Rousseau. The hippies, or so goes the cant, are working in their own way to shrug off the stultifying accretions of modern life, to search anew for that primitive purity which has been lost by the conventions of middle class, bourgeois life. There are those who believe that nonsense.

—ON THE RIGHT, Nov. 9, 1967

The stage notes are explicit. "Hair," which is called an "American tribal love Rock musical," is about "what's happening now. The tribes are forming, establishing their own way of life, their own morality, ideologies, their own mode of dress, behavior, and the use of drugs, by the way, has a distinct parallel in ancient cultures, in tribal spiritual tradition, both east and west." Indeed it does, and whoever said that the hippies are any different from the Adamites?

—ON THE RIGHT, May 7, 1968

James Hoffa

The judge seems to suspect there was something corrupt going on in the jury room, which is a most natural thing to suspect, considering that if Jimmy Hoffa actually sat in Memphis for nine whole weeks without corrupting somebody, it would probably be for the first time since he was six. Though the official announcement has not been made, no doubt the government will retry the case, hoping next time to find a jury all of whose members will do their duty, even if Diogenes has to be awakened to find them.

—*NRB*, Jan. 8, 1963, *p. 3*

Paul G. Hoffman

There is an indisputable seemliness in the nomination of Paul G. Hoffman as a representative to the United Nations. Indeed, the President might have done better to *commit* him to the United Nations, for that is the logical habitat for a restless ideologue who has for years looked to centralized political authority as the source of all effective social action.

—*NR*, Aug. 1, 1956, *p. 5*

House Committee on Un-American Activities

Professor S. says, "If the reputation of even *one* [his emphasis] honest, innocent individual has been tarnished by the Committee, then I feel that whatever good, if any, which the Committee might have effected has been more than counter-balanced, and the Committee has thereby outlived its usefulness"—and who knows, Professor R. may also believe that if even *one* honest, innocent individual has been sent to jail under the common law, we should abandon the common law, as having outlived its usefulness.

—*NR*, Jan. 16, 1962, *p. 17*

Housing

The government has practically nothing to do with houses, if you consider government-built or subsidized houses as a percentage of the whole. (Between 1950 and 1960, free enterprise built 18,000,000 housing units, while the government, net, destroyed 100,000.) The people of America come within reach of houses as a result of their own exertions, and as a result of the disposition of other people to save. What makes it difficult for people to build their houses is: a) taxes (taken by the government); b) inflation (caused by the government); and c) restrictive labor union policies (protected by the government). The most useful thing the government could do to place decent homes within the reach of its people, is go away.

—ON THE RIGHT, Jan. 23, 1968

[From Chairman Bill's advice to the platform committees of the 1968 Republican and Democratic conventions:] The public housing program and the urban renewal programs suffer from advanced bureaucratism, and from a failure to appreciate the reserves of the private sector. In 1940, 49% of American living units were judged below standard. In 1950, 37%. In 1960, 19%. By 1970, the number will be down to 7.7%. During the period 1950–1960, when nearly 18.5 million new dwelling units were being constructed, urban renewal supplied only 28,000 units, less than one-fifth of one percent of the whole. And during the period that the federal government built these, it tore down 126,000 units: so that the government during that period was a net destroyer of nearly 100,000 units of living quarters in which the poor had lived. The case grows for taking the government out of the housing business altogether, and permitting the poor to find their own quarters and pay for them if necessary out of funds that come in from general federal and state welfare subsidies.

—ON THE RIGHT, May 21, 1968

Irving Howe

"Blessed are the meek, for they shall inherit the earth." Suppose that were told today to a congregation of American Negroes and it were left to Mr. Howe to make comment. He would denounce the passage as false in fact (have the Negroes, meek for so long, inherited the earth?), inept in logic (how does it follow that meekness conduces to ownership of the earth?), impudent in morals (it is wrong to urge on a people acquiescence in their servile condition), and un-Christian in spirit (should not a Christian hunger and thirst after righteousness?). Passages which are allegorical, let along paradoxical in structure, are not written for social anthropologists to stare at dumbly.

—*NR*, Dec. 15, 1964, *p. 1102*

... Irving Howe, editor of the socialists' *Dissent*, takes his pleasures mostly from mugging the United States.

—ON THE RIGHT, Dec. 5, 1968

Hubert Humphrey

Senator Humphrey is a cynic of the kind who believes cynicism to be the only truly healthy political response. Rather like the morally unoriented man who, it is said, read *Uncle Tom's Cabin* through and concluded that Simon Legree was the hero.

—ON THE RIGHT, August, 1964

Mr. Hubert Humphrey announces that we should make love, not anti-Communism, and calls for a new era of international relations, which presumably would reach a climax of joy under a Humphrey Administration.

—ON THE RIGHT, July 18, 1968

The point is that the hard left has pretty well decided to say no to Mr. Humphrey, and he is quite desperate about it. So desperate that he is swivelling all over the place and, since he tends in any case to freneticism, has managed to appear like a nervous breakdown.

—ON THE RIGHT, Oct. 5, 1968

... it is certainly predictable that future schoolboy examinations will not include the question "Answer, true or false, did Hubert Humphrey advocate unilateral cessation of the bombing when he ran for President in 1968?" Or perhaps, in our permissive age, the question will be used. It is a fine student-coddler, because both answers are correct.

—ON THE RIGHT, Oct. 19, 1968

The Hungarian Revolt

The collapse of the Hungarian revolt and the failure of the United States Government overtly to assist the revolutionaries has made explicit a quandary that has for years implicitly plagued American foreign policy. West German and French newspapers have now published charges that the United States, through its semi-official Radio Free Europe, incited the Hungarians to revolt, and then refused to help them once they had done so. Mr. Frank J. Abbot, information director of Radio Free Europe, rushed forward to insist that his organization had done no such thing— had not, presumably, urged the enslaved peoples to exert themselves to regain freedom. "We have presented nothing but objective news and commentaries," he said. "We never urged anyone to revolt." Well then what *is* the policy of Radio Free Europe toward the satellite peoples? To re-enact the story of Tantalus? To hold out the objectively described joys of freedom to its listeners, but in a context that precludes their reaching for that freedom?

—NR, Nov. 24, 1956, *p. 3*

We do not minimize the tragedy of Hungary. But we warn against the highly predictable reaction to the catharsis we are now experiencing. In due course, weeks, or months from now, we shall be seeing Great Changes in the Soviet Union, as the result of this speech, or that defection, or the other "concession"; and, acting on the assumption of that change, we shall be lured, once again, to a common meeting place, to discuss our joint aspirations and pledge our mutual devotion to the cause of peace and freedom.

—NR, Nov. 24, 1956, *p. 5*

We wish a national moratorium could be declared on verbal and written criticism of Communism and Communists. We wish that every politician, every orator, every editorial writer, every preacher would, one morning, stop deploring any act of the Soviet Union, or aspect of Communism. In the sudden stillness, we would realize how empty has been our "opposition" to Communism, for in that stillness we would hear, in dreadful clarity, only the bustling wheels of normalcy, and know the absence of any meaningful act of resistance; and, without the solace of our rhetoric, we might be ashamed.

—NR, Nov. 17, 1956, *p. 4*

Huntley-Brinkley

The night John Kennedy was shot, we found ourselves staring, incredu-
lous, at Huntley and Brinkley, one of them saying to the other, What
could you expect except violence in a country in which a prominent
national magazine [*National Review*] "comes out for" hanging Earl Warren? "Of course," said David to Chet or Chet to David, "they pretended
they said it in jest. . . . but . . ." But?. . . Did Stephen Decatur *really* mean
to damn the torpedoes to eternal perdition? What did the torpedoes ever
do to him? Ah, my lords and oh, my lieges, what a dreadful time we are
going to have maintaining the robustness of the English language. It is
only obscenity that you can get away with these days. . . . Hang it all
(okay). Hang 'em all (no: Huntley-Brinkley no like).

—*NR*, July 2, 1968, *p. 644*

I

Immigration

... what is the point in encouraging immigration when, at home, we are encouraging birth control? We have the highest birth rate among the industrialized nations, and the highest capitalization per job; there is overcrowding in the cities, and unemployment always threatens. We are hardly in a position to help significantly any nation also suffering from unemployment or overcrowding by accepting twenty thousand of its citizens per year. But by accepting twenty thousand of everyone's citizens per year, we are in a position to damage ourselves; and there is no reason for a nation to seek to damage itself. No other nation whose population is deemed sufficient for its needs, does it—not England, not Italy, not Switzerland, not Germany, not France. Why us?

—ON THE RIGHT, Aug. 28, 1965

Impeach Earl Warren

Mr. Welch has called off a campaign which once he considered absolutely crucial to the success of his general enterprise. It remains for a lot of conservatives the bitterest pill of recent years that the prestige of Mr. Warren increased in direct ratio to the intensity of Mr. Welch's campaign against him. Not so many years ago just before Mr. Welch decided to impeach the Chief Justice, the reputation of the Warren Court had sunk so low as to have provoked the explicit censure of the majority of the justices of the supreme courts of individual states, and of such learned scholars as Edward Corwin and Learned Hand. But the proposal that Warren be impeached struck so many people as so patently inappropriate

115

that his critics found themselves muting their criticism lest by association they be linked with the fanatic from Belmont who believed that poor old Eisenhower was of all things a Communist agent ("Eisenhower isn't a Communist,"—Russell Kirk's rejoinder is still the classic—"he is a golfer"). When one thinks of all that energy spent, all those dollars squandered on speeches, and prizes, and literature, and billboards: it is a special irony that the situation contributed not to the weakening of the influence of Earl Warren, but to the consolidation of his power and prestige! If one were to proceed to analyse the whole episode by Birchite logic, one would conclude that the movement to impeach Earl Warren, which after nine years' effort was unable to enlist the support of a single Congressman, was a Communist plot intended to discredit the opposition to Mr. Warren.

—On The Right, Nov. 14, 1967

India

India's position, as spoken over the past decade, is that any form of Communist imperialism is perfectly okay except Communist imperialism against India. It was perfectly okay for the Reds to take over Eastern Europe, perfectly okay for Khrushchev to confirm his colonialism over Hungary by sending his tanks there, perfectly okay for the Red Chinese to overrun Tibet; but most definitely *not* perfectly okay for the Red Chinese to invade India, as they did in 1962, during which period the Indians salivated for those American weapons whose use they condemn whenever they are employed to keep people other than themselves free.

—On The Right, April 27, 1965

Individualism

Socialize the individual's surplus and you socialize his spirit and creativeness; you cannot paint the *Mona Lisa* by assigning one dab each to a thousand painters.

—*Up from Liberalism*, p. 228

Integration

It does not seem to occur to anyone to remark that the exodus of white middle class families from the cities, the rate of which has trebled in the past three years, is above all things an indication of the lengths to which people intend to go in order to avoid certain conditions. It is utterly useless to moralize about it: the people who dominate America have written their position on the matter of forcible integration with their feet. The father who is willing to leave the city where he grew up, where he holds down his job, to endure the expenses of moving, of reacclimation, of buying or renting a new home, is expressing himself about as directly as anyone can. To criticize him for being uncharitable, let alone to attempt to devise laws that would rob him of the economic freedom to make his decision, is as useless as to criticize politicians for seeking to please their constituencies, or to attempt to devise laws which would force politicians to speak the truth.

—ON THE RIGHT, March 11, 1969

Intellectual Probity

The intellectual probity of a person is measured not merely by what comes out of him, but by what he puts up with from others.

—*Up from Liberalism*, pp. 42–43

Intellectuals

... in this country there are two consensuses, that of the people (broadly speaking) and that of the intellectuals (narrowly speaking).

—*Rumbles*, p. 26

I am obliged to confess that I should sooner live in a society governed by the first two thousand names in the Boston telephone directory than in a society governed by the two thousand faculty members of Harvard University. Not, heaven knows, because I hold lightly the brainpower or knowledge or generosity or even the affability of the Harvard faculty: but because I greatly fear intellectual arrogance, and that is a distinguishing characteristic of the university that refuses to accept any common premise. In the deliberations of two thousand citizens of Boston I think one would discern a respect for the laws of God and for the wisdom of our ancestors such as doesn't characterize the thought of Harvard professors —who, to the extent that they believe in God at all, tend to believe He made some terrible mistakes which they would undertake to rectify; and, when they are paying homage to the wisdom of our ancestors, tend to do so with a kind of condescension toward those whose accomplishments we long since surpassed.

—*Rumbles*, pp. 134–135

I have always believed that the mental and spiritual health of the average American is far better than that of the American intellectual who spends his life disdaining his fellow countrymen. But I do not doubt that the poison diffuses from our poets to our centurions: that Lyndon Johnson, who would himself go for broke for this country, does not realize that he is under the influence of men whose ardor for America is no more kindleable than a misogynist's for the Venus de Milo. We are paying the price, in our foreign policy, for years of attrition against an honorable American self-pride.

—On The Right, Jan. 21, 1965

[De Gaulle] ceases, really, to be interesting. Instead, his influence is interesting, and we have now the extraordinary spectacle of complete puppetization of his cabinet. If it were the Politburo, whose unanimity was recorded by Josef Stalin or even Alexei Kosygin, that would be one thing. But de Gaulle's cabinet includes Andre Malraux, perhaps the principal genius of Europe: and for him to go along with de Gaulle's mischievous puerility concerning Canada is to record, for the millionth time, the infinite servility of the intellectuals.

—On The Right, Aug. 5, 1967

Internal Security

There *is* an issue bearing on Communists in government, and it is not wished away simply because all sides agree that they are against Communists in government. Everyone is against Communists in government. The question is how to keep them out. Painful and costly experience has taught us that the only way in which an effective security system can be maintained is by resolving all reasonable doubts as to an employee's loyalty or reliability in favor of the government.

—NR, Sept. 29, 1956, *p. 5*

A security program is not a civil rights program; it is a security program. Its purpose is not to affirm the rights of individual employees, but to put forward the claims of collective security. It is as foolish to speak about the rights of an individual to his job as superior to the requirements of security, as it is to speak of the rights of the soldier as superior to the demands of an order on the battlefield. ... When there are reasonable doubts about an employee's reliability or loyalty, they should be resolved in favor of the government.

—NR, May 22, 1962, *pp. 353–354*

International Negotiations

What matters about conferences isn't so much whether they're held; it's who we send there. If President Johnson were to send someone like Chester Bowles to argue with somebody like Chou En-lai, the entire nation might well get down on its knees and pray in our hour of peril. If we sent someone like John L. Lewis, we could hope he'd return with Mrs. Chou En-lai.

—On The Right, April 13, 1965

Irish Catholics

To Professor Eric Goldman, Princeton University. Dear Professor Goldman: You write in your review of *Senator Joe McCarthy* by Richard

Rovere that McCarthy's popularity was partly due to "the Irish Catholic's susceptibility to theories of conspiracy." Should one not reject the notion that the Irish believe in conspiracies just as one rejects the notion that the Jews participate in them? Eh, Goldman?
/s/ William Francis Buckley Jr.

—*NR*, August 1, 1959, *p. 229*

Israel

At this writing Israel has okayed the request of the State Department to permit American Army planes to fly over its territory to Jordan, but yesterday the answer was No, as it was a few months ago in connection with another similar request, and as it may be tomorrow. The United States has done enough favors for Israel, it seems to us, to entitle us to expect that any request for "overfly" rights should be automatically granted. We have, after all, the Ultimate Weapon. If Internal Revenue started to disallow tax exemption of gifts to the United Jewish Appeal, Israel wouldn't be able to pay the cable-cost of sassing our State Department.

—*NR*, Aug. 30, 1958, *p. 147*

Perhaps we should sign that mutual defense pact with Israel—if only for our own self-protection.

—*NR*, June 27, 1967, *p. 679*

The American people have been pro-Israel over the years for the best of reasons, admiring as we have those qualities in the Israeli enterprise which so closely correspond with those of the early Americans who doggedly established themselves on this continent.

—On The Right, Jan. 7, 1969

J

Jacob Javits

Jacob Javits, meanwhile, having not a chance in the world to wrest the Republican nomination away from Rockefeller, came to the end of *his* period of deliberation, and announced that, on reflection, he would not seek the governorship for himself. He had a condition, however. Rockefeller must not advance himself for the presidency or the vice presidency in 1968. Because the GOP needs "new faces." What would be a new face for the GOP? "Mine would be a new face" for the GOP said Javits. It certainly would. So would Mario Savio's.

—ON THE RIGHT, May 5, 1966

Senator Javits instantly did his best to discourage any discussion of Rockefeller as a presidential candidate. "Governor Rockefeller," he told a panel of experts, "is a 'man of his word,' so that"—and here Javits indelibly, though no doubt unintentionally, underscored the difference between the word of non-politicians and the word of politicians: "I think he means it." Javits went on to confess his widely known dislike for Nixon ("they rarely run race-horses after they're six or seven"). And to express what might be called a velleity for Governor Romney. The Senator's genuine enthusiasms are normally confined to himself.

—ON THE RIGHT, Nov. 15, 1966

Senator Javits of New York found in the election a triumphant repudiation of conservatism, though when pressed on the subject he started to dribble off into vacuities, in which he is greatly at home.

—ON THE RIGHT, Nov. 15, 1966

... Senator Javits is a splendid symbol of the diminution in the prestige of the ultra-liberal Republicans. And his anguish is especially acute in the light of his having so recently lost his heart to himself as Vice President in 1968. Indeed, Sen. Javits had told an interviewer earlier in the week that frankly, he believes himself "entitled to national consideration." Why? Because he has been—brace yourselves—the Republican Party's chief "ideologist" over the past twenty years (if indeed he were, he would be entitled to be tarred and feathered on national TV).

—*NR*, Dec. 27, 1966, *p. 1304*

... Senator Jacob Javits is bugging out as a sponsor of the Committee of One Million, which is devoted to the policy of maintaining pressure on Communist China—diplomatic, economic, and cultural—pending the liberation of the Chinese people ... "I do feel," says the Senator, "that the Committee has played a most useful role ... and whatever the decision as to its continuance, this should be gratifying to its officers and members." The planted axiom is that without Jacob Javits as a sponsor the Committee of One Million is likely to die. If so it will not be because it has lost its heart or its head; it has merely lost its liver.

—*NR*, Jan. 10, 1967, *pp. 14–16*

Talking of debates, the most competent, the most exciting, the most tense that could possibly be staged, is one between Mr. Javits when speaking downstate and Mr. Javits when speaking upstate. I cannot imagine which of them would win. Perhaps, as someone predicted about a previous presidential election, they would both surely lose.

—ON THE RIGHT, Oct. 29, 1968

Walter Jenkins

A man who does the kind of thing Mr. Jenkins did is unstable. "Instability" is more than a catch-all cliché. It is a psychic disorder which can result in distorted visions of reality, and the incapacitation of the individual's ability to govern his life around the conventional hierarchy of loyalties. A man who for the sake of a moment's gratification will risk his future, the happiness and honor of a wife and six children, the career of the President of the United States, who is also his beloved friend and patron, is a man whose capacity for misjudgment causes chills of apprehension in every American who meditates on the kind of damage that such a man, operating out of the very ganglion of Western strength in the White House, could do, when presented with temptation. The point is that Mr. Jenkins' nervous disorder, combined with his role in government, might very well have jeopardized the national security.

—NR, Nov. 3, 1964, *p. 947*

Pope John

How curious that, by and large, the same group of people who are busy condemning what they understood as the silence of Pius XII over the fate of the Jews under Hitler, acclaimed what they understood as the silence of Pope John over the fate of Christians and Jews under Khrushchev and Mao.

—NR, Aug. 25, 1964, *p. 713*

... Pope John appealed most strongly to "liberals," and Pope Paul is appealing more strongly to "conservatives." Pope John was so ardently admired, for instance, by Robert Hutchins, who is sort of the ultimate liberal, that he convened the clan last winter and, after a three-day ceremony, Pope John was ordained as a democratic institution.

—On The Right, Sept. 30, 1965

Lyndon Baines Johnson: After Two Weeks As President

The editors of *National Review* regretfully announce that their patience with President Lyndon B. Johnson is exhausted.

—*NR*, Dec. 17, 1963, *p. 509*

Lyndon Baines Johnson

It is widely known that whenever Senator Johnson feels the urge to act the statesman at the cost of a little political capital, he lies down until he gets over it.

—*NR*, June 21, 1958, *p. 6*

The new President of the United States gave a speech at the closing session of the General Assembly which—which, to quote Randall Jarrell's reaction to another speech—you had to hear it, not to believe it. It is only 1,500 words long, yet managed to exemplify almost every shortcoming in modern liberal expression: vagueness; pretentiousness; inelegance, rhetorical and intellectual. It did not come near to rivaling the more or less disciplined indiscipline of Mr. Kennedy's lofty bombast. Its reliance on the cliché must have affronted even the UN professionals, who preside over the greatest cliché-distillery the world has ever seen.

—*NR*, Dec. 31, 1963, *p. 554*

... Johnson's personality is not of the kind that demands lionization, any more than the omnicompetent president of the local Elks does; and for this too, many people are glad. For one thing it spares them the sense of profanation, that someone should so soon be occupying the dead hero's bed. For another, it spares them the necessity of a fresh emotional commitment, after the emotionally exhausting one they so recently endured.

—ON THE RIGHT, Feb. 13, 1964

Lyndon Johnson, for all his simplicity, is acquiring some kingly habits. Wherever he goes nowadays he seems to have got into the habit of making a royal gift, like the kings of yore who when visiting their provinces would scatter about a chestload or two of ducats among the peasants, as evidence of their royal favor. Considering how much Mr. Johnson is given to traveling about, there is some fear for the endurance of the patrimony. His trip to Appalachia cost the royal exchequer one billion dollars. When he went up to the World's Fair to speak to the Amalgamated Clothing Workers he was not in a munificent frame of mind, and dropped therefore a mere million dollar gift to the cause of juvenile delinquency in Harlem.

—NR, June 2, 1964, *p. 439*

Someone recently remarked that if America's liberals had been informed in 1960 that the race in 1964 would be between Lyndon Johnson and Barry Goldwater, they would probably have marched out into the ocean and drowned themselves. . . . But when Mr. Kennedy was killed, Lyndon Johnson recognized that he would be regarded by his most vocal constituents much as Hamlet's uncle was when he went to bed between incestuous sheets. Accordingly, a new Johnson was born. Within minutes, or so it seemed, he breathed life into the civil rights bill. He went to New York and gave a speech so far gone in UN-unction as might have struck even Mrs. Roosevelt as fulsome. Medicare . . . Anti-poverty . . . Increased social security . . . See the Yellow Pages of the ADA Directory; practically everything was quickly bought by Lyndon Johnson on becoming President.

—NR, Oct. 20, 1964, *p. 902*

. . . he wants to stop Communism by appearing on Russian TV—he would more likely stop whatever is left of the Resistance Movement. . . .

—NR, Jan. 26, 1965, *p. 56*

Malice is not necessarily the motive of Mr. Johnson's detractors. Some people consider it a charitable explanation for another man's dissent from their own point of view to say of him that he is not, poor thing, actually quite all there. . . . I do not deny that Lyndon Johnson's ego corresponds to his fearful appetite to run our lives for us, to arrange for our education, for our old age, for our poor, for our rich, for our culture, for our labor union policy, for our droughts, for our floods, for our bridges and for our subways; and conservatives in this country have every reason in the world to project from that vanity a true threat to the survival of our local institutions. But all conservatives must, I think, join in resenting the insinuations that Mr. Johnson is just plain off his rocker. We can do this safely without being drawn into the orbit of Mr. Jack Velenti's recent paean on Mr. Johnson, which he should indeed have saved for such a moment as it becomes relevant to nominate Mr. Johnson for sainthood.

—On The Right, July 17, 1965

He is a man of his most recent word . . .

—*NR*, Aug. 24, 1965, *p. 714*

But Lyndon Johnson has a way of convincing himself that whatever he does is transcendently right, and subsumes, in its higher morality, his previous positions.

—On The Right, Sept. 4, 1965

The Presidential Pride . . . surpasseth, in its magnitude, anything anywhere in America, from the mountains, to the prairies, to the oceans white with foam. For the Senate to do as it pleases, rather than as Lyndon Johnson pleases, could result in a reactionary convulsion in government; who knows, could result in a return to the separation of powers.

—On The Right, Aug. 31, 1965

What the President will have to do, he will in due course find out, is once and for all to shrug off the Left: or to capitulate to it. It is, as I started out to say, quite dangerous to feed it, because its tapeworm keeps it always hungry, never fully satisfied, and if it isn't telling us to get out of South Vietnam, it will tell us (as it did a few years ago) to get out of Quemoy and Matsu; or, as the Left was beginning to urge some time ago, to get out of West Berlin. What makes it sad—the ambiguities in our foreign policy apart—is that Johnson cannot bear not to be loved by any group as powerful as the Left. He is visibly troubled, and sometimes seems to have lost some of that old-time zest with which he used to toss out his clichés, never thinking he would run into them at bayonet point —in the UN, in the columns and editorials of his old pals, in the privacy of his Cabinet room. Who knows, he may even be having trouble with Lynda Bird.

—On The Right, Feb. 15, 1966

For all the talking he does, and he is apparently the most talkative President in the history of the Republic, he does not talk to us in order to communicate. He talks to us in the same way that a piano-tuner caresses a keyboard, to get the feel of its timbre, its shortcomings—to size up the nature of the impending operation. . . . What the President needs is a first-class balky Congress, a Congress of dug-in naysayers who will by gawd wrest information from Mr. Johnson about matters of public concern, or refuse to continue blankchecking him along his tortured odysseys. It would pay, in a word, for Congress to remind the President that we are other than a piano for him to strum, and improvise upon.

—On The Right, Dec. 13, 1966

The President, it is said, hand-wrote the version of the State of the Union address we all heard, and the credibility gap notwithstanding, it is altogether plausible that it is so. It was a pretty awful speech, awful in every sense. . . . Fortunately, the state of the union is better than the state of its President's mind.

—On The Right, Jan. 23, 1968

The President has quite understandably spoken of having reached his decision to withdraw Before Kennedy. Human pride requires that one withhold from one's enemy the satisfaction of confirming that he has accomplished his purpose. The net effect of Mr. Johnson's B.K. talk is, alas, merely to give us one final glimpse of the credibility gap in action. No doubt it occurs to everyone in high office, in moments of intense exasperation, to muse about the pleasures of private life. But people built like Lyndon Johnson do not voluntarily give up their power. They are pushed out.

—ON THE RIGHT, April 4, 1968

One wonders whether Lyndon Johnson is demoralized. Surely he isn't so angry with the United States that he will decline to interpose himself between his country and Robert Kennedy? Could it be that the President is in fact so much the sadist that he desires America to stew in a Kennedy administration? Have we dealt with him that unkindly? I do not endorse that explanation, but I yearn for another.

—ON THE RIGHT, April 20, 1968

We have now achieved a President of the United States who cannot deliver a speech except in an army camp.

—ON THE RIGHT, Aug. 3, 1968

Lyndon Baines Johnson: His Coronation

Atlantic City is well suited for the coronation of Uncle Cornpone. It is a resort without flavor, but with a well developed flair for celebrating its mediocrity.

Only four years ago Lyndon Johnson, hero of the forthcoming event, was being roundly denounced by many of the people who are here acclaiming him, because he was ideologically underdeveloped.

Senator John O. Pastore is in the tradition of Convention keynoters who are expected, like diplomats, to go out and lie for their country.

[The Democratic delegates] are as irrelevant, at this proceeding, as cattle at a beef auction. The delegates are not only here to be seen and not heard —there are not even ripples of life from them, let alone of irritation. One cannot get any idea of the sense of Democratic opinion out over the land from talking to them. If you were to ask a delegate whom would he truly like to see as Vice President, he would faint at the implied invitation to presumption. Nothing matters here, absolutely nothing, except the word of LBJ, which is, when you come to think of it, a strange evolution in the democratic way of life, at the hands of the Democratic Party. ... Freedom and dignity are something that the Democratic Party desires abstractly for Negroes. Not for convention delegates.

Queen Elizabeth could walk through Atlantic City and be untouched by its tawdriness. Uncle Cornpone can't: the salt-water taffy, instead of curtseying, tends to stick to him ...

And Big Daddy Bird is reputedly very pleased, very confident, in this the best of all possible worlds—which wouldn't have been possible, nossuh, without the help of Mommy Bird, and Lynda, and Luci, and one hundred billion dollars a year to spend.

—*NR*, Sept. 8, 1964, *pp. 763–765*

The Johnson Administration

The Great Society was merely the phrase that came out of this year's political can, as empty of content as the phrase "New Deal" was when it was first uttered by FDR, who hadn't the remotest idea what he wanted, other than to be President of the United States again and again and again. Lyndon Johnson knows that the chances are very good that he will die in the White House, and he desires to die, his biographers have told us, a great man, universally recognized as such. With that face, manner and background, he is going to have to work very hard at it. Someone like Warren Harding, or John Kennedy, with such noble mien, can slip into the golden books by coming up with a solution for the 30-day strike against the Shredded Wheat Trust. You have to be awfully bad, if you look like Harding—you have to be as bad as Harding—to end up in history's trash-heap. You have to be very bad if you look and act like John Kennedy—you have to be worse than John Kennedy was—to end up other than in the pantheon. Lyndon Johnson has got to do very special things to shake himself free from Uncle Cornpone of Johnson City, Texas, from the wheeler-dealer who got the FCC to hold away the competition while he made ten million dollars in Austin, Texas television; the opportunistic old gasbag, who cussed civil rights and the ADA in 1960, swooned over them in 1964. The chances are he will look to do something big. Brace yourselves.

—NRB, Nov. 24, 1964, *p. 1*

Poor Mr. Johnson. So many decisions to make. On the other hand, poor us, that so few people should all the time be making decisions involving us and our tranquillity.

—ON THE RIGHT, Dec. 14, 1965

Lady Bird Johnson

It is commonly suggested that the businessman in the family is Lady Bird, whose green thumb as a broadcaster and landbuyer makes her responsible for this heady accumulation of money. There are those who will buy that version, others who will remain skeptical. The former should immediately propose a movement to name Mrs. Johnson Secretary of Commerce, in the hope that she can do for her country what she has done for herself.

—NRB, Sept. 1, 1964, *pp. 1–2*

K

Estes Kefauver

Altogether, it was a bad day for Estes Kefauver. Old Keef has always had his trouble, but he never bargained on hell freezing over, or the cow jumping over the moon. . . . On a single day last week, the Senator a) told a crowd in Minnesota how glad he was to be back in Nebraska, b) effusively thanked the elders of a hamlet world-famous for its graniteware for the "beautiful marble" gift they had made him, c) accused the Republicans of stacking the National Labor Relations Board with "pro-labor" men ("You mean anti-labor, don't you Senator?" "I *said* Labor Relations Board," the Senator nodded), d) stressed the dissimilarity between Eisenhower and Diogenes—who "spent his whole life in search of an honest *ladder.*" Heaven only knows *what* would come out of an attempt by old Keef to take the Vice-Presidential oath of office! It might be worth finding out.

—*NR*, Oct. 6, 1956, *p. 3*

. . . the Senator's demagogy was as shameless as any our nation has known in recent years from men who were trained to know better, and must indeed have known better. He did not lose an opportunity to contribute to the notion that all men who were engaged in big enterprises were, at bottom, scheming against the little man, with whom he succeeded, notwithstanding his wealth, his position, his incredibly hedonistic habits, in identifying himself. Some say he was actually a sophisticate: all the more inexcusable his lifelong transvestism as the hick, at home only with the debasing formulations of class warfare. He built a career on patronizing the little man while rattling the hob-goblins with which he frightened them; and such men can only be said to have contempt for humankind.

—*NR*, Aug. 27, 1963, *p. 142*

Murray Kempton

... there is no issue touching the Communist problem that Murray Kempton cannot sentimentalize.

—*Rumbles*, p. 183

... Murray Kempton, pin-up boy of the Bohemian Left, who writes an impressionistic column for James Wechsler's *New York Post*. It is one of Kempton's convictions that one should never kick someone when he's down, provided he is a Communist.

—*NR*, Jan. 25, 1956, *p. 12*

In my judgment, Murray Kempton is capable of discerning and appreciating and communicating distinctions of considerable subtlety. He is endowed with the eyes, the mind and the pen which together can produce moving and important social criticism. Sometimes—not often, unfortunately—he appears, in a sentence or two, to be about to take advantage of the generous dispensations he is granted by the Establishment in recognition of his particular talent: sometimes he peers over into prohibited territory, and for a moment or two seems to be staring, horrified, at the metaphysical desert in which he and his friends are living out their lives. But undisciplined in every other respect—he writes, analyzes and muses, the latter being what he does most of, unevenly—here he always pulls himself back, and ends up well within the boundaries of the reservation.

—*NR*, Aug. 1, 1956, *p. 11*

Around here we have a high personal regard for Kempton. He is bright, and funny, and literate, and personable. He is also about the nearest thing to a walking Kreuttner cartoon.

—*NR*, July 5, 1958, *p. 55*

Murray Kempton, probably the most entertaining, possibly the most gifted, and certainly the most eccentric newspaper columnist in the country, recently delivered a sick-speech before a meeting of Communists gathered to protest the McCarran Act at Manhattan Center. Kempton was the only non-Communist there, and did his best to extinguish the difference.

—*NR*, July 17, 1962, *p. 12*

Mr. Kempton can't stand the FBI because the FBI can't stand Communists, and Communists are like Elizabeth Gurley Flynn, whose face belongs on American pie-mixes. Kempton cryptographers will know exactly what I mean; others will have to take my word for it that Mr. Kempton is absolutely and undeviatingly loyal in his disapproval of anyone engaged in concerning himself with the internal security: whence the source, if not the coloration, of his special dislike for J. Edgar Hoover.

—ON THE RIGHT, Dec. 17, 1966

But then some go to Kempton for thought, which is like heading south when in search of the North Pole.

—ON THE RIGHT, Dec. 17, 1966

Mr. Kempton, although in some respects he is innocent beyond the imagination of Walt Disney, is as a columnist the noblest of us all.

—*NR*, May 7, 1968, *p. 437*

Willmoore Kendall

Kendall has a capacity for infuriating liberals that makes this reviewer positively green with envy. ... He even makes sense, for instance, and for the very first time in America, of the whole McCarthy business (tempers got as heated as they got precisely because the fight involving McCarthy *was* a fight over Heresy). ... His chapter on pacifism [in *The Conservative Affirmation*] is stunning—did you ever see a metaphysical argument walking? Well I did. And so will you if you read Chapter Seven.

—NR, April 23, 1963, pp. 322–324

George Kennan

... George Kennan, a gentle, intelligent human being whose view of the Soviet Union has for a while been based on his famous statement that he no longer knows what a Communist is.

—On The Right, Dec. 5,1968

John F. Kennedy

John Kennedy ... was by nature a modest man, but in his campaigning he too came to sound messianic and in no time at all was confiding to his intimates, or so the story goes, that he knew no man better qualified than he to serve as President of the United States; and he so oversold some of his own apostles on the general subject, that some of them went on to commit sins of fulsomeness which, one hopes, deeply embarrassed him.

—The Unmaking of a Mayor, p. 84

His critique of American life seems to reduce to a profound dissatisfaction with his own non-occupancy of the White House.

—NR, July 16, 1960, p. 6

National Review has from the beginning maintained the undesirability of Senator Kennedy's becoming President of the United States. In the age of Communism we do not want as leader of the West a man who speaks in such faltering accents about the Soviet menace; a man whose instinct was to apologize to Nikita Khrushchev when the national honor was at stake. In an age when the machine, the bureaucracy and mass-culture threaten to dehumanize life, we do not want a man who seeks to accelerate the tendencies toward centralization; whose understanding of the intricate predicament of the individual is as mechanical and inhuman as his close adviser's, John Kenneth Galbraith. We do not want, in an age when heroic leadership is required, a man who will submit so passively to the presumptuous demands of a Walter Reuther; whose Brave New Frontier is symbolized by his call for a protective tariff for New England.

—*NR*, Sept. 24, 1960, *pp. 168–169*

Mr. Kennedy's cabinet will be described by the court historians as "representing a broad coalition of interests"; and other fancy things will be said about it, to disguise what it actually is, namely, an opportunistic patchwork, made up for the most part of men with undistinguished public records, but almost every one of whom meets the demands of one or more critical pressure groups within the country. . . .

—*NR*, Dec. 31, 1960, *p. 397*

. . . all discussions of why the reporters are leaving the press conferences with a feeling of emptiness are preceded by extravagant testimonials to Mr. Kennedy's undisputed quick-wittedness. And who would deny this? He talked himself into the Presidency of the United States, after all.

—*NR*, April 8, 1961, *p. 207*

... Kennedy after all has lots of glamor. Gregory Peck with an atom bomb in his holster.

—*NR*, July 16, 1963, *p. 9*

Our President emerges as the ultimate man in the gray flannel suit: the great accommodator, the weather vane on the perfect ball bearings— soul-free, immune from any of the frictions of reality.

—*NR*, Aug. 13, 1963, *p. 95*

... the gentlefolk of England, gathered to consecrate an acre of ground at Runnymede to his memory, heard Her Majesty remark Mr. Kennedy's "will of steel." It takes, one supposes, a will of steel to do nothing.

—ON THE RIGHT, May 20, 1965

John F. Kennedy: The Assassination

The rhetoric has gone quite out of control. The symbol of our emotional, if not neurotic excess, is the Eternal Flame at Arlington, a few hundred yards from the shrines we built to the memories of George Washington (86 years after he died), Thomas Jefferson (117 years), and Abraham Lincoln (57 years); who have no eternal flames. The lovely and tormented Mrs. Kennedy needs a gentle hand lest in her understandable grief, she give the air of the Pharaoh, specifying his own magnitude. . . .

What we need is a period of dignified mourning for a graceful human being who passed through our midst with style and energy, a mourning more intense in virtue of the treachery of his end; but less intense than that which degenerates into abject pity for ourselves, or that asks that we place our personal grief above the best interests of our country as we understand them; which interests many people thought of as calling for the retirement of Mr. Kennedy from public life one year from now. Jack Kennedy wouldn't want a caterwauling public besotted by its own tears for its own self, or accepting his program for sentimentality's sake. He asked us to keep the torch lit. And that means work, each one of us according to his own lights, to keep this country at least as strong and as free, stronger, we can hope, and freer, than it was when John F. Kennedy last knew it.

—NR, Dec. 17, 1963, *p. 512*

Moments after the assassination some of the most influential—and self-righteous—opinion-makers in this country jumped to the conclusion that an Extreme Rightist did It. In a matter of hours a Communist was apprehended, and it transpired that it was he who had done the job. That disappointing reversal meant only a change of tactic. It could no longer be said that a rightist assassinated President Kennedy; but lynchers do not give up easily. The story then became that the Right had 1) created an "atmosphere of hatred" which 2) generated the impulse which 3) galvanized the trigger-finger of 4) a Communist assassin. ("Mommy," the remark was made, "is it true that John Wilkes Booth was a member of the John Birch Society?") The argument—may I speak my mind?—is not in any moral sense different from the argument used by the Nazi genocides who excused the extermination of the Jews on the grounds that the Jews had, by their alleged venality, created an atmosphere which required their extermination.

—NR, Dec. 31, 1963, *p. 559*

Finally, there remains the idiot fringe, who will not be satisfied until a commission comes along that proves Kennedy was struck down by General Walker while H. L. Hunt was passing him the ammunition.

—ON THE RIGHT, Oct. 1, 1964

Kennedy Administration

GETTING THE RIGHT MEN FOR THE RIGHT JOBS, DEPT.: "The Administration has announced a policy of hiring, where possible, mentally retarded persons for federal employment."—A.P.

—NR, Oct. 8, 1963, *p. 263*

Kennedy and Cuba

WHEREAS, The Government of the Soviet Union has over a period of forty years sought by military and other means to undermine the peace and security of the world, and to enslave all the world's peoples; and

WHEREAS during these years the principal objective of the aggressive policies of the Soviet Union has been the Government and people of the United States towards whose debilitation and eventual enslavement all Soviet policy everywhere in the world is directed; and

WHEREAS the Soviet Union, by subversion and terror, has enslaved the Cuban people, at a point ninety miles from the coastline of the United States, and has used Cuba as a base from which to intensify its subversive operations in this hemisphere; and

WHEREAS the Castro satellite government has recently procured from the Soviet Union extensive reinforcements of military personnel, military technicians, and war material, which have greatly swelled the offensive potential of Cuba and now constitute an intolerable threat to the security of the United States and this hemisphere; and

WHEREAS the Government of the United States is committed by its covenant to guard the independence and security of its people by any means; and

WHEREAS under the Monroe Doctrine the United States undertook to protect all the peoples of this hemisphere from subjugation by a foreign power,

NOW THEREFORE I, John F. Kennedy, President of the United States of America, and commander-in-chief of its land, naval and air forces, do hereby

DECLARE, that the United States shall:

Do nothing.

Given at the White House

Sept. 5, 1962

—NRB, Sept. 18, 1962, *p. 1*

The President informed us that at the moment Cuba has acquired the weapons to deliver nuclear devastation ... What is Kennedy's reply? That no more weapons, than those the Cubans now have, will be permitted to enter. The Cubans will not, so long as Mr. Kennedy is President, be permitted to accumulate more than their fair share of nuclear weapons. Fair play for Cuba, our President believes, who staggered America tonight with the information that what Gromyko had told him last Thursday turned out to be false. Gromyko will be reported to the United Nations.

—*NR*, Nov. 6, 1962, *p. 342*

Robert Kennedy

Mrs. Clare Boothe Luce wondered out loud the other day what would happen if Jackie Kennedy, standing up to get her ovation at the Democratic Convention, should say, instead of "Thank you, thank you, ladies and gentlemen, from the bottom of my heart"—"I nominate Robert F. Kennedy for Vice President of the United States." The Convention delegates would go mad. So might their countrymen a few months later, surveying the wreckage. (Talk about the face that launched a thousand ships, talk about burning the topless towers of Ilium!)

—*NR*, June 16, 1964, *p. 481*

The prospect of another Kennedy era, dominated by Bobby, is enough to send the average New York conservative to a monastery. The only historical parallel that comes readily to mind is those few months of utter panic in 1949 when the astonishing victory at the polls of Franklin Delano Roosevelt Jr. suggested to American conservatives the horrible prospects of reincarnation.

—*NR*, Dec. 1, 1964, *p. 1050*

Mr. Johnson having colonized everyone from the militant Left to the easygoing Right, there's not a figure left in megalopolitan Washington who dares to sneeze in his presence. Except for Bobby. . . . He is back in Washington and owes no debt to LBJ. Moreover, he has a more intensely enthusiastic personal following than LBJ. It is always easier to be seduced by Don Giovanni than by Leporello. . . . God save us, Bobby Kennedy, for the time being, is the nearest thing we have to a two-party system.

—*NR*, Dec. 1, 1964, *p. 1050*

Thus Robert Kennedy last week—I am always left breathless by the sheer gall of the tribe!—criticized openly Lyndon Johnson's *Caribbean* politics! It is as if the younger brother of the head of Curtis Publishers were to criticize Henry Luce's business sense. Someone actually thought to ask Robert Kennedy whether the Bay of Pigs had been a more successful venture in Caribbean diplomacy, and the Senator answered, disarmingly, "I don't think we handled that one particularly well." To be sure. But what one *did* we handle particularly well?

—ON THE RIGHT, May 15, 1965

We find it difficult to believe that Mr. Kennedy is the cynical thinking machine he is sometimes described as being. It is easier, on the evidence, to believe that he thinks viscerally, at least when he speaks spontaneously, as he did a few weeks ago when he made the extraordinary suggestion that it was in the American tradition to send American blood anywhere it is needed, including to the Vietcong. That is visceral reasoning, of the kind Mrs. Roosevelt was famous for making; highly commendable as instinct. As thought, however, it flunks.

—*NR*, Dec. 14, 1965, *p. 1146*

Senator Kennedy's final remark—to the effect that he is willing to give blood to anyone at any time—I think he should be given an opportunity to think over, some time before election season 1970, when he will run again for the Senate. Because if nobody else gets around to it, I shall rise from the ranks of the garment industry workers at the regular outdoor rally and ask, "Senator, is it true you would have been willing to send your own blood during the war to the Nazis?"

—ON THE RIGHT, Nov. 13, 1965

Bobby Kennedy and Nelson Rockefeller are having a row, ostensibly over the plight of New York's mentally retarded, a loose definition of which would include everyone in New York who voted for Bobby Kennedy or Nelson Rockefeller.

—*NRB*, Jan. 4, 1966, *p. 1*

The movement of Bobby towards the left is now so plain that it is likely to be noted in the next issue of the World Almanac, under "Left, move towards. 1. Robert F. Kennedy."

—ON THE RIGHT, March 1, 1966

Bobby, Bobby, everywhere. It drives a man to drink.

—ON THE RIGHT, June 2, 1966

The Republic of South Africa, the leak has it, will not permit Senator Robert Kennedy to return again next year. Will he return anyway? Maybe wade ashore like MacArthur? But amphibianlandingwise Bobby isn't very good. What he should have done at the Bay of Pigs was make a speech. Might have changed the course of the cold war. Come on, Bobby. Smile.

—*NR*, June 28, 1966, *p. 605*

But in 1959–1960 there was no counterpart to Bobby Kennedy. (As a matter of fact, in the history of politics there has been no counterpart to Bobby Kennedy.) Rockefeller had a certain metropolitan popularity, and as a big-spender was always worth watching. But he was hardly mountainous, in the way Robert is. Sixteen-year-old girls had been known to pass by Rockefeller without fainting, whereas no such thing has ever been recorded about Kennedy.

—On The Right, Nov. 5, 1966

During the weekend, Senator Robert Kennedy went on a paralogistic spree. The occasion was a Democratic fund-raising dinner in San Francisco, the immediate purpose of which was to show the great big biceps of Speaker Jesse Unruh, who was recently worsted at the O.K. Corral by the deft gunmanship of Ronald Reagan. Senator Kennedy got his usual running ovation. But it was interrupted by a special ovation when he called on the American people to note the "monstrous disproportion of anyone willing to spend billions for the freedom of others while denying it to our own people." That is one of the political effusions which are the highest testimony to the moral and intellectual emptiness of the political idiom.

—*NR*, Aug. 22, 1967, *p. 894*

Who, now, will benefit from the cultivation of the mass approach? Bobby Kennedy, inasmuch as it is his technique to egg on hysterical adulation (could you imagine him saying to one of those audiences, "Oh cut it out and stop behaving like silly children").

—On The Right, April 6, 1968

And then Mr. Schlesinger goes on to recite the relative qualities of Senator Kennedy, whose apparent ruthlessness is really *decisiveness*, as the *Worker* used to say about old Joe Stalin.

—On The Right, May 11, 1968

Kennedy remains the celebrity, and it is as such that he will run in a celebrity-conscious state [California]. To cultivate that image he is, as usually, willing to do anything at all. Lately, he moved Jesse Unruh, the greatly competent speaker of the California Assembly, out of his conspicuous seat as campaign manager for Kennedy in California, the reason being that Mr. Unruh is thought of as a tough political operator, which he is, and that interferes with the desired vision of Kennedy rising like Venus from the springy dew, to save the children of darkness.

—On The Right, June 1, 1968

Robert Kennedy vs. Roy Cohn

... God help us, there we'll be again, with 45 consecutive days of TV, a Senate investigating committee, Roy Cohn, Bobby Kennedy, and the Executive Branch—a sobering prospect. But one we should nevertheless be prepared to put up with, if only to serve notice on Attorney General Trujillo down in Washington that it is not yet a crime, under the Penal Code, merely to displease a member of America's royal family. If you don't hear from me next issue, come and get me!

—*NR*, Oct. 8, 1963, *p. 272*

Robert F. Kennedy: Why He Wouldn't Appear on "Firing Line"

Why does baloney reject the grinder!

—Quoted in *Time*, Nov. 3, 1967, *p. 70*

Teddy Kennedy

There are reasons for voting against Ted Kennedy as numerous as the grains of surplus corn in Billie Sol Estes' granaries, but one of them is not that he is a brother of JFK. The anti-dynasty argument is an argument from dire weakness, and typical of the cowardly reluctance of many

Republicans to challenge the Kennedy Administration head-on. The argument against electing Ted Kennedy to the Senate is not that he is a brother of Jack Kennedy, but that he approves of Jack Kennedy.

—NR, Oct. 9, 1962, p. 254

It was only about a year ago that we went to all the trouble of passing a Constitutional Amendment prohibiting poll taxes in federal elections, on the grounds that the Congress had no authority whatever under the Constitution to remove them. Along comes Teddy the Transcender, with the news that such scruples are positively pre-Adamite—and comes very close to stampeding the Senate into accepting his rider. ... One wonders whether these gentlemen ever give a moment's thought to the concerns of the country, other than as they relate to the image they desire to create for themselves? I mean really. Can you picture Teddy losing sleep at night because you have to pay a buck and a half to vote in Virginia?

—ON THE RIGHT, May 15, 1965

Kennedy Family

David Bell, formerly director of the Bureau of Budget, has now been named to succeed Fowler Hamilton as administrator of foreign aid, thus disappointing those efficiency experts who had hoped the post would go to Sargent Shriver, JFK's brother-in-law. That way Jack could request the money, Teddy could appropriate it, Bobby could enforce its collection, and Sarge could spend it—keeping the whole operation in the family. Is Joe Kennedy losing interest?

—NRB, Dec. 11, 1962, p. 1

Really, the dynastic assertiveness of the Kennedys is a wonder of the world. ... There are conservatives around who are accused of wanting to put back the clock. But none that I know of who desires to restore the divine right of kings.

—ON THE RIGHT, Nov. 14, 1968

... disgraceful, the way our country forces Kennedys to fight for their throne.

—ON THE RIGHT, Nov. 14, 1968

Morningafterwise, what would you have thought if the mail had brought you a lapel button that read, simply, "E.M.K."? My reaction would have been that my name had got on the mailing list of a Greek terrorist organization, and I'd have tossed the thing away. But that is a sign of what sociologists might call Deficient Kennedy Awareness. Because— you guessed it—"E.M.K." stands for Edward Moore Kennedy. ...

—ON THE RIGHT, Nov. 14, 1968

The difficulty is that for every Communist incredibility there is in the West—a Kennedy.

—ON THE RIGHT, March 29, 1969

Khrushchev's Visit to the U.S.

I have not heard a "reason" why Khrushchev should come to this country that is not in fact a reason why he should *not* come to this country. *He will see for himself the health and wealth of the land?* Very well; and having confirmed the fact, what are we to expect? That he will weaken in his adherence to his maniacal course? Because the average American has the use of one and two-third toilets? One might as well expect the

Bishop of Rome to break the apostolic succession upon being confronted by the splendid new YMCA in Canton, Ohio. Does Khrushchev really *doubt* that there are 67 million automobiles in this country? What is he to do now that he is here? Count them? And if it is true that he doubts the statistics on American production and the American way of life, statistics that have been corroborated by his own technicians—then what reason is there to believe that he will trust the evidence of his own eyes as more reliable? And what will he do if there is a discrepancy? Fire Alger Hiss? . . . What reason have we to believe that a man who knows Russia and *still* has not rejected Marx, will be moved by the sight of Levittown? . . .

Ladies and gentlemen, we deem it the central revelation of Western experience that men cannot ineradicably stain himself, for the wells of regeneration are infinitely deep. No temple has ever been so profaned that it cannot be purified; no man is ever truly lost; no nation irrevocably dishonored. Khrushchev cannot take permanent advantage of our temporary disadvantage, for it is the West he is fighting. And in the West there lie, however encysted, the ultimate resources, which are moral in nature, Khrushchev is *not* aware that the gates of hell shall not prevail against us. Even out of the depths of despair, we take heart in the knowledge that it cannot matter how deep we fall, for there is always hope, In the end, we will bury him.

—Speech at Carnegie Hall rally opposing the Khrushchev visit, Sept., 1959

Martin Luther King

If we are henceforward to treat Martin Luther King as a saint, which is in some respects okay by me, I do believe he should try very hard to act like a saint. . . .

—ON THE RIGHT, Dec. 22, 1964

Dr. Martin Luther King, at this rate, will need to be followed about by a major truth squad. His demagogy is soaring, and he appears to feel no inhibitions at all in distorting the record. Never mind for a moment the rhetorical enormities in his New York speech of April 4, in which he would have won an anti-American shouting contest against the principal hog-caller for the Red Guards. Consider this one . . .

—NR, April 18, 1967, *p. 395*

He has lost much of his following, and increasingly he emerges as the Harold Stassen of the civil rights movement.

—ON THE RIGHT, Aug. 19, 1967

Word should be gently got through to the non-violent avenger Dr. King, that in the unlikely event that he succeeds in mobilizing his legions, they will be most efficiently, indeed most zestfully repressed. Ambassador James W. Girard, approached by the German foreign minister and reminded that there were five hundred thousand German-Americans who would rebel in the event the U.S. joined the Allies, replied: "We have five hundred thousand and one lamp-posts in America."

—NRB, Aug. 29, 1967, *p. 1*

Dr. King's flouting of the law does not justify the flouting by others of the law, but it is a terrifying thought that, most likely, the cretin who levelled his rifle on the head of Martin Luther King, may have absorbed the talk, so freely available, about the supremacy of the individual conscience, such talk as Martin Luther King, God rest his troubled soul, had so widely, and so indiscriminately, made.

—ON THE RIGHT, April 9, 1968

Kooks

It is strange how much the left can do and yet avoid embarrassing the Democratic Party. Two years ago the whole country roiled with a fabricated resentment over Senator Goldwater's refusal to bracket the John Birch Society with the Ku Klux Klan. Where are the complementary gestures from the Democrats? Let us hear Franklin Delano Roosevelt Jr. or Frank O'Connor on the subject of LeRoi Jones—or Adam Clayton Powell, Jr. Or hear Governor Brown on the Center for the Study of Democratic Institutions, or on his former Democratic associate Simon Casaday; on the peacemarchers and anarchists; on the attack on Earl Warren from the other quarter. But isn't it the problem that without the kook-vote no politician can win; and isn't it the technique in current politics to make that plain concerning Republicans, but never concerning Democrats?

—On The Right, Oct. 8, 1966

Ku Klux Klan

"This trial," Murphy thundered to the jury, "is nothing more than a conspiracy to smash the Ku Klux Klan!" (If such a conspiracy exists, put me down as an applicant for membership in it.)

—On The Right, May 13, 1965

Thomas Kuchel

And in California, they are saying that Senator Thomas Kuchel, the lame duck, will be named Secretary of the Interior. Without knowing much about what Mr. Kuchel knows about the Interior, it would appear that such an appointment would be calculated rather to help Mr. Kuchel than to help the Interior. . . .

—On The Right, Nov. 16, 1968

Erik von Kuehnelt-Leddihn

Again this fall our European correspondent, Erik von Kuehnelt-Leddihn, will lecture in the United States. . . . He is equipped to lecture on everything from aardvarks to zymurgy, and will be glad to talk to groups in German, Russian, French, Spanish, Italian, or Japanese. By special arrangement, he will learn any other language. However, for this he needs two weeks' notice.

—*NR*, May 22, 1962, *p. 356*

L

Labor Unions

The society that tolerates bullying is decadent, and inhuman. For many years, the great bullies in America have been the big, tough, cocky labor unions; yet those who cry out against their excesses are yawned away, dismissed as cranks, pests. Sometimes acid is thrown in their eyes. Only Senator McCarthy is a bully, and the House Committee on Un-American Activities, and the Citizens Councils. Walter Reuther, and David Beck, and James Hoffa, they're not bullies. They are agents of progress. They are in league with the future. That may be, in which case we hope the future is a long time in coming. At the present rate, the labor unions will own the future, lock, stock and barrel.

—NR, Sept. 8, 1956, *p. 4*

The principal objective of a new law . . . should be to break up the power of any labor union to dominate an entire industry. We suggest that thought be given to making it unlawful for a single union to represent workers in a) more than 10 per cent of an industry, or b) more than a single firm, whichever is greater, and c) to provide that no labor contract involving a company doing more than 10 per cent of the business in a particular industry shall terminate within 60 days of any other such contract.

—NR, Feb. 13, 1960, *p. 98*

One wonders, might there be, somewhere in the U.S., a little child wrapped in swaddling clothes, who one day will be President and have

150

the courage to stare the monopoly unions in the face and say: Gentlemen, your reign is ended? . . . Arise, people of the world, you have nothing to lose but your squalid oligarchs.

—NR, Jan. 29, 1963, pp. 52–53

It is an interesting coincidence that the strength of labor unions has ceased, during the past ten years, to grow with the population. It is for precisely this reason that the unions hunger more and more for artificial power, the kind of power only governments can confer. They want power to protect themselves against competition, and against the dawning realization by the preponderant non-union working class, that many of the labor unions have become associations for the extraction of relative advantages for a privileged class of workers at the expense of the consumers, most of whom are unprivileged workers.

—ON THE RIGHT, Dec. 1, 1964

What Labor has to fear is a courageous Republican voice of great influence, which is to say that it has very little to fear.

—ON THE RIGHT, Nov. 17, 1966

Extensive revisions of the basic labor law are greatly overdue. . . . 1) No corporation which can be shown to have lost money during the average of the preceding few years should be required to bargain collectively; which means that management would [be] free to negotiate directly with individual employees. 2) And no labor union contract should deprive management of the right to institute cost-saving practices and machinery; which means that management would [be] free to automate, trim its staff and overhead, without consulting the union.

—ON THE RIGHT, May 11, 1967

The labor unions . . . are dominated by old-line Democrats who tend to prefer orthodox Democrats to the beboppers.

—ON THE RIGHT, April 20, 1968

The other day a colleague of mine, a lady of bright disposition and middle years, went to her garage to fetch her car, only to find the garage doors closed and her car interred inside. A strike. She has asked the doorman of the apartment building to raise the garage door, but he has informed her that the striking garage attendants removed the spark plugs from the machine that hoists the doors, so that there is no feasible way to lift them. I spoke of "her garage" intending to be precise. She owns her apartment and, accordingly, a part of the garage which is a part of the building. So that *her* car is being detained in *her* garage against her will, and if you think that big brave courageous law-abiding people-loving John Lindsay is going to utter one word of reproach to the labor unions, let alone dispatch a unit of policemen to wrench open that garage door and restore a citizen's rights, you are a romantic, and a patriot, and out, out of this crazy world.

—ON THE RIGHT, Feb. 6, 1968

[From Chairman Bill's advice to the platform committees of the 1968 Republican and Democratic conventions:] It may well be too late, but before the country goes down, a major political party should call for removing from any one labor union the right to tie down the entire country or an entire community, as various of the unions have recently done. Needed: extension of the anti-trust principle to the labor movement, plus a bill of rights for management, exactly specifying the rights of management against the exercise of which, strikes are unlawful as conspiracies to deny civil rights. Also needed, laws that prohibit compulsory unionism. The labor union itself should be reviewed in terms of public policy. Research establishes that the unions are a means of increasing the wages for the better off (approximately 10–15% of the labor force by 10–15%) at the expense of the less well off (89–90% by 4%). It is accepted public policy that the government should enforce the country's anti-monopoly policies, the result of which removes the urgent necessity of labor unions, so many of which now serve purely extortionist functions which liberals look increasingly clumsy defending.

—On The Right, May 21, 1968

Latin America

Already American capital—the savings of American men and women— is the largest single employer in Latin America. But for the billions we have invested there, an estimated one-third of the Latin American labor force would be jobless. These are the facts that must be dramatized: not that Latin America has not received as much foreign aid as other countries, but that she has received, per capita, most of all; that the bulk of it was given without a penny of taxation in America; that it got there without bureaucratic boondoggling, and that it sought out those commercially rewarding and socially beneficial opportunities which only the freely moving dollar, with its uniquely sensitive antennae, can probe.

—*NR*, July 30, 1960, *p. 41*

Owen Lattimore

On Friday, April 9, the *New York Times* published an extensive letter from Professor Owen Lattimore ... The remarkable thing about the whole performance was his identification by the *Times:* "Mr. Owen Lattimore was a former assistant to Chiang Kai-shek." Rather like introducing Lucifer as a former assistant to God.

—*NRB*, April 27, 1965, *p. 3*

Law and Order

And then says the NAACP ominously, "There is the additional factor that responsible leaders who speak out against the extremists have been subjected to threats of violence." For example, Mr. Herman Ferguson has been indicted for conspiring to kill moderate Negro leaders. And of course nothing is more important than to guarantee the physical safety of such leaders from the ruffians, the muggers, the blackmailers. The NAACP will perhaps understand what some of us mean in calling for law and order.

—ON THE RIGHT, Nov. 26, 1968

Leadership in America

It is a key to the understanding of what has happened to this country that Dwight Eisenhower became President, rather than Douglas MacArthur. This is not the time to slight Mr. Eisenhower, whose principal fault, after all, lies in his intimate relationships with his age: the age is at fault, not Eisenhower; the age was not imaginative enough for MacArthur. The age was afraid of MacArthur, and well might it have been, because he stood above it, as de Gaulle stands above his own time. In France they turned, at last, to de Gaulle, but only because the deadly inefficiency of the French finally prevented recourse to yet one more mediocrity. We in America, being a little more efficient—a little more conservative—than the French, never felt the need to reach beyond a mediocrity, so we elected the affable Eisenhower, and let MacArthur go to his Colombey-les-deux-Eglises at the Waldorf Towers, there to fade away.

—*NR*, April 21, 1964, *p. 309*

Linda LeClair

It is now a national story that Miss Linda LeClair, 20, of Barnard College, has been living off-campus in New York with Mr. Peter Behr, 22, of Columbia, and that a general story on such practices by the *New York Times* flushed out the cohabitation and put the authorities of Barnard College on the spot. ... Miss LeClair's parents were finally consulted, and it transpires that they, being of the older generation of course, disapprove their daughter's habits, and have gone so far as to cease to send her money. Mr. Behr, who is a draft evader, is apparently unable to take up the slack; so that perhaps the indomitable Miss LeClair will list herself as an unemployed concubine and apply for relief from the City, which has never been known to deny relief to anyone who applies for it: and that should settle the economic exigencies of the matter. . . . One wonders whether, if Miss LeClair were plopped into the middle of Columbia's Union Theological Seminary, a single seminarian would trouble to argue with her, as Christ did the woman at Jacob's well, that her ways are mistaken?

—ON THE RIGHT, April 27, 1968

J. Bracken Lee

Now let me confess to a singular admiration for J. Bracken Lee, the Governor of Utah. Governor Lee, it seems to me, is an unusual man and an extraordinary politician. Having arrived at a set of principles of government, he announced them and succeeded in persuading the electorate to name him governor. On becoming governor, he turned out to be as good as his word, never moving from his position.

Which position is, notoriously, out of favor not only with all liberals, but also with the dominant members of his own party; so that Governor Lee ends up fighting Utah's Democrats, many of Utah's Republicans, all the nation's liberals, many of the nation's Republicans, and virtually all the nation's prominent Republicans; and yet Governor Lee proceeds about his business without demagoguery, without rancor (I have read three of his public speeches and I am dumbfounded by his good nature), always aware, in his heart of hearts, that he is on the wrong end of history, and that, ultimately, he will have to pay, with his career, for electing to align himself with the losing side.

—*NR*, Aug. 1, 1956, *p. 11*

If the earth still turns around the sun, and if anything should happen to *National Review*, and if we find ourselves emigrating to the West, and if we decide to settle down in Utah, and if we get there by 1958, and if we get around to registering as voters, we will vote for J. Bracken Lee for Senator.

—*NR*, Sept. 29, 1956, *p. 4*

Leftist Heroism

We should constantly remind ourselves that the price for heroism in the United States has been made very cheap by our torrid Justice Department. My favorite example continues to be the committee organized to persuade Very Important Intellectuals to refuse to pay that part of their income taxes which, it is calculated, would go to finance the Vietnam War. The executive secretary of the organizing committee appended a little note to the solicitation to sedition to the effect that it has not been the practice of the Justice Department to impose criminal penalties on fractious taxpayers—all they do is charge you 6% back interest on the unpaid balance. And since any bank will pay you 5% interest, you can become a hero at the cost of 1% of a part of your tax. Not bad, considering how expensive other things have gotten.

—On The Right, Jan. 20, 1968

Gen. Curtis LeMay

General LeMay, to use language he would find familiar, was a damn fool for consenting to run with George Wallace.

—On The Right, Oct. 12, 1968

The Lesser of Two Evils, Etc.

Who likes Nixon's Republicanism? We don't. But that does not mean as individuals we can't vote for Nixon for President, just as most though not all the editors of *National Review* voted in 1956 for Eisenhower. That didn't mean we let up the fire: indeed we had to go out in shifts, to leave one editor firing the machine gun at Ike, while another dashed out and voted for him. We must not confuse the verities with the political situation, but we must not, either, lose our vision of the good society merely because, year after year, it fails to materialize.

—*NR*, Oct. 22, 1960, *p. 233*

Fulton Lewis Jr.

Fulton Lewis had the capacity of driving people up a tree with frustration, indignation, outrage, and all those other qualities of despair that characterize the listener or the reader or the viewer at the receiving end of a tough polemicist. Lewis was the kind of person who could succeed in causing people to smash their radios and curse in their sleep. Fulton Lewis was a very good thing.

—ON THE RIGHT, Aug. 25, 1966

Libel

A lot has been done in recent years to define libel law as it concerns public figures, and the renowned *New York Times* vs. *Sullivan*, estopping public figures from suing unless they can prove actual malice, is in the right direction. But surely the reform most overdue would require the loser of libel suits to pay the cost of the winner?

—ON THE RIGHT, May 30, 1968

Liberal Establishment

... the Establishment here is not so much of the governing class, as of the class that governs the governors. ... The American Establishment seeks to set the bounds of permissible opinion.

—*Rumbles*, p. 23

What does the term mean? It means a loose and spontaneous association of the people who occupy most of the command posts in our society, who tend to react the same way to certain kinds of stimuli, and—because they are the style-setters of the age—pretty well succeed in planting their axioms on the public thought-process.

—ON THE RIGHT, Sept. 9, 1965

The Establishment in a Nutshell Dept.: the *New York Times*, describing (Feb. 8) the reception given a book on Marx by the English scholar Sir Isaiah Berlin: "Although the book is hostile to Marxism, critics liked it for its objectivity and its felicities of style."

—NR, Feb. 22, 1966, *p. 143*

The Liberal Millennium

What is the liberal millennium? So far as I can make out, it is the state in which a citizen divides his day equally between pulling levers in voting booths (Voting for what? It does matter; what matters is that he vote); writing dissenting letters to the newspapers (Dissenting from what? It does not matter; just so he dissents); and eating (Eating what? It does not matter, though one should wash the food down with fluoridated water).

—Up from Liberalism, p. 183

Liberal Republicans

. . . the point might be made that there *is* no extant Republican philosophy, and that Lindsay is its prophet.

—The Unmaking of a Mayor, p. 74

What the New Republicans needed was a great political shapelessness, an infinite ideological plasticity which, on approaching the great unresolved political problems that have arisen out of the growth of Communism and the omnipotent State, could be relied upon to ooze its way over those problems, without grind, or tear, or rasp or friction. The Eisenhower approach was designed not to solve problems, but to refuse, essentially, to recognize that problems exist; and so, to ignore them.

—NR, Jan. 18, 1958, *p. 59*

The new group, which is to be called the Republican National Citizens Committee, is, as Senator Goldwater immediately pointed out, tied down to the same worthies who went about the country in 1952 saying that Taft Could Not Win, and anyway, it had been proved in Texas that he was a Thief. That same group marched up the hill with Eisenhower, planted a few daffodils, and quickly hustled down again, leaving the nation no better off than it was before, for the simple reason that Dwight Eisenhower and his admirers and supporters never had, and do not now have, any idea of what is needed to dispose of the two great challenges to the republic: the Communist menace abroad, and the collectivist mania at home.

—NRB, July 24, 1962, *p. 3*

I resist the word "moderate" because it is a base-stealing word for the benefit of GOP liberals.

—ON THE RIGHT, March 21, 1967

Liberalism

Liberalism cannot *care* deeply, and so cannot be cared about deeply; and so it leans, altogether, on those whom it has infatuated, who cannot see far enough to see how nearby is the end of liberalism's world. There is nothing there of ultimate meaning to care for, though there is much there to despise. The large majority of students, angled as they are toward liberalism, are silent, reflecting the great emptiness of their faith.

—Up from Liberalism, pp. 141–142

The salient economic assumptions of liberalism are socialist.

—Up from Liberalism, p. 170

I have resolved not to read another history of liberalism unless my mother undertakes to write one.

—*Up from Liberalism*, p. 175

I do not understand liberalism as a historical continuum. I refuse to submit to the facile expositions of liberal historians who do not shrink from coopting for the liberal position any popular hero out of the past. Thomas Jefferson, a liberal when he lived, would be a "liberal" were he alive today because, so their argument goes, the principles he then propounded, *mutatis mutandis*, have evolutionized into the principles of the contemporary liberal. Thomas Jefferson, the humane, ascetic, orderly patrician, countenance the mobocratic approach to belly-government of Harry Truman and the Americans for Democratic Action? But why? What has befallen us, that liberalism should be, ineluctably, the only approach to democratic government, mid-twentieth century? And if what has befallen us is a historical imperative with which we must necessarily come to terms, must we do so joyfully, even to the sacrilegious point of arrogating for it the enthusiasm of Thomas Jefferson? It may be that, as James Stephens wrote, "the waters are out and no human force can turn them back"; but is it necessary, he wondered, that "as we go with the stream, we . . . sing Hallelujah to the river god"?

—*Up from Liberalism*, pp. 177–178

Democracy has no eschatology: no vision, no fulfillment, no point of arrival. Neither does academic freedom. Both are merely instruments, the one supposed to induce a harmonious society, the second supposed to advance knowledge. Now let me say that I, for one, would not willingly die for "democracy," any more than I would willingly die for "academic freedom." I do understand the disposition to die for the kind of society democracy sometimes ushers in; and I do understand the disposition to die in behalf of some of the truths academic freedom may have been instrumental in apprehending. There is the difference. And it is not lost on the undergraduate that there is no liberal vision. And so long as there is not, there is no call for that kind of passionate commitment that stirs the political blood.

—*NR*, Feb. 14, 1959, *p. 527*

And so we come to liberal proposition Three: *All the roads that lead to the recovery of freedom, or to the diminution of Communist power, are closed to us, because to follow them would mean to risk nuclear war.* This is the clinching argument in all liberal rhetoric, by which they seek to paralyze all purposive action, everywhere in the world, that aims at the improvement of the position of the Free World. This is the ultimate mischief that liberalism is capable of performing, and in this respect liberalism most clearly does the work of the Communists, the object of whose propaganda for years has been discernible, namely, to terrorize the West into inactivity by threats of nuclear war.

—NR, Feb. 27, 1962, *p. 127*

Liberals

I go so far as to say theirs is today the dominant voice in determining the destiny of this country.

—Up from Liberalism, p. xvii

I detect a little discomfort, here and there, when the word "liberal" is bandied about. Many people are not satisfied to be unique merely in the eyes of God, and spend considerable time in flight from any orthodoxy. Some make a profession of it, and end up, as for instance the critic Dwight Macdonald has, with an intellectual and political career that might have been painted by Jackson Pollock. But even discounting that grouping, an increasing number of persons are visibly discomfited by the appellation "liberal," and it can only be because there is in fact perceptible, even though the proper prisms for viewing it have not been ground, a liberal virus—and a corresponding liberal syndrome. . . .

—Up from Liberalism, p. 36

They are men and women who tend to believe that the human being is perfectible and social progress predictable, and that the instrument for effecting the two is reason; that truths are transitory and empirically determined; that equality is desirable and attainable through the action of state power; that social and individual differences, if they are not rational, are objectionable, and should be scientifically eliminated; that all peoples and societies should strive to organize themselves upon a rationalist and scientific paradigm.

—Up from Liberalism, p. 37

... though liberals do a great deal of talking about hearing other points of view, it sometimes shocks them to learn that there *are* other points of view.

—NR, Jan. 11, 1956, *p. 24*

The liberals are not willing to take the position of the Quakers and abjure the use of all weapons: they only want to lay down our nuclear weapons. They will not take the position of the Western world since the time of Christ and say that liberty is worth dying for; they simply want to die in some way other than atomically. They will not accept the ultimate conclusion of their argument, that physical survival of the species is more important than the enslavement of the species. Adrift in a sea of assumptions, too distraught to follow their ideas to the home port, they wash back and forth between fiction and contradiction—and, with their wonted self-conceit, call their hodgepodge a "contribution to the discussion."

—NR, Nov. 19, 1960, *p. 301*

Well, the irresponsibility of the ritualistic liberals is about as newsworthy as the sunrise.

—NR, June 30, 1964, *p. 524*

After all, if you can get, say, Richard Rovere, Arthur Schlesinger, Dwight Macdonald, James Reston, and Walter Lippmann to agree on something, and when can you not, the reading public has just about had it, considering the leverage of these gentlemen and their epigones on public opinion, and their extraordinary capacity to fill the nation's libraries, magazines, and newspapers with their thoughts. Indeed, whenever they belch synchronically, the lava flows, and one knows what were the thoughts of the wretched men of Pompeii as they saw their approaching fate.

—On The Right, Sept. 24, 1966

Sir Arnold Lunn once described a liberal as a man who defends the rights of conservatives, which definition would exclude a whole lot of ladies and gentlemen who think of themselves as liberals but would sooner die (though not to be sure in Vietnam) than extend to conservatives such rights as conventional courtesy.

—On The Right, Nov. 16, 1967

"Hey, hey, L.B.J.? How many kids did you kill today?" That slogan, which greets the President everywhere he goes, is countenanced, and indeed applauded, by men who used to tear out their hair in anguish because Senator Joseph McCarthy had said the day before that John Crinkley belonged to twenty-two Communist fronts when in fact everyone knew he belonged to only twenty-one.

—On The Right, Feb. 10, 1968

Poor Mr. Nixon. If only he would cease, forever and ever, trying to please these gentry. How he, and the country, would profit from it!

—On The Right, Nov. 23, 1968

Marvin Liebman

The magician in charge was, of course, Marvin Liebman, the Sol Hurok of the anti-Communist community.

—*NRB*, May 26, 1964, *p. 1*

John V. Lindsay

... his public positions have been, roughly speaking, as far removed from the GOP's as Wallace's have been from the Democratic Party's.

—The Unmaking of a Mayor, p. 65

John Lindsay tends to sound like a Commencement Address most of the time ... But Lindsay's chances, even in a City predominantly Democratic, are good, if only because people do desire a fresh face every now and then, and anyone who votes against Lindsay will feel that little twinge you get when you interfere with manifest destiny. Lindsay's manifest destiny is the GOP Presidential nomination in 1972.

—On The Right, May 18, 1965

To challenge Senator Javits for his seat in the Senate in 1968 would have been as inconceivable as a challenge by one to another member of the Blessed Trinity.

—On The Right, May 18, 1965

New York is going absolutely mad on the subject of John Lindsay. And the enthusiasm is quite other than that which would be justified by either a) the prospect of liberation from the rule of Wagner (it isn't all that bad; not that much worse than it would be under Lindsay); or b) the absolute irresistibility of John Lindsay (who is undeniably attractive, but after all New York has Barbara Streisand, and Rudolf Nureyev, and doesn't go ga-ga over big Ivy League types who go around making commencement addresses about the decline and fall of the Brooklyn Navy Yard); or any combination of a) and b). What is happening is that Mr. Lindsay is being paid off for his gallantry in refusing to endorse the Republican choice for the Presidency a year ago.

—NR, June 1, 1965, *pp. 451–452*

Meanwhile, John Lindsay seeks to avoid identification as a Republican, which is okay by a lot of Republicans.

—NR, June 15, 1965, *p. 490*

What has John Lindsay of New York decided to run on? One metropolitan newspaper has carefully and enthusiastically recorded his attributes, the most significant of which, some observers have noted, is the brilliance of his teeth. (Yes, that was a qualification solemnly remarked by one major newspaper.) When the press mulcted from Candidate Lindsay the specific ideas he had for New York, he temporarily deserted his Spenglerian observations about the decline and fall of the City and said that a) he feared the desertion of New York by private industry; b) he thought something ought to be done about the flourishing narcotics trade here; and c) he did not believe that sufficient effort had been made to save the Brooklyn Navy Yard. Back to the teeth.

—NR, June 15, 1965, *p. 498*

Mr. Lindsay's Republican Party is a rump affair, captive in his and others' hands, no more representative of the body of Republican thought than the Democratic Party in Mississippi is representative of the Democratic Party nationally.

—NR, July 13, 1965, *p. 586* (statement announcing his candidacy for Mayor
of New York City)

Mr. Lindsay did not win as a Republican. No one would stress this point more emphatically than Mr. Lindsay, who in the course of his campaign did everything he could to suppress his part affiliation. He did of course desire the Republican vote, and he voraciously consumed great draughts of Republican money: but he did not on any occasion advise the voters that the Republican Party was the party of liberation from Democratic politics. His literature omitted all mention of Republicanism. Rather it stressed his devoted allegiance to "the principles of John F. Kennedy and

Lyndon B. Johnson." He won at the outset the support of New York's Liberal Party whose bosses, Mr. Dubinsky and Mr. Rose, have never flagged in their devotion to a hard, dogmatic liberalism. He won the support of the Americans for Democratic Action. He won the support of the *New York Post*, the Peglerian voice of New York liberalism. And he even won, incredible to recount, the editorial support of the *Nation* Magazine, which is the leftwardmost journal of general circulation in the United States.

—NR, Nov. 16, 1965, *p. 1014*

During the campaign for Mayor of New York (1965) Mr. John Lindsay, to the relief of foreign affairs, said very little about foreign affairs, though on one or two occasions he did produce a platitude or two, lest he disappoint his trained audiences.

—ON THE RIGHT, Dec. 3, 1966

But seriously folks, as the comedians say: Mr. Lindsay's tactics are interesting. They suggest a reinforcement of the proposition that the medium is the message. That the way to communicate one's concern over rioting is simply to appear, shirt-sleeved, in a potentially riotous area. But then of course if the rioters are that easily tranquilized, the danger is remote. And if the Republican Party is that easily beguiled, the danger to the Democrats is similarly remote.

—ON THE RIGHT, Aug. 22, 1967

Recently, a worldly young editor of *Time* Magazine was shocked to learn from a former fellow student at graduate school that he could not join him for a weekend, because he had to write a book review for John Lindsay. The young editor knew, as all of us know, that ghosts have been with us for many years. . . . But to assign to a ghost a review of a book which one is not even going to read—well, that is a kind of job-automation which shocks even worldly young editors of *Time* Magazine.

—ON THE RIGHT, Nov. 28, 1967

Republicans who fancy Lindsay have every reason to be sheepish. They are, after all, Republicans who fancy the Democratic Party.

—On The Right, July 30, 1968

I do not need to be reminded of the shortcomings of Mayor Lindsay, a little birdie having told me about them years ago.

—On The Right, Jan. 9, 1969

Mr. [Charles] McWhorter is a longtime enthusiast for John Lindsay— they were young Republicans together back when the destruction of New York City was only a gleam in Lindsay's eye.

—On The Right, March 1, 1969

A witticism of John Lindsay is recorded that when he was the Congressman for Manhattan and voted on a single day against a subversive control bill and against an obscenity control bill, that he commented to an aide that Congress was trying to crack down on his constituency's two major products.

—On The Right, April 10, 1969

The prospects for Mr. Lindsay are not, then, so very bright. In this respect he perfectly symbolizes New York City.

—On The Right, April 15, 1969

... it is just possible as it now stands that no New York political party, not the Democrats, not the Liberals, not the Republicans, not the Conservatives—will endorse Lindsay. Handling an incumbent that way, particularly an incumbent who has always fancied himself as *presidentabili,* is a most serious setback even to a modest vanity, which is less vanity than Mr. Lindsay possesses.

—On The Right, April 16, 1969

The trouble with John Lindsay, fundamentally, is that he cannot think rigorously. The next trouble is that when he does think, he thinks in harrowingly penetrable liberal clichés. The third trouble is his genius for saying the inappropriate thing.

—On The Right, May 8, 1969

Manhattan is Lindsay's organizational stronghold, good-old-Manhattan, where, traditionally, Republicans will vote either for *Life with Father* (Barton, Coudert), or for *Hair* (Lindsay), nothing in between.

—On The Right, June 5, 1969

Walter Lippmann

. . . Walter Lippmann, whose consistent misreckonings on the subject of the Soviet Union have contributed much to the strategic impoverishment of our leaders.

—*NR*, May 7, 1960, *p. 286*

Something recently tickled Mr. Walter Lippmann's toes, and he looked down, and, lo and behold, there he saw the Goldwater Movement. . . .

—*NR*, Sept. 24, 1963, *p. 223*

The trouble with these subtle explanations of what John means to do to Smith by being pro-Smith, is that they are so subtle no one but John, Smith, and Walter Lippmann end up understanding what the entire public is supposed to have been led to believe.

—ON THE RIGHT, Oct. 26, 1965

Henry Cabot Lodge

It was apparently Lodge who, masterminding the fight for Eisenhower in 1952, decided it would be convenient to call Robert Taft a thief, a venture in inspired audacity, rather like denouncing Pope Pius XII as a playboy. But it worked ... he flatly refuses to give more than a single speech a day. For this act of fortitude I honor him deeply, and have no doubt that the friendly treatment given him by the press is directly the result of not having to hear him speak more often than once a day. Once a day is quite enough. ... He steadfastly refuses to leave South Vietnam to take part in the political race, on the grounds of the emergency in South Vietnam. No doubt there are Vietnamese who feel that if Lodge goes, so might the emergency, which after all came about the time Lodge arrived. But those are illogical thoughts, and we should suppress them.

—ON THE RIGHT, April 11, 1964

Logan Act

There is a law on the books, the Logan Act, passed in the earliest days of the Republic, which makes it an offense for an individual to negotiate with a foreign government. There have never been any prosecutions under that law, primarily because the law can be construed either so loosely as to be dangerous to anyone who writes a Christmas card to Mao Tse-tung, or so narrowly as to apply to practically no one at all.

—*NR*, Feb. 8, 1966, *p. 105*

Loyalty-Security Hearings

At a loyalty-security hearing (as distinct from a criminal trial), the government is, and ought to be, given the benefit of any reasonable doubt. That being the case, it is important not to suggest that a security system's casualties are *disloyal.* They are, merely, *risks,* and such risks are not, in these apocalyptic times, worth taking. If the civil libertarians succeed in grafting full jurisprudential rules onto security operations, they will have succeeded in investing a security proceeding with the moral authority to determine guilt and innocence; this would damage civil rights far more than occasional arbitrary rulings by security panels.

—NR, March 12, 1960, *p. 159*

Clare Boothe Luce

NEW HAVEN: The unsinkable Clare Boothe Luce has left town with her reputation—as writer, *raconteuse*, political tactician and female female—just a little bit more secure than when she arrived six hours ago. She firmly put the lie to that scoundrel in the Bureau of Records who is reported to have reported that Mrs. Luce has passed the green side of sixty. An *NR* spy got the irreverent impression that she was actually flirting with undergraduates at dinner, and with astonishing success. She told stories on Walter Lippmann and Arthur Krock, and lightly deflected the insistent young men who wanted her to disparage Barry Goldwater. To another obvious question, she replied, "I had hoped to demonstrate to Mr. Keating the essential value of party unity in pursuit of victory— for which there is no substitute in politics." To a particularly tendentious question on civil rights: "Perhaps you should read my book on that subject. Which I wrote before you were born. When I wasn't running for office." Then, in a formal address, in a packed Yale Law School auditorium (than which there is no more implacable academic audience) she gave a sharp analysis of the problems—political, psychological, historical—which now beset the GOP. Her arresting delivery produced seven interruptions for applause, nineteen for laughter. What next for Mrs. Luce? Harvard, of course.

—NR, Dec. 29, 1964, *p. 1134*

Henry Luce

Henry Luce is a complex man. To show you how complex he is, he said a couple of weeks ago at Belgrade about Tito that he is "one of the authentic heroes of the twentieth century." It takes a man who is either a Titoist-Communist, or extremely complex, to make such a statement about a man with as bloody a history as Tito's ... What *can* Mr. Luce have meant? He should elucidate. What Mr. Luce needs is a medium through which to reach the public.

—*NR*, Nov. 29, 1966, *p. 1199*

Staughton Lynd

Staughton Lynd of Yale University is assistant professor of radicalism, in pursuit of a first-hand knowledge of which, you will remember, he went off to Hanoi eighteen months ago and mooed his solidarity with the Communists there, returning to Yale to display proudly all the new hair on his revolutionary chest.

—ON THE RIGHT, Sept. 14, 1967

[To Staughton Lynd on *Firing Line*:] Surely, as a Marxist, you don't seriously believe that your little vacation to Hanoi would have midwived some sort of a dialectical reconciliation which would not otherwise have taken place? Surely Hanoi isn't dependent upon Yale's vacation schedule for deciding how to press its foreign policy?

—Quoted in *Time*, Nov. 3, 1967, *p. 70*

M

Douglas MacArthur

MacArthur was the last of the great Americans. It isn't at all certain that America is capable of producing another man of MacArthur's cast. Such men spring from the loins of nations in whose blood courage runs: and we are grown anemic. That is why so many have spoken of an age that would die with MacArthur. An age when, occasionally, heroes arose, acknowledging as their imperatives the Duty, Honor, and Country which MacArthur cherished, but which the nation that rejected him has no stomach for, preferring the adulterated substitutes of the Age of Modulation, approved by the Pure Food and Drug Act, and adorned by the seal of *Good Housekeeping* Magazine.

—NR, April 21, 1964, *p. 310*

Dwight Macdonald

Many people are not satisfied to be unique merely in the eyes of God, and spend considerable time in flight from any orthodoxy. Some make a profession of it, and end up, as for instance the critic Dwight Macdonald has, with an intellectual and political career that might have been painted by Jackson Pollock.

—Up from Liberalism, p. 36

Anybody ambitious to please Dwight Macdonald had better be prepared to devote full time to it, given the fact that one cannot count on pleasing

172

him tomorrow by adhering to the position that pleases him today. Verily, Dwight Macdonald is the Tommy Manville of American politics; he has been married to just about every political faith.

—NR, Aug. 1, 1956, *p. 8*

Norman Mailer

I welcome Mr. Mailer's interest in the American right wing. On behalf of the right wing let me say that we, in turn, are interested in Mr. Mailer, and look forward to coexistence and cultural exchanges with him in the years to come. I hope we can maintain his interest, though I confess to certain misgivings. I am not sure we have enough sexual neuroses for him. But if we have any at all, no doubt he will find them, and in due course celebrate them in a forthcoming political tract, perhaps in his sequel to the essay in which he gave to a world tormented by an inexact knowledge of the causes of tension between the Negro and the white races in the South, the long-awaited answer, namely that all Southern politics reflects the white man's resentment of the superior sexual potency of the Negro male. Mr. Mailer took his thesis—easily the most endearing thing he has ever done—to Mrs. Eleanor Roosevelt, to ask her benediction upon it. She replied that the thesis was "horrible," thus filling Mr. Mailer with such fierce delight that he has never ceased describing her reaction, commenting that he must be responsible for the very first use of that overwrought word by that singular lady in her long, and oh so talkative career.

—Rumbles, p. 71

Not only do I not know anyone whose dismay is more fetchingly put down, I do not know anyone whose dismay I personally covet more; because it is clear from reading the works of Mr. Mailer that only demonstrations of human swinishness are truly pleasing to him, truly confirm his vision of a world gone square. Pleasant people, like those of us on the right, drive him mad, and leech his genius.

—Rumbles, p. 72

... if only he would raise his eyes from the world's genital glands ...

—*Rumbles*, p. 75

We shall always have moral perverts among us—sometimes they will go on to explode, as Norman Mailer has—and there is nothing much that can be done about it.

—*NR*, Dec. 17, 1960, *pp. 369–370*

In every categorical sense, Norman Mailer is an utter and hopeless mess. If there is an intellectual in the United States who talks more predictable nonsense on the subject of foreign policy, I will pay a week's wages not to have to hear him. ...

As a philosopher, however, Mailer is—dare I say it?—in his own fashion, a conservative. Wrestling in the twentieth century with the hegemonies of government and ideology, the conservative tends to side with the individualist. In his savage novels, Mailer's titantic struggles are sustained by the resources of his own spirit (plus booze). In his most recent novel, *An American Dream*, a hero as screwy as Mr. Mailer lurches from Gomorrah to hell and back, but always depends on himself to get out of the jam. ... it is a relief—sort of a halfway house to the proper blend of the individual and tradition—to read a novel in which the protagonist doesn't depend for his salvation on life rafts cast out into the sea of Hope by Marx, Freud, or U Thant.

—*NR*, Nov. 2, 1965, *p. 969*

Mailer ... decocts matters of the first philosophical magnitude from an examination of his own ordure, and I am not talking about his books ...

—*NR*, July 2, 1968, *p. 667*

Herbert Matthews

... he is a scholarly, subtle man who makes and continues to make supercolossal mistakes in judgment, but whose loyalty to his misjudgments renders him a stubborn propagandist ... and an easy mark for ideologues on-the-make. So well know is he as doyen of utopian activists that when in June of 1959 a Nicaraguan rebel launched a revolt, he wired the news of it direct to Herbert Matthews at the *New York Times*—much as, a few years ago, a debutante on-the-make might have wired the news of her engagement to Walter Winchell. Matthews was once, to use his own phrase, an "enthusiastic admirer of fascism." He turned away from fascism while in Spain covering the civil war, where he took up the cause of the Popular Front with the same ferocious partisanship that earlier he had shown for Mussolini's Italy, and later was to show for Castro's Cuba.

—Rumbles, p. 67

Eugene McCarthy

It looks as though Senator Eugene McCarthy of Minnesota is the chosen instrument through which left-leaning Democrats will commit damage on President Lyndon Johnson, and of course Senator McCarthy is splendidly qualified. On the one hand he is meticulously liberal—never ever has he erred in the direction of common sense, when the alternative was to vote liberal.

—ON THE RIGHT, Nov. 18, 1967

What it comes down to, I venture, is that Senator McCarthy will not likely again, in his lifetime, command a substantial political movement. I mean, he's through.

—ON THE RIGHT, Nov. 2, 1968

Joseph R. McCarthy

Whatever else Senator McCarthy did, he brought liberalism to a boil. Everything he did that was good, everything that he did that was bad, added together, do not have the residual sociological significance for our time of what his enemies were revealed as seeing fit to do in opposing him. Let us concede that if ever a man in America crossed the liberal ideology, or at least gave the impression of doing so, McCarthy did, which is why the McCarthy years are a cornucopia for the sociologist doing research for a *Middletown* on American liberalism, and for the psychiatrist looking for what I have called his syndrome.

—*Up from Liberalism,* p. 40

... the Senator caused more people to make bloody asses of themselves than anybody in the history of the world. People like Robert Hutchins, I mean: who, during the heyday of McCarthyism, gravely reported that such was the reign of terror that it required an act of physical courage to contribute money to Harvard University. Senator McCarthy said some foolish things. But none so foolish as those of his principal detractors.

—On The Right, Aug. 22, 1968

I am prompted to make public for the first time the only little piece of history to which I was ever an eyewitness. Senator McCarthy was in my home one day in the fall of 1952, when Eisenhower was running against Stevenson, and Representative John F. Kennedy was running against Henry Cabot Lodge, who was then Senator from Massachusetts. The phone rang for McCarthy, and when he came back to the dining room he told us glumly that he had just been confronted with a dilemma. The caller was a member of Lodge's campaign staff, with a request to McCarthy that he go to Boston and make a speech in behalf of Lodge's re-election. McCarthy felt that as a dutiful Republican he had a formal obligation to go. On the other hand, he explained, Lodge had always opposed him in the Senate, most noticeably during the period of the Tydings investigation. By contrast, Jack Kennedy had always been friendly to him, and he counted him as a covert supporter—and Mr. Joe Kennedy, he said, had contributed money to McCarthy's campaign. ... Suddenly he shot up, went to the phone, came back with an expression of overwhelming self-pleasure. "I cracked that one," he said impishly. "I told them I'd go to Boston to speak if Cabot publicly asked me to. And he'll never do that—he'd lose the Harvard vote."

And so McCarthy stayed out of Boston, and so Kennedy won—by a tiny majority, which almost surely McCarthy, had he gone to Boston, would have overcome, for he was then the number one hero of practically all the Boston Irish. And if Kennedy hadn't won in 1952, he wouldn't have become President in 1960; and Teddy couldn't have run for Senator in 1962. ... Which makes McCarthy a dynasty-maker, doesn't it? His enemies must remember to add that to the list of his sins.

—NR, Oct. 9, 1962, p. 254

McCarthyism

... there has never been much doubt that in the great game of anti-McCarthyism, the end justifies any means.

—NR, Feb. 29, 1956, p. 4

A local girls' preparatory school, in an effort to establish beyond peradventure its belief that *all* sides of every issue should be openly discussed, recently posted a topic for debate which represents a solid advance down the road of academic freedom: "Resolved, that Senator McCarthy's un-American activities are justified." There, now. Can any little witch hunter object to that?

—NR, March 21, 1956, p. 4

Mrs. Annie Lee Moss is one of the symbols of our age. A middle-aged, sad-faced, distracted, harassed colored woman, plucked from the obscurity of her government job and publicly terrorized by Senator McCarthy and his inquisitorial agents: accused, would you believe it? of being a Communist. Have you read the writings of Karl Marx, Senator Symington asked her? Karl Marks? I don't believe ah know who he is, suh, she said sadly; and when it was over, Senator Symington said, I believe you, Mrs. Moss, and if they fire you, come to me and I'll give you a job. From that moment, Mrs. Moss became a symbol, here and abroad, of the typical victim of the wanton human destructiveness of the McCarthy machine.

And now, four years later it develops (the Subversive Activities Control Board has assessed the data, which even the Communist Party cannot deny) that Mrs. Moss *was* an active member of the Communist Party: and there goes a towering liberal myth. Only just about nobody was there to record the demise. No editorial writers to speak of, no banner headline men, no social historians. Perhaps they thought a part of them was being buried, along with the myth?

—NR, Nov. 22, 1958, *p. 326*

Robert S. McNamara

. . . are we really prepared—all the men, women and children in the United States—to simply turn over our defense policy to Robert McNamara, subject to the pleasure of the President—whose faith in him appears to be if not unthinking, at least unlimited? Suppose McNamara is wrong? Not merely about the Reserve, but about the manned bombers, the moon program, the overseas bases. Hell—literally, hell—there would be to pay. How are we to inform ourselves about Mr. McNamara's performance, if he succeeds in intimidating all his subordinates, lifetime students of the discipline of war, among whom we must suppose resides a relevant sum of knowledge about, and experience in, military and strategic matters which Mr. McNamara, for all his agility, has presumably not been able to surpass during his four years in the Defense post. . . . Mr. McNamara may be the greatest military genius since Alexander the Great. But then again he may not be: and if he isn't who . . . is going to start finding out for us? The Russians?

—NR, May 4, 1965, *p. 361*

Secretary McNamara's use of English is odd. It certainly isn't idiomatic, and yet it isn't by any means Bureaucratic-Exact, or even Just Plain Functional. I fear there is a trace of Newspeak in it.

—ON THE RIGHT, May 26, 1966

The strength of McNamara's mind, moreover, is highly limited. He is the type who would score up in the stratospheric reaches in any test of intellectual dexterity. But—see his Montreal speech—as a philosopher he is jejune, banal. The kind of person who is satisfied to say that poverty is the cause of the war. Mr. McNamara is a man the liberals have been aching to lionize, because they feel the sweet vibrations of great technical competence combined with liberal platitudes.

—ON THE RIGHT, Dec. 2, 1967

It has even been whispered that Mr. [Clark] Clifford will pursue the objectives of victory in Vietnam more wholeheartedly than Mr. McNamara did, about whom the insiders tell of great agonizing over the entire matter, an agonizing which cannot compare with the agonizing of American soldiers as they hear shells drop over them which were manufactured in the Soviet Union and found their way to the war front because Mr. McNamara—and Mr. Johnson—agonize over world opinion.

—ON THE RIGHT, Jan. 25, 1968

The Meaning of Life

It is, to be sure, hardly fair to blame Mr. Johnson for the decline in the meaning of our lives. Though one half suspects, half fears, to judge from his hunger to commit goodness, that he is quite prepared, if the idea should cross his mind, to set up a new Cabinet post to concern itself with the meaning of our lives. People may lose the meaning of their lives as a result of action or even inaction by government. But their lives don't very often acquire meaning as the result of government action. The young pro-Communist idealists lost much of the meaning of their lives, at least temporarily, when the governments of Hitler and Stalin came together in 1939. But nothing the Soviet government ever did gave meaning to their lives. Mostly you lose the meaning of your life not at Moscow or Munich or Yalta, but at other places, remote from the concern of government if not, necessarily, from the reach of government. Some lose it on reading Nietzsche. Others on taking a deep lungful of air at our most sought-after academies. Some absorb their meaninglessness from the meaninglessness of others. Ortega's mass-man, even 35 years ago, was more and more without the meaning of existence, and correlatively more and more insistent that the mere fact that he lived required that others bestow great favors on him, but even as they pour down, in greater and greater volume, man chokes with boredom—and sweats up with envy; and rollicks down the halls of pleasure, in pursuit of the self-centered self whose odyssey, Dean Fitch has taught us, is the voyage of our time.

—Book Week, July 11, 1965

Krishna Menon

... the misanthropic little West-hater Krishna Menon, a man so warped in guile and bitterness that the Indian people finally rose and told their beloved Nehru that this was the single emolument of office he would not be permitted.

—ON THE RIGHT, June 4, 1964

Menus

A message from a West Side restaurant: the manager desires to name a dish after me, and the menus are going to press, would I like to be a chicken or a rice pudding? A chicken, thank you.

—NR, Jan. 30, 1968, *p. 71*

Method

How can one feel passionately about method? And what is it other than method that one is encouraged, in the relativist academic surroundings of liberalism, to feel passionately about? There was much more excitement over Senator McCarthy's methods (did he or did he not, in his interrogation of Civil Servant Jones, observe approved methods of interrogation?)—than over the putative revelations that ensued upon the interrogation (did Civil Servant Jones in fact whisk away that atomic secret?). There are many more allusions, in college campuses, to the fact that Antonio Salazar governs Portugal undemocratically—than to the fact that he has governed it well. (Can't you hear it?—"How *can* you govern well if you don't govern democratically?") The central concern of higher liberal education being for method, *qua* method, the excitement, when there is any, is over method: over Democracy—not "is democracy yielding desirable results"? Over Academic Freedom—not is "academic freedom advancing the truth"? Over Scientific Method—not "where is it applicable"? Over Education—not "what shall we teach"?

Democracy . . . has no eschatology; no vision, no fulfillment, no point of arrival. Neither does academic freedom. Both are merely instruments, the one supposed to induce a harmonious society, the second supposed to advance knowledge. Now let me say that I, for one, would not willingly die for "democracy," any more than I would willingly die for "academic freedom." I do understand the disposition to die for the kind of society democracy sometimes ushers in; and I do understand the willingness to die in behalf of some of the truths academic freedom may have been instrumental in apprehending. There is the difference. It is not lost on the undergraduate or on the adult public that there is no liberal vision. And so long as there is not, there is no call for the passionate commitments that stir the political blood.

—Up from Liberalism, pp. 140–141

Minimum Wage

. . . the pity of it is that so many people continue to defend the minimum wage idea as a humanitarian concept. Which, as it happens, the minimum wage simply is not. If there is a reputable economist in the United States who defends the minimum wage law in terms of its pretended benefits for the poor, he has yet to surface. The minimum wage law is an instrument by which the middle class worker, precisely at the expense of the poor, effects a redistribution of income to his benefit.

—NR, Sept. 20, 1966, *p. 922*

Mississippi

What is needed in Mississippi is not in any way different from what is needed in New York: it is education in right thought.

—*NR*, July 14, 1964, *p. 575*

If only the channels of communication were open to Mississippi, one could hope that the decent citizens of that state, no doubt an overwhelming majority, would rise to carry out justice themselves. But the trouble is that by its fanatical egalitarianism, by its pseudo-laws, by its abstract moralizings, the Federal Government and the Supreme Court and the moral intelligentsia have made such communication almost impossible. Even citizens of Mississippi who most profoundly abhor the Beckwiths in their midst will not stir to find them out and punish them when they reason that to do so is finally to surrender to Eastern ideologues who have no understanding of the best part of Southern life—the part that caused William Faulkner, on one occasion, to say that he would take up a rifle and shoot at any federal marshal whose presence challenged Mississippi's right to govern itself.

—*NR*, Dec. 29, 1964, *p. 1137*

Mob Rule

There are mobs, and mobs. There are mobs that lynch people. And there are mobs, yes, which, transported by idealism, will march into the withering gunfire of oppressive governments, as the mobs did in Budapest. But the mob moved by a balanced righteousness is the rarity. The mob is generally a negative, even a nihilist instrument. The mob seldom serves as an architect of civilizations. The more typical mob will throw stones at a visiting Vice President, string up a Negro, torture and kill a deposed prime minister, sing a chorus of hate upon the proddings of a bearded madman.

—*NRB*, May 14, 1960, *p. 1*

"Moderates"

One way to become a moderate is to walk a few feet away from the furthest wall, and say something appropriate. Another way to become a moderate is to stay right where you are and find someone who will extend the wall out beyond where you are leaning, thus marking the new limits of extremity.

—ON THE RIGHT, August 11, 1964

Our Modern Age

It is a specially unpleasant hour we live in, in an unpleasant age, an age I am proud to despise. A lady columnist whose hatred for the American right wing has got the best of her, or I should say driven the best out of her, finds that Goldwater is a monstrous and ambitious mountebank with a "heart as cold and dry as the desert night." And she concludes that Senator Goldwater attracts those who "resent the swift tides of history." Well, I resent the swift tides of history. One of those tides serves at one and the same time to drown intemperates on one side of the political fence, while baptizing maniacal intolerance on the other side of the fence. A Frenchman dubbed it: *Pas d'ennemi à gauche*—there can be no enemies on the left. The waters of history are running fast, and they deal ruthlessly with those who seek to dam them. Who meanwhile will instruct the moralizers in good manners? In charity? That too, perhaps, is for another age, the age that many Americans hunger for, as a replacement for their own.

—ON THE RIGHT, Feb. 27, 1964

It only remains to be charged, as I think I said on another occasion, that God is really a Communist—which allegation has the advantage of accounting for the strange behavior of the world in recent times.

—ON THE RIGHT, May 7, 1964

We live—as all men have ever lived—in two worlds. Roughly speaking, it is the world that makes the newspapers, and the world that doesn't. The world of the unusual and the world of the usual. In the journalistic world they define a news story as man bites dog, that is, the reverse of what is normal. In the plain and ordinary world, dogs bite men. In the newsworthy world, the man bites the dog. A world structured on common sense recognizes the difference between the two acts, ignores the one as commonplace, remarks the other as an occasion worth commenting on. Something special is happening in our world that blurs the old distinctions between the commonplace and the unusual. We are departing from realism so much as to make one wonder whether we are not entering an age of surrealism. An age when it is considered far more remarkable that a dog should bite a man than vice versa. An age, here in New York, where it is considered far less extraordinary that a criminal should break a law, than that a criminal should be apprehended for doing so. . . . What goes on here? My friends, we live in a world in which order and values are disintegrating. In which sometimes in order to view reality, to hope to understand, one needs to take the printed page and read it backwards, as off a mirror. Every age in which values are distorted, an age like our own—in which truths are thought either not to exist, or to exist only as quaint curios from the dead past—the wrath of the unruly falls with special focus on the symbols of authority, of continuity, of tradition.

—*NR*, April 20, 1965, *pp. 324–326*

Modern Republicanism

Boy oh *boy* oh boy, does that Arthur Larson bear keeping one's eye on! Mr. Larson . . . is the dauntless intellectual who undertook a labor more difficult than those of Hercules: he undertook to infuse into the Republican record of the past three years a sense of order, a coherent philosophy. To that end he wrote a book, *A Republican Looks at His Party.* It is a brilliant book—but should be read as a *tour de force;* which, by definition, any effort to philosophize Progressive Moderation is bound to be. But the book—and its author—have become enormously influential. For one thing, it is rumored that *the President has read the book!*

—*NR*, Sept. 8, 1956, *p. 5*

Wayne Morse

Listening to Senator Wayne Morse last week, it was for the first time really believable to us that he once spoke, in the Senate, for twenty-two hours without stopping. It also becomes believable that, during those twenty-two hours, he said nothing whatever that could not have been better said in as many minutes. How sad that a man whose training and instincts entitle us to expect of him a respect for intelligence and logic should end up a banal and utterly undisciplined scold, with nothing to say that would not have sounded stale to a Fabian twenty years ago.

—NR, Aug. 25, 1956, *p. 3*

Senator Wayne Morse said last week on the floor of the United States Senate that sending U-2 planes on spy missions over Russia was an "act of aggression on the part of the United States," and added that if any President ever does such a thing again "he should be impeached." Senator Morse seems to have lost completely his grip on reality. The gathering of intelligence information for defensive purposes is not and never has been considered an act of aggression, and a former dean of a law school should know that. And then to say that he would vote to impeach any President of the United States who takes peaceful measures to guard the security of this nation: *i.e.*, to impeach any President of the United States who faithfully discharges his responsibility to serve as executor of the nation's defense policy, is—is to talk as though one had been kicked on the head by a horse.

—NR, July 16, 1960, *p. 4*

N

National Conference for New Politics

A new committee has been founded called, with divine ineptitude, the "National Conference for New Politics"—a meaningless tongue-twister of a title which instantly stiffens the healthy voter's skeptical hackles. As well it should. The NCNP is a committee headed by four kneejerk-lefties who seek to use their influence in the fields of their specialities to urge all Americans to vote for candidates as innocent as themselves in national affairs. There is, to begin with, and almost necessarily nowadays, the babyologist Spock, Co-Chairman of the Committee for a Sane Nuclear Policy. Then the Reverend William Sloane Coffin of Yale, an eloquent professional sit-in who cannot understand why we worry about North Vietnam when we could be sending our air force to bomb Alabama. And Julian Bond, whose principal accomplishment has been to maneuver an unsophisticated legislature in Georgia to disqualifying him because of his pacifist inclination. And finally Simon Casady of California, who was eased out of his position in the California Democratic Council for overweening leftism.

—On The Right, June 4, 1968

National Goals

Every editor or foundation head in America worth his salt has during the past year commissioned his subordinates to find him a national objective, allowing, in the case of an opulent journal, as much as three months for the job. The need is patently there. It is a felt need, and that much is good. Fr. [John Courtney] Murray wonders whether it will be found in time,

186

and whether those who search for the public philosophy will turn, no doubt with anguished resignation, to the natural law: the neglected, tatterdemalion lode from which, if we set out to do it, we can mine a public philosophy which will bring the West out alive.

—NR, Jan. 28, 1961, *p. 57*

National Review

It stands athwart history, yelling Stop, at a time when no one is inclined to do so, or to have much patience with those who so urge it. *National Review* is out of place, in the sense that the United Nations and the League of Women Voters and the *New York Times* and Henry Steele Commager are *in* place. It is out of place because, in its maturity, literate America rejected conservatism in favor of radical social experimentation.

. . . .A vigorous and incorruptible journal of conservative opinion is— dare we say it?—as necessary to better living as Chemistry.

We begin publishing then, with a considerable stock of experience with the irresponsible Right, and a despair of the intransigence of the liberals, who run this country; and all this in a world dominated by the jubilant single-mindedness of the practicing Communist, with his inside track to History. All this would not appear to augur well for *National Review*. Yet we start with a considerable—and considered—optimism.

. . . .We have nothing to offer but the best that is in us. That, a thousand liberals who read this sentiment will say with relief, is clearly not enough! It isn't enough. But it is at this point that we steal the march. For we offer, besides ourselves, a position that has not grown old under the weight of a gigantic, parasitic bureaucracy, a position untempered by the doctoral dissertations of a generation of Ph.D's in social architecture, unattenuated by a thousand vulgar promises to a thousand different pressure groups, uncorroded by a cynical contempt for human freedom. And that, ladies and gentlemen, leaves us just about the hottest thing in town.

—NR, Nov. 19, 1955, *p. 5*

Just at the moment when the protests about this or that trait of the magazine are about to break our back, Providence moves in. A couple of weeks ago, someone wrote in to say *he was receiving his magazine regularly!* That saved the circulation manager. This week, amid protests about the language we sometimes use, a correspondent wrote us, "Baroque being of course the high style of our civilization, a reader salutes you as editors in the words of [W. H. Auden, who thus] defends his new baroque mode:

> Be subtle, various, ornamental, clever
> And do not listen to those critics ever
> Whose crude provincial gullets crave in books
> Plain cooking made still plainer by plain cooks.

That saved Frank S. Meyer.

—*NR*, Feb. 22, 1956, *p. 6*

National Review is neither supine nor irrelevant. It does not consult Arthur Schlesinger, Jr., to determine the limits of tolerable conservative behavior, nor does it subsist on mimeographed clichés describing The Plot to Destroy America. It has gathered together men of competence and sanity who have, quietly and with precision, gone to work on the problems of the day and turned over many stones, to expose much cant and ugliness and intellectual corruption. It is to be expected that They should set the hounds on us.

—*NR*, Aug. 1, 1956, *p. 12*

... alas, the President [Eisenhower] is probably not even aware of our existence, since we do not get mentioned in the works of Eric Hoffer, Zane Grey, or Chester Bowles.

—*NR*, Sept. 1, 1956, *p. 5*

Would you believe it, last week a Scotsman canceled his subscription (come to think of it, he waited till it ran out and then declined to renew) on the grounds that *National Review* is *predictable!* Of *course* we're predictable! We'll be peddling the same principles on our fiftieth anniversary as on our first—and they'll be just as bright and shiny then as they are now. The principles *National Review* affirms—again and again and again—have weathered all kinds of crises, even man's passion to change his gods every little while. We have suggested to our Scotsman that if he wants variety he subscribe to whatever journal it is that publishes the platforms of the Republican Party.

—NR, Dec. 7, 1957, *p. 512*

National Review has a problem—and the devil's own time solving it. We take for granted, we hear sometimes from our critics, a familiarity with people and events that we have no right to take for granted. To which we have been replying: repetitions are tedious, and the problem is how to find the golden mean between tiresome repetition of known facts, and esoteric references to data which mean nothing to many readers.

. . . .The problem becomes more than mere *identification:* should we not characterize? *Time* magazine solves the problem by selective physical description, *e.g.,* "tall, straight-backed, graying" *(Time* likes), or "squat, bleary-eyed, nose-picking" *(Time* no like). If one eschews this method, characterizations must be by other means. . . .

How do other publications solve the problem as regards *us?* Our readers will be glad to know that more and more our humble journal is referred to *not* as *"National Review,* the magazine of the Neanderthal Right," or *"National Review,* the magazine of the extreme right," but more and more by the use of the single dirty term, *"National Review"* (snarl).

—NR, Aug. 2, 1958, *p. 104*

National Review was not founded to make practical politics. Our job is to think and to write; and occasionally to mediate. We are tablet keepers.

—NR, Oct. 22, 1960, *p. 234*

With this issue, ladies and gentlemen, *National Review really* goes public. For years we have had mail: Why can't I find *National Review* at my newsstand? To which we have replied: Because we cannot afford to send it to your newsstand. We used to distribute only in Washington and New York, and at a few college newsstands. But during the summer and fall, we slowly, stealthily, increased the ration we gave to the newsstand suppliers, and to our amazement found that the percentage of sales did not diminish. Thus did we soar from 2,000 distribution to 7,000. Along came a distributing entrepreneur, a Madman Muntz type, who caught us in just the right frame of mind, and said: "Let me have 30,000 copies of *National Review!* I think I can sell them!" Tremblingly, we gave the order to the printer: and the copies should now be all over the United States. Ladies and gentlemen, please eat *National Review* for breakfast, lunch and dinner.

—*NR*, Jan. 16, 1962, *pp. 13–14*

Ladies and gentlemen. A Very Reverend and most estimable monsignor in Los Angeles has made to *National Review* a gift which, if all goes well, could relieve us of the necessity for a 1969 Fund Appeal. Cross your fingers on June 29, which is the day of the Irish Sweepstakes, that the winner will be X B Q 35435.

—*NR*, July 2, 1968, *p. 644*

And then there is the subscriber who canceled his subscription because a recent letter from the Circulation Department was franked with an FDR postage stamp. (And quite right.)

—*NR*, Oct. 22, 1968, *p. 1052*

National Review: Its Tenth Anniversary Dinner

I am on the one hand most grateful to you for being here, and on the other most disconcerted that, after the most recent *National Review* Fund Appeal, there should be so many of you left with seventeen dollars to spare for a dinner ticket.

—*NR*, Nov. 30, 1965, *p. 1127*

National Student Association

There is a very rigid hierarchy of disapproval in the glossary of the NSA. When the disapproval is really swinging, one "condemns"—as, for instance, one "condemns the House Committee on Un-American Activities." Next to that, one "deplores"—as, for instance, the landing of the Marines in the Dominican Republic. Still further down, one " regrets" —as, for example, one might "regret" the excesses of Fidel Castro. And, finally, one "does not condone" the students who "may have acted irresponsibly" in imprisoning a policeman sent out to imprison someone else. On these distinctions, worlds hang, at lively conventions.

—NR, Sept. 21, 1965, *p. 810*

Negativism

At the political level, conservatives are bound together for the most part by negative response to liberalism; but altogether too much is made of that fact. Negative action is not necessarily of negative value. Political freedom's principal value is negative in character. The people are politically stirred principally by the necessity for negative affirmations. Cincinnatus was a farmer before he took up his sword, and went back to farming after wielding some highly negative strokes upon the pates of those who sought to make positive changes in his way of life.

—Up from Liberalism, p. 219

Negro Advancement

We cannot help the Negro by adjourning our standards as to what is, and what is not, the proper behavior for human beings. Family irresponsibility; lawlessness; juvenile delinquency—whatever subtle explanations there may be for the pressures that conduce to them—are nonetheless deplorable, and a matter of urgent social concern. ... It is the ultimate act of condescension to suppose that merely because a man is a Negro, one may not denounce him; that because he is a Negro, it is hardly surprising that he is a poor husband, or an absent father, or a delinquent child. Mr. James Baldwin has said that the Negroes in Harlem who throw garbage out on the streets do so as a form of social protest. It is a much higher form of social protest to denounce such reasoning and the men who make it.

—*NR*, July 13, 1965, *p. 587* (statement announcing his candidacy for Mayor of New York City)

Negro Militants

The stories of black militants booing non-conformists are now legion: they proceed as if they have the rights of union leaders, to bully and to intimidate those who do not want to join.

— ON THE RIGHT, Jan. 25, 1969

Negroes

[From Chairman Bill's advice to the platform committees of the 1968 Republican and Democratic conventions:] The Negro community must be encouraged to exert itself in every field of endeavor, and to do this, subject itself to minimum standards of civility, even if this means indulging impulses to separatism. For instance, the continuing exclusion of Negroes by the prosperous and oligopolistic construction trades unions should be met by encouraging the formation of Negro unions. Negro-dominated schools where there is community pressure for them, should be encouraged as tactical experiments leading to a strategic integration of the kind that tends to occur between people of similar economic and intellectual achievement. Such emphases as Judge Skelly Wright of Washington, D.C. has put on checkerboard integration are exercises in abstractionist lunacy. Granted the danger of autarky, it is a significant statistic that in their respective New York communities forty times more Chinese than Negroes had traditionally patronized businesses operated by members of their own race. Deflate the rhetoric of racial utopianism. It is worse than useless, it is mischievous, and frustrating. We shall not overcome tomorrow, or the day after. Hold out realistic hope; tranquilize; bring calm. Emphasize order.

—ON THE RIGHT, May 21, 1968

Jawaharlal Nehru

From the time of the first attacks by Soviet tanks on Hungarians, it took Jawaharlal Nehru, well-known moral preceptor to mankind, exactly thirteen days to express a word of disapproval.

—*NR*, Nov. 17, 1956, *p. 3*

Nehru was the anti-colonialist who moved tanks against the little Portuguese settlement in Goa, smashing the local, and utterly contented 500-year-old regime. Nehru was the great moralizer who refused to rebuke Russia when Russia sent her tanks in to run over students in Budapest who clamored for their liberties. Nehru was the anti-nuclearist who made no motion, at the famous Belgrade conference of the neutralist powers, to criticize Russia for her unilateral resumption of atom testing in 1961. Nehru was the champion of Asian freedom who welcomed the coming to power of the greatest genocidal maniac in the history of the world, the same Mao Tse-tung who has killed four times as many Chinese as Hitler killed Jews. The great believer in peaceful relations with the Communists, who sat by impotent, depending finally on military help from the West he abhorred and contemned, to shore up his northeastern frontier against the Red Chinese aggression; and declined to help Tibet, or even protest against its annihilation. It is Nehru whose taste in men was expressed by his devotion to the misanthropic little West-hater Krishna Menon, a man so warped in guile and bitterness that the Indian people finally rose and told their beloved Nehru that this was the single emolument of office he would not be permitted.

—ON THE RIGHT, June 4, 1964

Nehru once said that in modern times there is no justification for war, any time, any place, over any issue. He said that about nine months before sending in troops to make war against little Goa.

—*NR*, Sept. 21, 1965, *p. 802*

Neutralist "Third World"

It is correctly predicted that Mr. Nasser will succeed Nehru as leader of
the neutralist world, and although that cannot make things much worse,
it does not make them much better, as Mr. Nasser's recent treatment of
Khrushchev so dramatically symbolizes. Like Nehru, Nasser is a socialist; like Nehru, a compulsive nationalist and anti-colonialist; like Nehru,
a racist of sorts, though the politer term, preferred by anthropologists and
others with syllables to spare, is an "ethnocentrist"; like Nehru, Nasser
hasn't the slightest moral appreciation of the struggle for the world.

—ON THE RIGHT, June 4, 1964

New Frontier

There are those, including myself, who have difficulty locating the so-
called New Frontier. But one thing is clear: As we have said in *National
Review*, in Laos, the New Frontier is five hundred miles closer to the
United States than it used to be.

—*NR*, Feb. 27, 1962, *p. 126*

New Hampshire Primary

A civic-minded group, and Lord knows there are enough of them around
with nothing very important to do, should break the hold of New Hampshire, and it would be very easy to do. A matter merely of persuading
three or four states around the country to advance their primary date to
coincide with New Hampshire's. The idea should be as appealing to
Democrats (who from time to time also fight in primary contests) as to
Republicans. The success of such a movement would ensure that candidates sculpt their programs without over-emphasis on the New Hampshire situation. And, besides that, would humanize the whole grisly
process, which up until now has required the candidates to visit every
grocery store in New Hampshire.

—ON THE RIGHT, Aug. 12, 1967

New Isolationism

We are moving towards a new isolationism in this country, as a result only in part of the limitations of our resources. Mostly it has to do with the demoralization of the anti-Communist alliance.

—On The Right, Oct. 17, 1968

Jack Newfield

I pause to record that in the current issue of the *Evergreen Review* Mr. Jack Newfield, whose conscience is so refined that the gentlest wind will sear it, notes that he voted for Eldridge Cleaver for President, which is rather like a staff member of President John Kennedy voting for Oswald for President, inasmuch as Newfield was a fervent follower of Senator Kennedy, and Eldridge Cleaver calls Kennedy a pig and Sirhan Sirhan a hero.

—On The Right, Nov. 26, 1968

Have you ever heard of him? I mean—other than you curators of the ideological zoos? Well, Mr. Newfield thinks you have: thus he writes matter-of-factly in a recent book review, "Everyone knew I was a personal friend of Robert Kennedy's." "Everyone" being, so far as I can figure it, everyone except everyone who didn't know that Jack Newfield was a friend of Robert Kennedy, indeed, who didn't know who Jack Newfield *was* a friend of; indeed, who didn't know who Jack Newfield was or, for that matter, is.

—On The Right, Feb. 1, 1969

Newspaper Columnists

... when in doubt, try servility. We column writers are, I am led to believe, the original Toms.

—*NR*, May 7, 1968, *p. 436*

New York City

... the Simon-pure left-ideologists who breed in New York like jackrabbits ...

—ON THE RIGHT, Sept. 17, 1966

... almost every problem in New York that doesn't have to do merely with maladministration arises out of a series of capitulations to special interests.

—The Unmaking of a Mayor, p. 29

A modern Justine *could*, in New York City, wake up in the morning in a room she shares with her unemployed husband and two children, crowd into a subway in which she is hardly able to breathe, disembark at Grand Central and take a crosstown bus which takes twenty minutes to go the ten blocks to her textile loft, work a full day and receive her paycheck from which a sizeable deduction is withdrawn in taxes and union fees, return via the same ordeal, prepare supper for her family and tune up the radio to full blast to shield the children from the gamy denunciations her next-door neighbor is hurling at her husband, walk a few blocks past hideous buildings to the neighborhood park to breathe a little fresh air, and fall into a coughing fit as the sulpher dioxide excites her latent asthma, go home, and on the way, lose her handbag to a purse-snatcher, sit down to oversee her son's homework only to trip over the fact that he doesn't really know the alphabet even though he had his fourteenth birthday yesterday, which he spent in the company of a well-known pusher. She hauls off and smacks him, but he dodges and she bangs her head against the table. The ambulance is slow in coming and at the hospital there is no doctor in attendance. An intern finally materializes and sticks her with a shot of morphine, and she dozes off to sleep. And dreams of John Lindsay?

—The Unmaking of a Mayor, pp. 30–31

... the trouble is, once you give in to a Voting Bloc, you become an addict. Just about every politician in New York is a political junkie.

—ON THE RIGHT, Oct. 6, 1964

New York City's finances are currently paralyzed because of the divine right of the 15-cent transit fare. Everybody knows the fare has got to go up, but nobody within the reach of New York City voters wants to be the man who pushed it. Accordingly, the two most prominent New York City politicians are locked in mortal combat to establish which is the more irresponsible. John Lindsay being mayor, and therefore having the biggest lever on public opinion, is the presumptive winner. Frank O'Connor, as president of the Democratic-dominated City Council, is a hot contestant. If it weren't for an obscure state senator in Albany, critically situated in the legislature, who has flatly refused to consider any relief for New York City until the transit fare is raised (every other major city in the country charges at least 25 cents), it is altogether probable that New York's elected representatives would see the City fold up before doing what obviously needs to be done.

—*NR*, June 28, 1966, *p. 610*

New York City—The 1965 Mayoralty Race

I had working for me, I repeat, an invaluable advantage, namely that I did not expect to win the election, and so could afford to violate the taboos. Lindsay and Beame had taboos' mother to observe: Beame could not afford to criticize Boss Powell or Boss Steingut; Lindsay could not afford to criticize Boss Rose or Boss Dubinsky. Neither would breathe a word of criticism against John Kennedy, or Mrs. Roosevelt, or Herbert Lehman, or Lyndon Johnson, the welfare state, the press, the voting population, labor unions, universal suffrage, or the Statue of Liberty. That left them precious little to criticize except inexperience (Lindsay's), fatigue (Beame's)—and of course (all together, boys), me, Goldwater, and the nineteenth century.

—*The Unmaking of a Mayor*, pp. 272–273

The differences between Mr. [Abraham] Beame and Mr. Lindsay are biological, not political.

—*The Unmaking of a Mayor*, p. 242

Mr. Lindsay is insufficiently aware of the problems of internal security, and . . . by his record, he shows that if he were Mayor, not only would there be no witchhunting, there would be no Communist-hunting.

—*The Unmaking of a Mayor*, p. 246

Mr. Lindsay says of Mr. Beame that he "promises not progress but procrastination, not ideas but indifference, not energy but evasiveness, not advancement but apathy."

What is wrong with that sentence—other than its suicidal search for alliteration? What is wrong with it is that it is unintelligible. How can an orderly mind maintain that Mr. Beame "*promises* procrastination"? And in what sense is "evasiveness" the opposite of "energy"?

As for your servant, Mr. Lindsay accused me of seeking "to downgrade and vitiate, to divide, to negate, and to prey upon the tensions and fears among our people." Now (a) I would be very happy, indeed, to "vitiate" the tensions and fears of our people—that, in fact, is why I am running for office. So why should Mr. Lindsay (unless he favors *validating* the fears of the people) criticize this? And, (b) How on earth does one "divide" a "*tension*," let alone a "*fear*"? And how can one *simultaneously* "vitiate a tension," and "prey upon it"? Is Mr. Lindsay seriously concerned about the educational standards of New York City? How would he know if they were inadequate? Mr. Lindsay is constantly criticizing me as the candidate from Connecticut. I don't know why he is so hostile to Connecticut. Perhaps because he went there to be educated and, for manifest reasons, is displeased with the results.

—*The Unmaking of a Mayor*, p. 264

On leaving the *Times* building [during the 1965 mayoralty race] I found a television crew waiting outside to question me. . . . Gabe Pressman of

NBC, the cameras still rolling, asked me jocularly how I felt on emerging from the *Times* building and I said—the kind of thing, I fear, that makes some people gray with anger—that it was as though I had just passed through the Berlin Wall. "What is the first thing you would do if elected?" he pressed. "Hang a net outside the window of the editor." If I had been more conservative, less impulsive—more civic-minded?—I suppose I would have recommended a commission to investigate the desirability of suspending such a net.

—The Unmaking of a Mayor, pp. 302–303

I do envy some people their cachets with the press. If the Mayor-elect, in the next few months, succeeds in removing one double-parked car, he will be hailed as the dawn of a new municipal era. We might meanwhile discover that, on soberer analysis, E doesn't actually equal mc squared and for our pains be denounced as anti-Semitic.

—NR, Nov. 30, 1965, *p. 1128*

New York City—The 1969 Mayoralty Race

Four years ago, when Mr. Wagner left office after three terms as mayor, it was generally believed that providence itself had separated New York City and Mayor Wagner. But the experience of the last four years has caused many New Yorkers to think back on the Wagner years as the Age of Pericles.

—On The Right, April 3, 1969

New York City Republican Party

. . . being tapped by the Republican organization in New York City is not to be compared with marrying the boss's daughter.

—The Unmaking of a Mayor, p. 65

New York City School Decentralization

As so often is the case, it is a pity that the more obvious solutions do not suggest themselves. For instance the old conservative alternative, of encouraging the growth of private schools by a system which would remit to the parents municipal vouchers exchangeable for education at the school of the parents' choice. There are difficulties in a transition to this system of individuated education, but it is already clear that such difficulties could not exceed those that have caused the present paralysis. The beauty of it is that such a system would instantly accommodate those who are primarily dissatisfied. Because they would have almost instant recourse to schools of their own devising. As it now stands, the militants on either side cannot win the right except as they dominate the opposite side. This way, both sides could win.

—On The Right, Feb. 6, 1969

New York City Schools

The lieutenants of the New York public school system are so ruddy terrorized by pressure groups of every kind that they respond to simple questions like eight-year-old schoolboys explaining away lateness in getting to school. They go on and on and on, not making very much sense, but making all the right noises. Call up an influential member of the Board and say something like, "I say, what is your policy on God?" and you can hear bells ringing and horns blowing; and then you get shunted from person to person, each more evasive than the last, but all of them dutiful in reminding you of the solemn responsibilities of everybody to everything, and of the democratic nature of democracy.

—NR, Nov. 26,1955, *p. 5*

New York Conservative Party

And then there was the young Conservative, running for the State Assembly in Harlem. A Negro woman advanced on him and growled that he was a Nazi. "Look, madam," the young and engaging Yale graduate said, "it's not right to call me a Nazi, anymore than it would be right for me to call you a Communist." "But I AM a Communist!" she answered exultantly.

—On The Right, Nov. 15, 1966

New York Herald Tribune

... the *Tribune* of New York, which heralds any publication that suggests that the Goldwater movement is extremist and dangerous as though it were a freshly discovered Dead Sea Scroll.

—*NR*, Oct. 6, 1964, *p. 856*

New York Post

Mr. William Shannon, a servant of American liberalism, had a convulsion last week in his column in the *New York Post*—a good place to have a convulsion, by the way, since no one is likely to notice anything unusual.

—*NR*, Dec. 20, 1958, *p. 395*

New York Republican Party

... there are the cynics who say that Javits was dismayed when Rockefeller went on, against great odds, to win the election. If he had lost, Javits would have been the indisputable No. 1 Republican in New York State. As it stands, he is disputably No. 2. Disputably because there is the androgynous Mayor Lindsay who, if you catch him at exactly the right exposure, with the lens opening exactly set, comes up a Republican.

—On The Right, Jan. 31, 1967

New York Review of Books

... the last court of appeal for highbrow screwballs.

—On The Right, Feb. 18, 1969

The New York Times

... we can take the *New York Times—any* day. For the editors of *National Review*, it's like swatting flies.

—*NR*, Jan. 25, 1956, *p. 30*

The publishing firm of Devin-Adair endeavored to advertise one of its recent books in the *New York Times*. Most of the ad copy consisted in an extended quotation from a review of the book published in *National Review*. The reviewer summarized Mr. Reuther's career, as depicted in the book by Eldorous Dayton (*Walter Reuther: Autocrat of the Bargaining Table*), in language the *New York Times* found unfit to print. The ad was returned to the publisher. The offending passages were: 1) "Mr. Reuther is committed to making his union into a mammoth monopoly, even to the point of averting his eyes when his goons slug workers in a Wisconsin plumbing factory which hasn't the remotest connection with the automobile business." And 2) "What all this [Reuther's program for the U.S.] adds up to is a world of slavery. There could be no rights in a Reuther-dominated system. The worker would join the union and keep his mouth shut in the union, or else." The reviewer? John Chamberlain, who once served as daily book columnist of the *New York Times*. Sad when you think of the moral and intellectual deterioration of Mr. Chamberlain, since Mr. Sulzberger took over at the *Times*.

—*NR*, Dec. 6, 1958, *p. 357*

Speeches can be made to say pretty much what you want them to say, if you have a lofty platform available whence to plant your exegesis. The *New York Times*, for instance, is to Presidential pronouncements what the Supreme Court is to the Constitution. A speech means whatever the *Times* says it means.

—On The Right, April 13, 1965

In New York there was quite a furore caused by the obituary editorial published in the *New York Times* on Francis Cardinal Spellman. "Public controversy," the editorial said in part, "engaged the Cardinal on his

weakest side. He backed the late Senator Joseph McCarthy in his demagogic excesses, and he made a dismaying attack on Mrs. Franklin D.
Roosevelt when she upheld separation of church and state in education.
. . . Whether he was trying to ban the motion picture *Baby Doll* or block
the reform of New York's divorce laws, Cardinal Spellman sometimes
squandered his own and his church's prestige on trivial issues and lost
causes." Most of the objections centered on the question of taste, and
with most of the objections I myself happen to disagree. Obituaries
should strive (in the manner of *National Review*'s) to be generous, but
not distorted.

What is striking about the *New York Times* syllabus of errors is that
such research as we have been able to do indicates that the great big brave
New York Times didn't criticize the Cardinal for exactly those of his
faults which, now that it is too late for him to reform, they signal out for
posthumous anathematization. When he uttered a kind word about Senator McCarthy: silence. When he criticized Mrs. Roosevelt: silence. When
he criticized *Baby Doll*: silence. Obviously the *New York Times* should
have added to its obituary: "What is more, Cardinal Spellman so terrorized *us* that the *New York Times* did not dare to criticize him for these
delinquencies at the time he committed them." Now that we know the
cause of the *Times'* restraint over the years, we mourn the Cardinal's
passing even more.

—NR, Dec. 26, 1967, *p. 1418*

It was at about this moment that poor General Eisenhower . . . delivered
a speech, by TV-relay, to the [1968 Republican Convention] warning
against a relaxation in our attitudes towards the Communists. . . . The
New York Times was so stunned by the General's warning that its headline read, "Eisenhower Talk / Scores Red 'Foe'." The editor, perfectly
reflecting sophisticated public attitudes, obviously reasoned that a mere:
Red Foe would strike the reader as, somehow, wrong, rather as if you
said: Wicked Walt Disney. Obviously it must be 'Wicked' Walt Disney.
Anyone who speaks of the Reds as 'Foes' has to be carefully explained.
Even at the Republican Convention.

—On The Right, Aug. 7, 1968

The *New York Times*, whose editorial department sounds like Cotton Mather rewriting Eleanor Roosevelt ...

—On The Right, May 22, 1969

Richard M. Nixon

Richard Nixon has driven Max Lerner, *New York Post* columnist and self-proclaimed atheist, to prayer. Mr. Lerner concludes his post-election lament by pledging, "I hereby serve notice that during the next four years I shall pray every night for the health and strength and life of the President of the United States." On top of everything else, Mr. Eisenhower can now be called the Instrument of the Lord.

—*NR*, Nov. 17, 1956, *p. 3*

It goes without saying that the editors of *National Review* endorse the bid of Richard M. Nixon for the Presidency. ... Mr. Nixon has conducted himself well. He is freed of the subservience to doctrinal middle-of-the-roadism that made Mr. Eisenhower so—never mind. The point is that Mr. Nixon is clearly his own man now, and during the past few years he too has shared some of the disillusions with liberalism which are the waystations to political maturity. He is not as passionate a believer in the ingenuity of the free marketplace as, for instance, Barry Goldwater or Ronald Reagan. He is not such a counter-revolutionary as, in one's dreams, one has going to Washington to dismember the bureaucracy and return the country to that energetic independence which belonged to us back before we became a nation of individualists manqués.

But as Professor Milton Friedman pointed out at a banquet last week ... Richard Nixon is capable of giving the country the impulse it needs on the way back to sobriety. Little things, initiated by Richard Nixon, could mean a great deal, if they set into motion a new spirit of the age. Such reforms as could lead towards the stabilization of the dollar, the reform of agricultural chaos, the restoration of local control, a reduction in taxes, an impatience with crime and civil disobedience, and towards the de-utopianization of government. If Mr. Nixon is elected, there will undoubtedly be plenty to criticize in his administration of the nation's affairs. But there will be cause for gratitude that the nation's affairs are in his hands, rather than in those of his amiable opponent whose loquacious romance with orthodox liberalism will not be sundered in this world.

Concerning Mr. Nixon's human qualities, we confess to a great respect for the way he has conducted himself and his campaign. His rise from 1962, at which point he touched a low as low as Harold Stassen's, is nothing less than heroic, and it is good to see heroism rewarded; and good, also, to know that non-telegenic heroism still happens to stand a chance in the modern age.

So then, let us hope. For the best.

—*NR*, Nov. 5, 1968, *pp. 1097–1098*

Thus the striking passages of his [inaugural] address had to do with the human spirit. These passages he could speak feelingly because he is the primary American exemplar of the triumph of the human spirit over adversity. The astronauts never had such dark and lonely moments as Nixon had, and out of that experience he fashioned a philosophy which is, essentially, hopeful.

—ON THE RIGHT, Jan. 23, 1969

Nixon Administration

It is a most interesting thing to contemplate the number of people who are coming forward these days to advise Mr. Nixon on how to proceed. They have in common their opposition to Nixon's policies, and their loathing of Nixon personally.

—ON THE RIGHT, Dec. 5, 1968

The world has not come to an end. I judge this to be an extraordinary achievement of President Nixon, having been taught over the years that his induction into office would quickly be followed by third world wars, atomic holocaust, and who knows, after that, maybe even a revival of McCarthyism. . . .

Mr. Nixon may one day be scorned for failing to take us on the roller coaster rides which his predecessors specialized in. But there are those who will be grateful, who already are grateful for the opportunity to go one day—sometimes as many as two days—without waiting for the White House to give us the lead. That is a great contribution to the rediscovery of what Herbert Spencer identified as social energy. Maybe we will realize, under Mr. Nixon, that it is we who have to rebuild the cities, restore order to the campuses, seek reconciliation among the races, oversee the education moral and intellectual of our children. The failure of the future will be ours, not his; so also will the achievement be ours, not his. That I judge to be a healthy relationship between a free people and their president.

—The New York Times Magazine, July 20, 1969

Nobel Prizes

The Nobel Committee is, to begin with, a semi-mysterious group of intellectuals and bureaucrats who appear to be influenced alternately by sentimentalism (the award to Cordell Hull), pseudo-cosmopolitanism (Halldor Laxness of Iceland), literary proletarianism (Italy's Quasimodo), and out-and-out left-pacifism (Linus Pauling). Any redblooded Westerner should think twice before accepting a Nobel award, precisely because to do so is to lend the recipient's prestige not merely to the idiosyncratic criteria the Committee uses, but to its political relativism.

—NR, Nov. 17, 1964, *p. 1004*

1968 Nominations

General James Gavin has announced that he is ready to move towards the presidency. If he had some ham, he could make a ham sandwich, if he had some bread.

—NR, Oct. 31, 1967, *p. 1153*

Nuclear Non-Proliferation Treaty

Once again we have moralized ourselves into a situation of relative weakness, even as when we promised to stop the testing of nuclear weapons we abandoned the advantage of a technical lead which had we exploited it, might have endowed us with such a scientific breakthrough —a new weapons system, perhaps—as would have made unnecessary our current concern with the multi-billion dollar ABM system. All of this in order to deny the atom bomb to a future Hitler. A remote concern, surely, considering that the present Hitlers have the bomb already, and can, whenever they feel disposed to do so, give that bomb to future Hitlers.

—ON THE RIGHT, March 18, 1969

What the Soviet Union wants, pure and simple, is to prevent West Germany from getting the bomb, because it is West Germany perhaps alone that has the stamina to use the damned thing if necessary to keep the Soviet armies at bay.

—ON THE RIGHT, Feb. 11, 1969

Nuclear Test-Ban Treaty

The pressures on Mr. Kennedy to make an agreement are very great. They come mostly from the emotional school of international affairs (Norman Cousins—Pres., N. Khrushchev—puppetmaster), and from the fetishists, who believe that cessation of tests has something to do with securing peace, which in fact it has not.

—*NRB*, Aug. 21, 1962, *p. 3*

"Dear Senator Clark,"—the Senator introduced into the *Congressional Record* a letter which he considers the "most succinct comment" in favor of the test ban—"I saw you on the 'Today' program debating with another man. I asked Mommy who was right. Mommy said, 'You tell me.' I said that you were right. Mommy was pleased that even a 9-year-old girl could tell that it was a good idea to ratify the test-ban treaty. Love, Elizabeth May." Dear Senator Clark: Would you please give us the reasons why we should back the test-ban treaty? We are over nine years old. Love, The Editors, *National Review.*

—*NRB*, Sept. 17, 1963, *p. 1*

We owe Mr. Kennedy this much: a vote of gratitude for taking the matter to the Senate in the first instance. Granted the constitutional require-ment, it is nevertheless ignored, time after time, by Presidents who have convinced themselves that they are really above the Constitution. When General Eisenhower decided on a test ban, he simply instituted it, unilat-erally. At least President Kennedy went to the Senate and persuaded it to ratify his foolishness. How's that for finding a silver lining?

—*NR*, Oct. 8, 1963, *p. 265*

Nuclear War

Granted if there were a war today, there would be more deaths—far more deaths—than were caused by yesterday's war. But what is the meaning of that statistic to the individual dead man? None—he knows not whether he died alone, or in company with a hundred million others. What is the meaning of it for the survivor? None that goes beyond that abysmal grief of personal loss experienced well before the nuclear age by, for instance, the frontiersman's wife whose husband and children were massacred by the Indians. And individual human being can sustain only so much grief, and then bereavement becomes redundant. . . .

It is necessary, when we listen to a Norman Cousins or a Steve Allen or a Sidney Lens or a Bertrand Russell or a Kenneth Tynan going on and on about the horrors and scale of nuclear death, to force ourselves to face explicitly what we know intuitively. And that is this: that if it is right that a single man is prepared to die for a just cause, it can be argued that it is right that an entire civilization be prepared to die for a just cause. . . . Better Dead than Red is an inaccurate statement of the American position, listing, as it does, non-exclusive alternatives. Properly stated it is: Better to face the *chance* of being dead, than the certainty of being Red. And if we die? We die.

—*NR*, Dec. 4, 1962, *p. 424*

Nuclear Weapons

. . . our fundamental belief [is] that nuclear weapons are, at this point in history, a blessing, not a curse. Without them, as Winston Churchill has pointed out, there would not today be a free man on the continent of Europe.

—*NR*, June 18, 1963, *p. 483*

The use of limited atomic bombs for purely military operations is many times easier to defend on the morality scale than one slit throat of a civilian for terrorism's sake; and yet, incredibly, the Vietcong seem to win all the propaganda victories, and the moralizers' inveighing is against us, not against them.

The tactical nuclear weapon is a weapon designed to increase the efficiency of warmaking, and warmaking, when conducted by the good guys, is supposed to be preferred to, let us say, permitting Hitler to kill millions of Jews and conquer Europe; preferred to, let us say, turning Berlin over to the Soviet Union; preferred to ushering in an age of misery and bloodshed in Southeast Asia. We are constantly being reminded about Confucius, or whoever it was, who warned the U.S. against a land-war in Asia, but we are practically never told about how to multiply those advantages that are naturally ours, advantages by which we might stand to offset the enemy's advantages in potential manpower, and in ubiquitous ruthlessness. Even as we never dare to talk about economic blockades against the major suppliers of the Vietcong, we are not permitted to talk about the use of tactical nuclear weapons. Not allowed to speculate, even, on whether the careful use of them, years and years ago, might not have saved us, and the South Vietnamese—and the North Vietnamese—years and years of misery.

—On The Right, Feb. 22, 1968

Conor Cruise O'Brien

Conor O'Brien is the kind of person who would sooner uphold the proposition that Nkrumah is divine, than that Christ was. His idea of cool. ... O'Brien is an ideological swashbuckler, a nose-tweaker who doesn't know the bounds of taste, nor cares much for the hurt he inflicts. He is most likely not a Communist, although he does their work for them. And he is not unique, although he is brighter than most.

—ON THE RIGHT, Oct. 23, 1965

Oil-Depletion Allowance

I have always thought that the oil depletion allowance is positively the easiest thing around to handle: if the Department of Commerce reasons that there is overproduction in oil (there is, by the way), well let the Department recommend that oil discovered after 1 January 1970 shall not be subject to depletion benefits.

—ON THE RIGHT, March 22, 1969

Ombudsmen

It has recently crystallized that in Washington, D.C. the administration of the government is chaotic. That is in part because President Johnson is a poor administrator, in part because his eyes are bigger than his stomach, and the Great Society has evolved in gargantuan proportions out of correspondence with the capacity of Mr. Johnson or the federal government to oversee. No doubt in due course it will straighten out a little bit. But even then, we shall be finding that every time we turn a corner, read a schoolbook, drink a glass of water, we will rub up against some federal regulation or aid program. And then we will need a friend. A free friend. One wonders why the Republican Party waits another moment before coming out, as a party objective, for Ombudsmen at all levels, state and federal.

—ON THE RIGHT, Nov. 29, 1966

P

Jack Paar

I tried thinking on his program, instead of emoting, and he was so traumatized it took him two and one-half shows, several gag writers, half a dozen bald lies, and a couple of character assassins to restore his composure. . . .

One must bear in mind that Jack Paar is given to expressing *his* feelings for humanity by weeping publicly, thereby setting standards of his feelings for humanity by weeping publicly, thereby setting standards of demonstrable humanitarianism with which those of us not trained in show *biz* find it difficult to compete.

—NR, March 27, 1962, *pp. 205–206*

Pacifism

. . . the Constitution was devised, among other things, to defend the United States from its enemies, foreign and domestic. There is plenty of ground for argument on how best to achieve that objective, but none at all, under the Constitution, for argument about whether we should defend this country, which of course means by force if necessary. In other words, the argument is at least defensible, at most conclusive, that a pacifist cannot serve his own ideology, and also the Constitution of the United States.

—ON THE RIGHT, Jan. 20, 1966

Parents

The government has the responsibility to declare hopelessly irresponsible parents unqualified to bring up children, who should then be turned over to charitable organizations to bring them up. The axiom that bad parents are better than no parents at all is a bad axiom, which is worse than no axiom at all.

—On The Right, May 18, 1968

Pay-TV

If we had a comprehensive development program for reaching the moon comparable to the FCC's program for pay-TV, we might expect to reach there sometime after the Communists become worried about the moon's population explosion.

—*NR*, June 4, 1963, *p. 442*

It is one of the best subdued scandals of our time that the major networks have succeeded in keeping pay-TV off the air—for all intents and purposes. Their arguments against it have been dressed up in the most high-faluting humanitarian rhetoric: but they break down, under the assault of rudimentary analysis, to a desire to retain a commercial advantage. The original, and still the best idea for a program of liberation from the tyranny of television by Nielson, is pay-TV.

—On The Right, April 28, 1964

... the movement by a bloc in California to outlaw pay-TV is ... an epochal attempt to stop progress, interfere with the First Amendment, secure monopolies, and abort the most encouraging cultural exploitation of the photo-electric formulas Einstein thought through years and years ago, making television possible.

—*NR*, Sept. 22, 1964, *p. 806*

Peace

All civilized men want peace. And all truly civilized men must despise pacifism. ... Pacifism is a Christian heresy that springs from critical misunderstandings. *Peace on earth* is a plea for those conditions on earth —love, charity, temperance—which make peace thinkable. Peace is unthinkable in a community in which plunderers have hold of the city at night; and the prayer for peace is not a prayer that the elders of the community maintain the peace by yielding every night to plunderers: rather, it is a prayer that men be helped in finding the strength to suppress their acquisitive and aggressive instincts sufficiently to make unnecessary armed resistance to man by man. In praying for peace, we pray that grace will settle in the hearts and minds of those bellicose people in the world who are critically situated, and cause them to exercise that restraint which makes peace possible. If peace were the first goal of man, you would not have to pray for it: you could have it. The price is to yield. If you are prepared to yield your family, your property—your honor— it is generally safe to assume that you will be ceded your life: that you will have gained "peace."

—*NR*, Oct. 24, 1959, *p. 427*

The point is that the surest way to have peace is to show our determination to wage war if necessary. ... Any sign of weakness by the Free World increases the appetite of the enemy for more war and more conquest as surely as the progressive revelations of the stripteaser increase the appetite of the lecher.

—*NR*, Feb. 27, 1962, *p. 127*

Shouldn't it be made a little bit more evident to the peace-breakers that the price of peace-breaking is very high, higher than a reproachful editorial in the *New York Times?*

—*NRB*, June 6, 1967, *p. 1*

Peace Corps

The nation's youth are treating the idea as though it were a call to go to Africa for a mass sit-in. There is no doubting that genuine altruism is involved: a desire to help other people. What one cannot help but wonder is why American youth are so caught up in the enthusiasm for bringing electric dishwashers to the Angolese, while remaining so perennially indifferent to the idea of bringing freedom to the slaves of the Communist Empire; or even to keeping the frontiers of slavery contained. Why are the youth clamoring to go to South America, and Africa, and Asia, to counter the activities of the Communist apologists who continue to pour out of the Soviet Union to sow their mischief? Why aren't they clamoring for the so-called Freedom Academy, which would train American youth in the tactics of non-military warfare? By a resourceful and devoted use of the weapons of political and psychological warfare, our idealists could hope to do more than raise the GNP of underdeveloped nations by one or two per cent. They might save whole nations from succumbing to the blandishments and conspiracies of the slavemasters who roam about the world, seeking the destruction of souls.

—*NR*, March 25, 1961, *pp. 171–172*

"Peace" Rallies

And from somewhere, and one should not exclude a local casting office, a withered old Indian chief was gathered and introduced by Dr. Spock who warned that we were doing to the Vietnamese population what our forefathers had done to the Indian population (incidental intelligence department: there are more American Indians alive today than when Columbus discovered America). "Say ugh and sit down," an impatient television camera man muttered silently from a safe fifty feet away. But Big Chief Hatum War muttered a few husky lines and then summoned his 100-year-old squaw and another veteran of the battle of Little Big Horn and the three of them began to bellow into the microphones what one supposes was an old Indian peace cry, which though atonal and ear-piercingly loud was infinitely soothing by contrast with, say, the words, uttered in English, of Stokely Carmichael.

—*NR*, May 2, 1967, *p. 470*

Drew Pearson

... there are those who conclude that to worry about Pearson's irresponsibility is rather like worrying about illicit sex: as long as there is human
lust, there will be human panderers.

—ON THE RIGHT, Aug. 13, 1966

It is very difficult to overestimate the gentleman's power, which is de-
cocted from pertinacity, odium, specious moralizing, mendacity and lots
and lots of readers, even as *Confidential* Magazine has lots and lots of
readers and for the same reason. Who will deny that the thought passed
through the minds of some of the senators who sat down to judge Senator
Dodd that any failure by them to vote censure might be rewarded instantly by torrential abuse from Drew Pearson. And having examined the
remains of Senator Dodd under glass, after more than one hundred
columns about him by Drew Pearson, it is not just any senator who is
willing to disobey the Quaker scavenger whose lies and contumely have
been deplored by every American President within living memory.

—*NR*, May 16, 1967, *p. 507*

What most senators and congressmen mostly care about is not that a full
disclosure of their financial affairs will leave them prey to the dragons of
Internal Revenue or the Justice Department: but that they would forever
after be grist for the Drew Pearsons of this world, who grow fat from the
business of malevolent distortion, which by the way ought to be listed on
the stock exchange, and count me in for a hundred shares.

—*NR*, July 11, 1967, *p. 751*

And a bulletin from the National Committee to Horsewhip Drew Pearson, from the Executive Whip: Everything is in the mail. However, some
of you have unclear handwriting, or else you wrote in such haste to
inscribe yourselves as charter members of the Horsewhip Committee
that your fingers trembled. In case your name appears wrong, please send
in your certificate, and we'll give you another one, free, gratis. And oh

yes, you will find, when you begin wearing your buttons, proudly, that lots of people will approach you and, almost invariably, ask:

"Why do you want to horsewhip Drew Pearson?"

To which there is one and only one answer authorized unanimously by the Committee, to wit,

"Because of what he said about Shirley Temple."

Now don't go and gild the lily. That's ALL you should reply. Then tilt your head up just the least little bit, heavenward, and permit, perhaps, a lazy tear to make its way slowly down your idealistic cheek, chick.

—*NR*, Dec. 26, 1967, *p. 1418*

Westbrook Pegler

Westbrook Pegler has had his final feud with the Hearst press—out he goes, not only out of the Hearst-owned King Features, but out of the Hearst newspapers, also. The long account of the divorce in the wire service story mentioned all sorts of things about Pegler—his beginnings as a sports writer, his Pulitzer Prize in 1941, his legendary temper, his costly legal engagement with Quentin Reynolds—everything except what most wants mentioning in any account of Pegler, surely, namely that he is easily the greatest satirist in American journalism, and probably in American letters; that he is the most vigorous, and sometimes the most amusing polemical journeyman in the country. Who knows the inside story of the rupture? We don't, and don't particularly want to hear about it. But there isn't anybody else like Pegler writing for Hearst these days, and no one around who can replace him.

—*NR*, Aug. 28, 1962, *p. 126*

Charles Percy

... a Liberal Republican who recently went so far as to decline to say whether he had himself voted for Senator Goldwater for President—thus endearing himself to those who seek candidates free of original sin.

—*NR*, June 14, 1966, *p. 563*

Philosophy

... note to all writers, everywhere: one cannot be a Communist and a philosopher, if you will permit an ipsedixitism.

—ON THE RIGHT, Sept. 30, 1967

Plebiscitary Government

The conservative fears plebiscitary government, for the very same reasons given by Burke and Adams. Instant guidance by the people of the government means instability, and instability is subversive of freedom. If Lyndon Johnson has to step down because 45 per cent of the Democrats in New Hampshire, half of them unable to reply accurately to the question whether Senator McCarthy was for or against the Vietnam War, voted for McCarthy, and because tens of thousands of college students moo over Bobby Kennedy who has delusions of being Ringo Starr, there is something somehow unsettling about it all.

—ON THE RIGHT, April 6, 1968

Police

In appearing before you [the New York Police Department Holy Name Society] today, in the general atmosphere of hostility towards the police force, I feel a little like the man in Madrid a few years ago who was asked at a sidewalk cafe, "What do you think of Franco?" "Come with me," he spoke mysteriously. The questioner got up and followed his quarry, who led him silent through the streets, past the park, to the shore of a lake. Wordlessly he drew up a rowboat, beckoned the man in and rowed silently to the middle of the lake, looked suspiciously about him, and whispered: "I like him."

—Speech of April 4, 1965; in *NR*, April 20, 1965, *p. 324*

The doctrine that a man is innocent until proved guilty seems to have been stretched to mean that the apprehending officials are guilty unless proved innocent. . . . Policeman, they say, should be human. But when they act human, it is deeply resented that they are not inhuman.

—Speech of April 4, 1965 before New York Police Department Holy Name Society; in *NR*, April 20, 1965, *pp. 324–325*

Negro militants have taken to calling whites "whitey" or "honkey." But surely the liberal would disapprove the white who called a Negro "blackey," or "nigger"? Policemen are being called "pigs" to their faces by both whites and blacks who resent them. Freedom of speech entitles them to their opinion and to the selection of their own descriptions. But it does not entitle them to insult people to their faces. Should the community allow its officers to be insulted with impunity? Should a policeman be required to permit others to call him a pig in public? The intent is certainly provocative and the intended purpose is to reduce the authority of, and respect for, the law. Policemen, unlike judges, cannot punish people directly. Insults to an officer of the law in the performance of his duties are, however, every bit as detrimental to public order as insults to a judge, and they should be treated as misdemeanors and legally punished. Moreover, if the law fails to provide this protection, we are inviting policemen, who have normal human feelings and failings, to retaliate by less desirable means. They are human, and have the same right not to be insulted *qua* policemen, as Negroes and whites have not to be insulted *qua* Negroes and whites.

—ON THE RIGHT, Sept. 28, 1968

The point of this lesson is that policemen are, in certain circumstances, precisely the agents of civilization and humanity. Their availability is something that the forces of reason and enlightenment should celebrate, rather than deplore. The dogmatic rejection of the police by so many members of the Harvard faculty is sad testimony to their ignorance of the necessity, under certain circumstances, of the use of force. One wishes, forlornly, that the Weimar Republic had had more policemen, and that they had succeeded, back when it might have worked, in rescuing those who were so permanently, so tragically, victimized by the uproarious students who fought and bled for Hitler.

—ON THE RIGHT, April 17, 1969

Police Civilian Review Board

In New York it is said that the backlash was responsible for abolishing the civilian review board. But what the people of New York, the nation's most liberal community, said, almost 2-1, on election day, was that the mere invocation of the racial issue is simply not enough to destroy their critical judgment. The great majority said in effect that they would not be intimidated by threats of racism to sanction an administrative contrivance which they judged not only irrelevant (it pursued defective conduct among policemen, rather than among criminals, who are rather widely misbehaving in New York), but impudently so (it was headed by a man of vast inexperience in worldly matters—the kind of man who could vote for Henry Wallace for President; and indeed did so). On CBS, nervously surveying the returns, Walter Cronkite asked one of his co-adjutors how could he account for the extraordinary high vote against the civilian review board in New York's Jewish, i.e., liberal, residential areas. Never before having been thrown a ball quite that raw, the junior mumbled something about "Jewish taxi drivers and Jewish mothers" and was quickly taken out of his pain by Mr. Cronkite who nervously turned the spotlight on a startling electoral development in Minot, South Dakota. The point, however, had been made. That not even the most adamantly liberal elements in New York were being swung, by threats of backlash, to defy their better judgment.

—*NRB*, Nov. 22, 1966, *p. 1*

Political Conventions

It is sometimes necessary to sloganize the political order if only to maintain one's sanity. Factional politics is an opiate, as necessary to occasional serenity of the mind as sleep is for the health of the body. A national convention is where judgments and discrimination are officially suspended (unless the convention features a Goldwater, in which case everyone is supposed to react as keenly, as questioningly, as skeptically, as students of Socrates at a session with the master in his garden). Gaiety in our time demands, after all, a considerable exercise in spiritual isolationism.

—NR, Sept. 8, 1964, *p. 764*

And, finally, on the matter of the demonstrations. I myself do not mind them. Granted, I do not look at them; but I do not even mind other people looking at them. There are those who deem them undignified. Quite so, and therefore they are perfectly appropriate to politics.

—ON THE RIGHT, Aug. 17, 1968

One way to cut down on the number of favorite sons would be to decree that the one with the fewest votes at the end of the first ballot would be publicly executed.

—ON THE RIGHT, Aug. 17, 1968

Political Demagoguery

It is difficult to discourage young demagogues when the record is there that a mere four years went by between the time that President Truman accused Candidate Eisenhower of being anti-Semitic and anti-Catholic, the Republican Party of being influenced largely by fascists, and the time when Mr. Truman received a doctorate of humane letters, *honoris causa,* from Oxford University.

—Up from Liberalism, pp. 50–51

Political Semantics

We conservatives are bowed down under the load of demands that we act "constructively" (or, if you like, "affirmatively," or "creatively," or "positively"). If we happen to say, to give an example, "We are *against* hiring Communists in government," we can expect to be accused of negative criticism, because there is a negative word in that sentence. Our critics have won an enormous advantage, through repetitious criticism of our "negative" approach, for they have convinced many members of the community that dissent (if it flows from the Right) is necessarily crabbed and shrill—in a word, useless. . . . The only safe way for conservatives to put their case affirmatively is "We give up, you win, have it your way." That formulation, we guarantee, will be greeted throughout liberaldom as a very constructive position indeed. . . .

—NR, May 30, 1956, *pp. 6–7*

Politics

It is the final curse of politics that nothing, but nothing, is permitted to be spontaneous. *Everything* one does is supposed to have been done with reference to votes. And the pressure sets up a counterpressure: no one will treat you other than on the assumption that that is what you are up to.

—The Unmaking of a Mayor, p. 258

Mr. Harry Truman once remarked that if you can't stand the heat, you should get out of the kitchen. I think he implied by that something a little different from the truism. He implied that no normal man—no virile man —would want to get out of the kitchen. I should like humbly to question Mr. Truman's planted axiom. I do not, to begin with, understand why any normal person should enjoy the heat of the kitchen, and especially I don't understand why a verile man should desire to expose himself to a heat which he cannot, under the terms of Mr. Truman's metaphor, insulate himself against. The normal thing for a normal man to do is to step outside the kitchen, and let the heat rage on within it. And a virile man takes matters into his own hands, and reduces the heat to a point of toleration. Politics, it has been said, is the preoccupation of the quarter-educated, and I do most solidly endorse that observation, and therefore curse this century above all things for its having given all sentient beings very little alternative than to occupy themselves with politics. It is very

well to say that we will ignore the Great Society. But will the Great
Society ignore us?

—*NR*, Nov. 30, 1965, *pp. 1127–1128*

Quite apart from moral grounds, which politics is mostly quite apart
from ...

—ON THE RIGHT, March 12,1966

... the delegates will begin to feel—or so it is programmed by Mr.
[Robert] Kennedy's strategists—that an irresistible force is moving
through the land. And in politics what you do about irresistible forces is
lie down and enjoy them.

—ON THE RIGHT, April 16,1968

Politics—Principles

Now, we are all for principles, and the more deep-seated the better; and
whenever a politician discovers principles, it is, or should be, cause for
national rejoicing—though to be sure there are those others who believe
that any politician who is about to come down with an incipient case of
principle should lie down until he gets over it.

—ON THE RIGHT, Sept. 3, 1964

Politics and Television

They say that TV is a useful democratic instrument because it reveals the
true character of a man to the voters. One wonders whether that in fact
is true, under the developing circumstances. Perhaps the Federal Com-

munications Commission should take a role here? After every appear-
ance of Mr. Lindsay on TV, the credit lines. "Mr. Lindsay's Speech by
David Carberry, Mr. Lindsay's Make-up by David Garth. Mr. Lindsay's
Ad Libs by Harry O'Donnell." Now there is a proposal for lodging more
power with the federal government which Mr. Lindsay could quite consistently support, if Mr. Carberry will permit him.

—ON THE RIGHT, Nov. 28, 1967

The Politics of Voting Blocs

... government designed to placate voting blocs, precisely does so at the
expense of individuals. It hardly satisfies the labor union member who is
granted special privileges, special immunities, that permit him special
advantages, to live in a city where his wife and daughter are not safe
because special privileges, special immunities, are granted in turn to
another voting bloc. It hardly benefits a man who can earn an average
of 415 an hour wiring a new apartment building, to find that he cannot
rent an apartment in that building except by paying a rent that reflects
the crushing cost of paying $15 an hour to electricians.

—NR, July 13, 1965, p. 586 (statement announcing his candidacy for Mayor
of New York City)

Politics—Vote-getting

A good debater is not necessarily an effective vote-getter: you can find
a hole in your opponent's argument through which you can drive a coach
and four ringing jingle bells all the way, and thrill at the crystallization
of a truth wrung out from a bloody dialogue—which, however, may warm
only you and your muse, while the smiling paralogist has in the meantime
made votes by the tens of thousands.

—The Unmaking of a Mayor, p. 272

Pope Paul VI

Resentment also came on account of the nature of the Pope's recent Christmas message, wherein he took the ground from under the same theologians and church activists who have come very close, in recent years and months, to unlicensing war under any circumstances. The Pope bore down very hard on pacifism, and in the course of doing so, acknowledged what many people know, but dare not say, namely that the motives of some, repeat some, of the young opponents of the Vietnam War are to say the least ignoble. What is more, in the very same passage, the Pope re-introduced into the analysis of specific wars certain conventional terms which the relativists have been getting away from. The Pope spoke about good and evil, about justice and injustice, freedom and the lack of it: and did so in such a way as to endorse the official view of what we are doing in Vietnam. This was a considerable moral setback for those who refuse to distinguish between the two causes. . . . it would appear that in his continuing commitment to the cause of pacifism he is showing the tenacious concern for the end of genocidal activity in the Far East which Pope Pius XII was accused of not having shown when it was the Jews who were being victimized by Nazi Germany.

—ON THE RIGHT, Jan. 4, 1968

Pornography

Our own notion is that to attempt to draw the line for adults is a practical impossibility, and that therefore it is better to go the way of permissiveness, than the way of Comstock. As regards minors, it does not greatly matter if a particular judge should err on the side of prurience: the underprivileged youth can catch up on his pornography in due course, when his emotions will have settled down a little.

—*NR*, Dec. 14, 1965, *p. 1148*

Poverty

Tax *all* the luxuries of the rich and you don't have enough money to buy all the Vatican treasures—it is the middle class and the lower middle classes who are shouldering the great economic load today, for the simple reason that the rich, if you took away everything they had, could not relieve the world's poor for a single week. The peace is not most usually disturbed by the poor, but by the power-hungry, rich or poor: the great peace-breakers of this century, Russia, Japan and Germany, were not poor nations by common standards.

—*NR*, April 18, 1967, *pp. 392–393*

Mr. Norman Thomas, on one occasion when I debated with him, said not less than three times that 17 million Americans "were not earning a living wage." After the third repetition of this, I was driven to asking him why, under the circumstances, they weren't dead? That obvious observation had a magical purgative effect on the evening's discussion and, rhetoric having de-escalated, we proceeded happily into effective argument.

—ON THE RIGHT, July 15, 1967

Adam Clayton Powell Jr.

The relationship between corruption and Adam Clayton Powell Jr. would appear to be something like the relationship between typhoid and Typhoid Mary.

—*NR*, March 26, 1960, *p. 191*

Well, Adam Clayton Powell Jr. has had his testimonial dinner, and if anyone gagged, it did not make the news columns. We thought of sending a reporter, but our instinct against voyeurism prevailed—we only wish unbuttoned political rituals would be conducted in total privacy.

—*NR*, Feb. 11, 1961, *p. 69*

Our hero Adam Clayton Powell Jr. was sued by the lady—by the rich lady, I guess we should say at this point—whom he had labeled the "bagwoman" *(i.e.,* the one that travels about from grafter to grafter with the little black bag); and last week the jury voted to sock the Reverend Adam two hundred and ten thousand post-tax bucks, which is a lot of bucks, even for Adam, and even though he sometimes seems to confuse his own financial resources with those of the federal government. Well, a couple of sermons over at the Abyssinian Church, a couple of extra collections, and, presto, the non-bagwoman is paid off. But before then, Powell's attorneys will appeal to federal courts to throw out the judgment, pleading immunity: on the grounds that in telling lies about the lady on television he was simply doing the kind of thing he does in the halls of Congress. A good point.

—NR, April 23, 1963, *p. 306*

I am advised by my conscience that I have not done my duty this season, not until I pay my respects to Adam Clayton Powell Jr. I confess that I need to drag myself to the typewriter to perform the ritual. In days gone by, when the Reverend Powell was a hero to significant members of the liberal community, it was different. I have expended, in my lifetime, as much first-class indignation on the rascal as on anybody in the world, regardless of race, color, or creed. And it was not, by the way, all that long ago that everyone agreed to hate Adam.

—NR, June 29, 1965, *p. 540*

Meanwhile, back in Washington, Mr. Powell was busily engaged, as ever, in hedonism, junketing around the world with curvaceous amanuenses, while maintaining a wife in Puerto Rico to whom he pays $18,000 per year out of congressional funds and whose usefulness to the United States is somewhat less than that of Madame de Gaulle, who at least pays the U.S. a visit every few years and spends a dollar or two in this country, thus stimulating commerce. So far as is known, Mrs. Powell, who is supposed to work on the congressman's staff, hasn't ever been in Washington since she got married and thereupon qualified for her high salary.

—NR, Oct. 4, 1966, *p. 975*

... Meanwhile there is plenty to do in Bimini, as long as there are fish unhooked, and whisky undrunk, and, of course, souls to be saved.

—On The Right, May 30, 1967

Pravda

Pravda's coverage of the first Glassboro conference between Kosygin and LBJ was confined to thirty-seven (37) words, about as much space as a major metropolitan newspaper devotes to the day's weather. The same front page of *Pravda* announced proudly in an editorial that the millionth Volga car had come off the assembly line at the Gorky auto plant, a news item comparable to something the Ford Motor Company put out along about, say, 1911. The front page also announced "nationwide support" (there is never any other kind of support in the Soviet Union—non-nationwide support, e.g., in favor of free speech, expresses itself in Siberia) for the Soviet Central Committee's denunciation of Israeli "aggression."

—On The Right, June 29, 1967

Prayer in Public Schools

It was Mrs. Murray who brought the action to impose a silence on the subject of God on all the children of the United States who study in public schools, because her moon-faced son's rights are otherwise trampled upon. She was the perfect plaintiff, poetically speaking, for this case. Just before the decision, Mrs. Murray gave an interview to *The Realist.* Her opening sentences were: "If I can't come through this case the same offensive, unlovable, bullheaded, defiant, aggressive slob that I was when I started it, then I'll give up now. My own identity is more important to me. They can keep their gawd-damn prayers in the public schools, in public outhouses, in public H-bomb shelters and in public whore-houses." Those, as we say, are the words not of the Supreme Court that wrote this decision, but of Madalyn Murray, who brought the case to the Court. You do understand that what has been accomplished, net, is to shield Mrs. Murray's son from exposure to religion in the schools. Religion is for the home.

—*NR*, July 2, 1963, *p. 521*

Ours is the *only* country in Christendom which officially forbids voluntary prayer in its public schools. Truly this is a land of fundamentalist passions. Cotton Mather obviously would not have approved of the program of the separatists, but their relentless arguments, their unflagging zealotry, would have warmed his flinty heart.

—*NR*, June 2, 1964, *p. 437*

The Presidency

In psychological terms, the office is so majestic that it is 1) impossible to conceive of almost anyone who is not President as being President without being faintly ludicrous; and 2) impossible to conceive of someone who is in fact President as altogether ludicrous. . . . when all is said and done it is impossible truly to train for the Presidency. Like using a parachute, it is something you have to succeed at the very first time. . . . The more complicated and powerful the job, the more rudimentary the preparation for it. You cultivate the essential virtues: high purpose, intelligence, decency, humility, fear of the Lord, and the passion for freedom.

—*NR*, April 23, 1963, *p. 312*

Mr. Coolidge used to take a very long nap every afternoon, and then go to bed very early after dinner. Mr. Mencken wrote that there is much to be said for any president who turns the White House primarily into a dormitory, but that was back in the pastoral age, when Americans did not demand that their president fill the role of king, God, and hero, in addition to chief executive.

—On The Right, Oct. 8, 1968

The Press

I have always wondered at the temerity of the American press. I did not view the interment of President Kennedy on television for fear that NBC would poke a microphone into Jackie's face and ask her what did she think of the eulogy?

—On The Right, Jan. 23, 1969

Privacy

Do you want your son or daughter to apply for a college scholarship? If so, you begin by filling out a standard form devised by the College Entrance Examination Board. The form is called "Parents' Confidential Statement," and asks your salary before taxes; other income; annual home expenses; extraordinary expenses; federal income tax paid; life insurance face value; value of home; fire insurance and unpaid mortgage on same; other real estate; capital value of your share of business or farm, cash, notes, accounts receivable, inventories, equipment, other fixed assets, mortgage, net fixed assets on said business or farm; the nature of your retirement plan; estimate of any gifts that might be given your son during school year from other sources, relatives, friends, organizations, government, foundation or veteran grants; family insurance policies; and, of course, make and year of family automobiles. How many gold teeth do you have? Heh! Heh! Heh! *They'll* never know! Until they think to ask.

—*NR*, Nov. 22, 1958, *p. 337*

Conservatives are presumptively opposed to the passage of laws telling people they can't do things. But here is a classic situation where the affirmation of an individual's right overpowers the presumption against the passage of new laws and indeed dictates their passage. More and more it becomes plain that privacy is the key to liberty. Privacy considered in the larger sense, as the right not only to insulate yourself against the importunities of a bustling, hustling order, but to preserve to yourself the ground within which to maneuver. ... Let us, then, have yet another law. Rather, fifty state laws (why a federal law?), forbidding the sale or purchase or ownership of anti-privacy devices, with a penalty attached that will guarantee to any miscreant user thereof the privacy of a jail cell for a couple of months.

—NR, June 1, 1965, p. 455

Reasonable folk agree that the FBI should utilize all technological inventions available to it in order to safeguard the national security and to frustrate the assassin or the kidnapper. The trouble is that once it sets up a bug, the FBI becomes a sort of omnium-gatherum, because the bug does not distinguish between conversation about how to steal a state secret, and conversation about how to make contact with a lady of easy virtue. Inevitably, other branches of the federal government hunger to know whether the bug has picked up information of particular interest to it. For instance, Internal Revenue. . . . Surely a law should be passed, and one assumes the FBI would welcome it, to the effect that no information should be given to collateral divisions of the government which is picked up by wire tap, unless it is necessary to prevent acts of violence?

—ON THE RIGHT, July 26, 1966

Private Schools

No one now doubts that what maintains the majority of American students in the public schools in the major cities is economic pressure. Let us admit that if the state were to give each child a voucher, on the order of what is given to veterans under the G.I. Bill of Rights, cashable for sum X at any accredited school, that there would be massive redeployments of children in all the major centers of the United States. And not only the children of the upper middle class. Also poor Negro children, for instance—to private schools especially designed to give special assistance to meet special needs. . . . It is the dawning realization that everybody would be better off under a mixed system in which public schools remained—for those who chose to patronize them. It is even suggested now by pedagogues of great reputation that it might be sound for the public schools to employ private contractors to teach the art of reading to individual students aged four and five and six. Indeed, the day may not be far away when it becomes possible—one is breathless at the prospect—to advocate the voucher system, and take education away from the bureaucrats and the egalitarians and the politicians and return it to the teachers and to the parents.

—ON THE RIGHT, Jan. 13, 1968

Progress

Every day, in every way, things are getting worse and worse.

—*NR*, July 2, 1963, *p. 519*

Americans always associate physical movement with progress, indeed it is sometimes a substitute for thought, as witness the endless bebopping about the globe of John Foster Dulles, the marches of the civil rights leaders, the travelling, for the sake of it, of the gypsy generation brought up on Jack Kerouac's admonitions to go on the road.

—ON THE RIGHT, April 11, 1968

Property Rights and Human Rights

There is no distinction between the two classes of rights. What are property rights, if not human rights?—Animal rights? Vegetable rights? All rights flow from the right of freedom. All rights are susceptible of abuse—including the right of free speech. So also can the rights of private property be abused; but the concept must not, on that account, be impeached.

—ON THE RIGHT, Feb. 1, 1964

Prosecution by Government

If the government assaults a citizen, puts him through grand jury meetings and public trials—and then fails to make its case, leaving the intended victim exonerated but exhausted, why shouldn't the government assume at least the financial burden of the exonerated defendant?

—ON THE RIGHT, Dec. 3, 1968

The Pueblo

Do we have, aboard the Pueblo, vital security information the removal of which by the enemy would seriously affect the national interest? Is that information . . . the refined electronic machinery aboard the Pueblo? In [that] event, the United States Navy ought not to have deliberated overnight. A bombing raid should have gone over to Wonsan with orders to sink our own ship, which surely it is our right to do: and if the marksmanship of our pilots is a little rusty and it turns out that we also sank the North Korean boats that brought in the Pueblo, why, you can't win them all.

—ON THE RIGHT, Jan. 30, 1968

Still, let the court martial proceed. It will presumably vindicate Mr. Bucher, but expose at meticulous and dismaying length the ineptitudes of powerful men whose conduct in the Pueblo affair was a perfect complement to the foreign policy which made the whole awful episode possible.

—ON THE RIGHT, Jan. 30, 1969

And then the strange question arises, Why wasn't the ship scuttled? The answer given was that it would have required two and one-half hours to sink the ship. I find this datum fascinating, since as a small-boat skipper I have spent considerable energy over the years keeping boats afloat, the sinking of which I have always assumed would be extremely easy to contrive, should the spirit ever move me.

—ON THE RIGHT, Jan. 30, 1969

R

Race Riots

Rioting in the ghetto is merely the slum variant of what Drs. Martin Luther King, Benjamin Spock, and William Sloane Coffin are busily engaged in doing, to the applause of a significant sector of the intellectual community. The riot in Detroit was merely a proletarian version of well-fed, well-housed white students preventing McNamara from speaking at Harvard, or a police car from leaving the premises of the University of California. One would have thought that the old stomach-argument about how to prevent riots would have died for intellectual undernourishment after the riots in New Haven and Detroit, model cities from the positivist point of view which guided the thinking of the Kerner Commission. What caused the riots isn't segregation or poverty or frustration. What caused them is a psychological disorder which is tearing at the ethos of our society as a result of boredom, self-hatred, and the arrogant contention that all our shortcomings are the results of other people's aggressions upon us. . . . The problem is bi-racial, and nothing said by the Kerner Commission is relevant to its solution.

—ON THE RIGHT, March 16, 1968

Racism

But mention the fact that Negro illegitimacy is a grave social problem, mention such a thing in front of, say, Mr. Beame, and Mr. Lindsay, and they will either simply vanish from the room in a cloud of integrated dust; or else they will turn and call *you* a racist! The very same gentlemen who believe that you can't *hope* to appeal to a Catholic voter unless you

235

present yourself alongside a Catholic running-mate; who believe that no
Jew in New York will vote for you unless you prop up a Jewish running-
mate and show him off, and chew away on a blintz, morning, noon, and
night; these same gentlemen are pleased to condemn as racist those who
could not care less what is the race, or the religion, of those who appear
on the ticket; or who do not for a moment suppose that merely because
a family is Negro, there is a congenital disposition to promiscuity.

—*The Unmaking of a Mayor*, p. 155

Railroads—Nationalizing Them

We do not suppose there are a great many people around more opposed
than we, for reasons historical, political, economic, and even spiritual, to
the nationalization of industries. But we do believe that the time has
come for the government to nationalize the railroads—*or* to permit them
to function as privately managed enterprises. As it stands, the railroads
cannot perform usefully and efficiently because everywhere they turn
they run into government. It is important to understand that the problem
of the paralyzing labor union is essentially the problem of government.
It is government that immunized labor unions from the anti-monopoly
laws.

—*NR*, May 5, 1964, *p. 345*

Rash Proposals

Of all the candidates [for Mayor of New York City] . . . I am the *most*
anxious not to make any rash proposals, because I have, looking over my
shoulders, not only the voters, but also my muse; to whose service I have
been devoted for lo these many years.

I am, then, against rash proposals. My God, I sound like John Lindsay!
Although I suppose he'd have added, "On the other hand, society must
take its share of responsibility for the plight of rash proposals. I have a
fountain pen given to me by President Johnson after signing the Act,
which I co-sponsored, to provide better living conditions for rash proposals."

—Mayoralty speech printed in *NR*, Nov. 2, 1965, *p. 978*

Ronald Reagan

Los Angeles—It is generally conceded that Ronald Reagan will announce his candidacy for Governor of California in the early future, and the guns are being oiled to shoot him down. The Democrats are not saying anything yet, at least not publicly; but they are passing around the word that Reagan will be easy to take. It must be understood that they would pass around the word that Abraham Lincoln would be easy to take, it being in the nature of the political business that one should scoff at the possibilities of the challenger, particularly a challenger the sound of whose name sends the butterflies of the stomach into hyperactivity.

—ON THE RIGHT, Dec. 16, 1965

[Reagan] is developing a political know-how which astounds the professionals, who believe that it is immoral that an actor, as distinguished from a haberdasher, should be a good politician.

—ON THE RIGHT, Dec. 16, 1965

Reagan has been doing disconcertingly well in his campaign for governor of California, to the distress of those who would dearly like to see him foam at the mouth and come out for the repeal of the internal combustion engine, or something.

—*NR*, April 19, 1966, *p. 344*

... when simultaneously Reagan voted with the majority to dismiss Kerr, and came out (via a subordinate who spoke out ahead of schedule) in favor of uniform reductions (10 per cent) in state spending, and in favor of charging tuition at the University of California and the state colleges, all the educators felt the tug of class solidarity that Karl Marx, Eugene Debs, and James Hoffa never succeeded in eliciting from the proletarian classes.

—*NR*, Nov. 28, 1967, *p. 1321*

Red China

[Senator] Javits wants to "chip away at the wall of hostility that separates us" from Red China by seeking out "areas of agreement in the interest of peace." The trouble is that when one seeks and does not find, it often happens that hostility increases; and rightly so. Let's make a list of things on which Red China and the U. S. agree. And send the list to Senator Javits. (My list: E equals MC^2.)

—On The Right, Jan. 5, 1967

Red China: Admission to the UN

To suggest at this moment in world history the advisability of throwing the diplomatic weight of the United Nations and, derivatively, of the United States, towards the stabilization of Mao's regime is, to put it gently, crooked. But the whole episode was symbolic of the fetishistic attitude of some Americans towards the United Nations. Membership in the UN is, as far as some of them are concerned, a baptismal experience: grace instantly follows, and wonderful things lope in over the horizon.

—*NR*, Oct. 31, 1967, *p. 1161*

... the sentimentalist rationale that Red China will dissolve into peacefulness immediately upon imbibing one chocolate milk shake at the UN.

—On The Right, March 29, 1969

Red China: Recognition

If "law and order" is a code word for racism, I divulge the code word for let's-recognize-Red-China ... to wit, "The participants will represent a spectrum of viewpoints on the various issues involved in our relationships with China's 700 million people." Anytime you see a reference anywhere to China's having 700 million people, believe me, that means we should recognize Red China. Try it.

—On The Right, Jan. 28, 1969

Why don't the liberals cut out the tergiversations and just say, plain and simple, to all of us, what they say to themselves in the privacy of their workshops (how do we know what they say in the privacy of their workshops? Because we know how their minds work), namely: We ought to recognize Red China, and the sooner the better. They should show some of the guts American soldiers showed when exchanging machine gun fire with Red Chinese.

—NR, April 8, 1961, *p. 211*

Reform

Reform is *not* a synonym for leftward ho!, and the first Democrat in power who recognizes this will go down big in the history books.

—ON THE RIGHT, Nov. 14, 1964

Relativism

We conservatives, I think ... know that just as the educational experience of recorded civilization has yielded certain scientific conclusions, it has yielded certain conclusions in the realm of values. We are as certain that Communism errs as we are that the whole is equal to the sum of its parts. And we wonder at the anti-intellectualism of those who, in the name of intellect, show so little respect for the human mind that they cannot credit it with the power to come to any reliable conclusion.

—NR, April 20, 1957, *p. 382*

Religion

All kinds of people are, these days, urging that we "re-examine" religion. ("Re-examine," as used by the social scientists, is the polite and fastidiously open-minded euphemism for "junk.") It is not merely the Communists who join Marx in dismissing religion as the opium of the people, or the doddering, reactionary naturalists and humanists; Christianity is under fire on a number of diverse, up-to-date fronts. Arnold Toynbee, for example, goes busily about from sect to sect, bent on synthesizing a religious Esperanto satisfactory to all, offensive to none. Colin Wilson wants a New religion. (Voltaire knew how to accomplish *that*. Asked how by a young disciple, he instructed him: "First you go and get crucified; then you rise again from the dead.") Dr. Lawrence Kubie of Yale, forecasting an end to human mortality, can't see where there will be room left for the "remote hereafter" of orthodox religions. Aldous Huxley informed us the other day that religion must be "re-examined" in the light of the discovery of drugs that can "alter human behavior." Why not take a vote on religion in the United Nations, and be done with this talk, talk, talk?

—*NR*, Nov. 17, 1956, *p. 7*

Religion and Politics

We have come a long distance from the way of Hilaire Belloc when he ran for Parliament, to the way of John F. Kennedy when he ran for the Presidency of the United States. In the terms I speak of, we have unprogressed. In 1960 John F. Kennedy pleaded with his fellow Christians, of Protestant denomination, not to take seriously the fact that he was by "accident of birth" a Roman Catholic. Hilaire Belloc was asked by a lady, while answering questions from a platform in 1906, whether it was true that he was a "papist." "Madam," he roared out his answer at the top of his voice, reaching into his pocket and drawing out a rosary, "do you see these BEADS? I say them every MORNING as soon as I get UP, and every NIGHT before I go to BED. And if you object to THAT, Madam, I can only PRAY to God that He will spare me the IGNOMINY of representing YOU in Parliament!" Belloc won, and achieved something more than his own election.

—*Saturday Evening Post*, Oct. 17, 1964, *p. 12*

The problem of how far churches and churchmen should probe into political issues is a vexed one, on which the finest moralizers have split hairs for centuries. I once discussed the whole issue on a television network with Mr. Charles P. Taft, brother of my late lamented hero the Senator. I remember asking him, intending to understand just where he thought the churches might establish useful limits against political factionalism, whether he didn't at least agree that churches should not take a stand for or against fluoridated water. He replied by accusing me of desiring the nation's youth to mature with rotted teeth.

—On The Right, May 21, 1964

Rent Controls

The only excuse for rent control is situations of temporary emergency, caused for instance by over-crowding in cases of war, famine, or plague. Lyndon Johnson guarantees us we won't have war, Orville Freeman guarantees us we won't have hunger, and Earl Warren has declared plagues unconstitutional under the 14th Amendment: so why rent control? —which as a matter of fact is mostly exploited by middle-income salary earners? Who authorized the city to single out apartment building owners as a class whose property was to be conscripted for the commonweal? The result of these laws is serious deterioration in fine old buildings, and the discouragement of new building, which cannot compete with the artificially low prices of the rent-controlled building.

—On The Right, Oct. 6, 1964

Repression

Repression is an unpleasant instrument, but it is absolutely necessary for civilizations that believe in order and human rights. I wish to God Hitler and Lenin had been repressed. And word should be gently got through to the non-violent avenger Dr. King, that in the unlikely event that he succeeds in mobilizing his legions, they will be most efficiently, indeed most zestfully repressed. In the name, quite properly, of social justice.

—On The Right, Aug. 19, 1967

It seems to me that the United States has lagged behind in developing the art of repression. There are now enough eyewitness reports to the activities of the mob—in Watts, Harlem, Detroit, Cleveland, Cincinnati,

New Haven, Newark—to justify the generality that we are suffering much more from violence and disorder then we are suffering from inadequate opportunities for dissent.

—On The Right, Nov. 23, 1967

The term "repression" is being used tendentiously by the left, which seeks to invest it with fascistic overtones. In fact repression is exactly what we need, repression of those who wake up every morning and decide which laws they are going to obey, which disobey. Repression is exactly what a healthy society needs against its aggressors.

—On The Right, Feb. 18, 1969

Republican Party

... the Eastern priesthood, who have acted as the Curia for the GOP for two generations ...

—On The Right, April 25, 1964

Mr. [Ray] Bliss will find, in the days ahead, that he must encourage a policy that satisfies the conservatives within the Republican Party, or else wind up with total control of a vast Republican National Headquarters composed of empty rooms with cobwebs on the typewriters, into which only those Republicans stroll who, for reasons of personal eccentricity, choose to call themselves Republicans even while holding views copyrighted by the Democrats.

—*NR*, July 27, 1965, *p. 630*

What Labor has to fear is a courageous Republican voice of great influence, which is to say that it has very little to fear.

—On The Right, Nov. 17, 1966

Republican Politics, 1964

. . . Scranton, if nominated, would leave San Francisco having created the largest body of defectors since Constantine committed Rome to Christianity.

—ON THE RIGHT, June 18, 1964

Republican Politics, 1968

A few stickers crop up on Waikiki Beach and elsewhere reading: "Rocky!" That exclamation point, clearly the work of the highest-priced professionals at Madison Avenue, probably cost the Rockefeller people a hundred thou. Compare "Rocky!" with just plain "Rocky" and you will understand the importance of professionalism. For instance, one wouldn't want, say, "Rocky. Ugh." On the other hand, "Rocky! A-ah!" might be slightly overdoing it. You have to give these matters a lot of thought before you come out sufficiently admiring the craftsmanship of the social engineers.

—ON THE RIGHT, July 6, 1968

Mr. Rockefeller is due to entertain munificently at breakfast, and make his pitch. My advice to one invited guest was: Order caviar, and then say No.

—ON THE RIGHT, July 6, 1968

The script called for a very considerable investment of money in newspaper advertisements, radio, and T.V. spots calculated to flush out latently pro-Rockefeller sentiment, or latently anti-Nixon sentiment, whichever was least constipated ...

—ON THE RIGHT, July 16, 1968

There was plenty of opportunity, Romney having retired, for his principal sponsor Mr. Rockefeller to stand in as challenger in the ensuing primaries. But Mr. Rockefeller chose this period to succumb to a severe case of the vapors, from which he recovered only just in time to miss all the primaries, and disparage Mr. Nixon's victories in them as of no consequence.

—ON THE RIGHT, Aug. 8, 1968

Such a case against [Spiro Agnew] as was attempted was to the effect that his nomination was done "in order to appease the South." By some people, this charge is deployed as a dreadnought. There are those, however, who pause to recall that the South, like other sections of the country, is inhabited by Americans, and until we hear otherwise from the Supreme Court, they too are entitled to political consideration. ... It is ironic that the principal opponents of the choice of Agnew, most of them advocates of the nomination of John Lindsay, were using arguments in Lindsay's behalf which were most readily translatable as suggesting the imperative need of appeasing the North and the cities.

—ON THE RIGHT, Aug. 13, 1968

Walter Reuther

Mr. Reuther may deplore General Motor's hold on the automobile industry, as rising on 60 per cent. He has never been heard to deplore his own control over the automobile industry, which rises on 100 per cent.

—ON THE RIGHT, Jan. 27, 1966

Rhetoric

... the dominant theme, as explicitly handled by the chairman of the history department of the University of Vermont, was "Religion and Communism—Parallel or Antithesis." Now, everybody knows enough about the structure of rhetoric to know that when you set up a question in just that way, your objective is to promote the minority point of view. If you see an essay called, "Tobacco—Pleasure-Giver or Death-Dealer?" —you can be absolutely sure that the article will come out on the side of tobacco as Death-Dealer.

—ON THE RIGHT, Dec. 4, 1965

Rioters

... now we are experimenting, or so the word leaks out from ingenious laboratories, with all kinds of new devices, some of them having, it seems to me, the distinctive virtue of contributing a little ignominy to the situation. My favorite is a form of glue, which I would most willingly shower down upon, let us say, an aggregation of sit-ins cluttering up the public corridor of an administration building. The glue in question takes many hours to remove, and during those hours the sit-ins are literally glued together, in a state of *Gemütlichkeit* that goes much further than anything they had contemplated. Another is a form of soap, banana-peel like, which upsets the balance of even the soberest rioter, making him look positively ridiculous. And who knows, contact with soap might have such an effect on the rioter as water is said to have on witches, who are fearfully afraid, knowing that if it should touch their skins, they will fade, fade forever away.

—ON THE RIGHT, Nov. 23, 1967

Ripon Society

... a little group of Cambridge intellectuals whose mission in life is to extirpate every trace of difference between the Republican and the Democratic Parties. .... If the Ripon Society desires to liberalize the YRs [Young Republicans], it had better liberalize youth in general. Why not urge Harvard to hire a few liberal professors?

—*NR*, July 11, 1967, *pp. 726–728*

Jackie Robinson

One of the rights the Negroes in New York have which nobody has got in the way of their exercising, is the right to tell Jackie Robinson to go back to the Hall of Fame and sit on his throne there, and stop discrediting the cause of interracial progress by threatening violence on any community whose members disagree with Robinson's own undeveloped political views.

—ON THE RIGHT, Nov. 4, 1965

The hold of Jackie Robinson on Governor Rockefeller is a point of minor interest. Two years ago, William Miller, Mr. Goldwater's vice-presidential candidate, volunteered to help Rockefeller achieve reelection as governor, and Rockefeller, on the prowl for conservative support, gratefully accepted. Whereupon Jackie Robinson served public notice that if Miller came in, Robinson would go out; and Rockefeller, missing a historical opportunity, capitulated. There must be something undeniable in Robinson. Perhaps President Rockefeller would send *him* to Hanoi?

—ON THE RIGHT, June 27, 1968

... Jackie Robinson, the baseball player who along the way decided he was really born to play Walter Lippmann.

—ON THE RIGHT, Dec. 19, 1968

Nelson Rockefeller

Governor Rockefeller ... has long since developed the knack of trans-
forming expedience into an act of transcedent principle. ...

—*NR*, Aug. 27, 1963, *p. 136*

Bobby Kennedy and Nelson Rockefeller are having a row, ostensibly
over the plight of New York's mentally retarded, a loose definition of
which would include everyone in New York who voted for Bobby
Kennedy or Nelson Rockefeller.

—*NRB*, Jan. 4, 1966, *p. 1*

Mr. Rockefeller is meanwhile reduced to heading up a vast draft-
Rockefeller movement.

—ON THE RIGHT, April 20,1968

But it takes men of archaeological passion to find Mr. Rockefeller's ideas
in Mr. Rockefeller's current prose. Next time, he should furnish his
audience with a trot.

—ON THE RIGHT, April 23, 1968

Nelson Rockefeller on Vietnam

Rocky! (as Madison Avenue has taught us to think of him) has come out
with his solution for Vietnam. It is absolutely unexceptionable. That is
to say, we're for it. All that is required, in order to promulgate it, is to
elect Nelson Rockefeller as President of North Vietnam. ... The political
and practical meaning of Mr. Rockefeller's plan is 1) vagueness on Vietnam is at a premium politically; 2) anything can be made to appear

serious if it is spread over two pages in the *New York Times*; and 3) he does not know what to do in Vietnam, or at least if he does, he knows that it is unwise to say what.

—NR, July 30,1968, *p. 734*

George Lincoln Rockwell

It is, one supposes, necessary to cover the most conspicuous exploits of Mr. Rockwell. Hardly necessary, I should think, to treat them with that sober-seriousness that encourages the wild exaggerations of his importance and that of his handful of fellow cretins, that some foreigners attach to them. . . . It is, as I have suggested, impossible to ignore Rockwell, even as it is impossible to ignore a bedbug. But bedbugs do not the headline make. They are things to be flicked off, forcefully, and with resignation, but at some distance removed from the spotlight at center stage.

—ON THE RIGHT, Jan. 26, 1965

George Romney

The excuse then was that inasmuch as Governor Romney was the anointed instrument of Republican moderation, Rockefeller should stay out of the way, lest he utter thoughts on foreign policy that would compete with Romney's, as indeed any thoughts would have.

—ON THE RIGHT, April 13, 1968

Don't you see, the analysis of Mr. Romney's failure as based on his personal limitations is now crucial to the liberal Republicans. They must perforce dwell on the startling personal limitations of Mr. Romney, which limitations they never informed us about before. What liberal-oriented observers are greatly reluctant to acknowledge is that the Republican Party of the United States of America, four years after the ignominious defeat of Senator Barry Goldwater, is more conservative—

more conservative by far—than it was in 1964. . . . What Mr. Romney's experience has shown is that this is not the season for liberal Republicanism, and that is the principal lesson of his defeat.

—ON THE RIGHT, March 7, 1968

Eleanor Roosevelt

. . . following Mrs. Roosevelt in search of irrationality was like following a burning fuse in search of an explosive; one never had to wait very long.

—*Up from Liberalism*, p.42

Mrs. Roosevelt's statement several years ago that she would "never cross any picket line," stood for years as the highest monument to contemporary anti-rationalism. But now she has come through with a rival. "I was shocked," she writes, "to hear not long ago that in one of our schools some older boys beat up their teacher." The explanation? "When this happens, you can be sure that the blame does not lie with the young people. Somehow or other such a teacher failed to build up the respect and interest of her pupils and did not arouse a feeling in the children that she could be trusted and could understand things which perhaps the youngsters would not even talk about at home." Whatever happened to the suggestion that, her residence having been ascertained beyond peradventure, patriotic citizens institute a 24-hour picket line around Hyde Park?

—*NR*, Aug. 11, 1956, *p. 4*

If the Declaration of Human Rights ever becomes the supreme law of the land, there will ensue in America 1) a Hundred Years War during which the courts labor to find out what on earth it all means; 2) a net diminution of the liberties guaranteed by the Bill of Rights. In the slave world, the Covenant, though duly ratified, would be as dead a letter as is the United Nations Charter, with all its exalted talk about freedom and peace. The

only reason for celebrating the Human Rights anniversary is that the
Commission that drafted the rights absorbed Mrs. Roosevelt's energies
for three whole years.

—NR, Jan. 3, 1959, *p. 422*

I have been sharply reminded that I have not written about Mrs. Roosevelt, and that only a coward would use the excuse that when she died,
he was in Africa. There, there are lions and tigers and apartheid. Here,
there was Mrs. Roosevelt to write about. Africa was the safer place.

. . .she treated all the world as her own personal slum project; and all
the papers, of course, remarked on that fabulous energy—surely she was
the very first example of the peacetime use of atomic energy. But some
publications (I think especially of *Time*) went so far as to say she had a
great mind. Now is the time for all good men to come to the aid of Euclid.

. . . "With all my heart and soul," her epitaph should read, "I fought
the syllogism." And with that energy and force, she wounded it, almost
irretrievably—how often have you seen the syllogism checking in at the
office for a full day's work lately?

—NR, Jan. 29, 1963, *p.58*

Franklin Delano Roosevelt Jr.

The reason why FDR Jr. is something less than a spiritual experience,
is that insiders know that his career in politics is something like Murph
the Surf's in the outside world: opportunize, sing, grovel, opportunize,
etc. FDR Jr. the liberal idealist called Hubert Humphrey a draft-dodger
when stumping for JFK in the West Virginia primaries, worked for Rafael
Trujillo to help sweeten the General's image, spurned the Liberal Party
in the forties after the Party had got him the seat in Congress, and now
accepts its designation for governor.

—ON THE RIGHT, Sept. 17, 1966

S

Sacco and Vanzetti

What matters now is less whether Sacco and Vanzetti were guilty than whether they were fairly dealt with. If it should prove they were innocent —if, say, the real criminal is still alive, and will one day establish that Sacco and Vanzetti were not the murderers—to what extent would the adamant defenders of Sacco and Vanzetti, or rather the adamant critics of the men who sent them to death, win justification? I should say, Not at all. For their obligation would still be to point back to the trial and say why the jury should have voted otherwise; or tell us where the prosecution failed to follow a lead; or show where the trial judge abused his role as arbiter; or indicate why the appellate courts should have suspected it was not Sacco and Vanzetti, but someone else, because there was compelling reason to believe the evidence had been rigged. But no such demonstration has been made.

—The American Legion Magazine, Oct., 1960, *p.49*

Sailing

Sailing has always had an allure for me which I have found irresistible. At 12, I persuaded my indulgent father to give me a boat. Cautiously, he gave me a boat *and* a full-time instructor.

—Motor Boating, April, 1958

SANE (Committee for a Sane Nuclear Policy)

It is headed for cuckooland. ... One cannot wish SANE, and the free world, luck, at one and the same time.

—*NR*, Jan. 14, 1964, *p. 11*

Jean-Paul Sartre

Sartre calls himself an existentialist. He is primarily a super-verbalist, who spins his teeming thoughts into plays, novels, autobiography, creative philosophy, biography, essays, criticism. He is one of the foremost creative literary men of our time, and although at the center of his philosophy is the importance of the individual, he is stubbornly atheist —and so denudes the individual of the divine spark that is his surest claim to individuality; and he is stubbornly socialist—and so denudes the individual of the privacy which best reflects the dignity of the human condition. It is these philosophical and social confusions which render Sartre ultimately a dull man, a man truly disoriented, whose concern for individualism tends to reduce to a kind of ascetic hedonism; it is not so strange that his life-long mistress would have written the definitive defense of the Marquis de Sade, or that he should have undertaken the definitive defense of the pervert Genet.

—*NR*, Nov. 17, 1964, *p. 1004*

Arthur Schlesinger Jr.

I shall always be glad to give publicity to any lapse by Professor Schlesinger into sanity, and do not worry that such a guarantee will heavily mortgage my future time.

—*NR*, May 8, 1962, *p. 316*

Schlesinger's great creative mind was assigned to the problem of Cuba 18 months ago. Another failure of foreign aid.

—*NRB*, Oct. 16, 1962, *p. 5*

... he thought to curry the opposition's favor by handing me, as their spokesman of the evening, a most redolent bouquet. Quoth Arthur: "Mr. Buckley has a facility for rhetoric which I envy, as well as a wit which I seek clumsily and vainly to emulate." The crowd (or my half of it) purred with pleasure. As an old debater, I knew exactly what he was up to, and determined, when my turn came to rebut, to say something equally oleaginous about Arthur. But I had only fifteen minutes, before getting up to speak, during which to compose a compliment, and my imagination failed me.

—*NR*, April 9, 1963, *p. 271*

Mr. Arthur Schlesinger Jr., God bless him—if there is a God, if not never mind—is still capable of a surprise or two. His native cunning prevented him, last week, from signing one of the hawkier statements calling for instant military intervention in the Mideast. ... he gave as his second reason for not signing the statement that his views on the Middle East are nobody's business. Now that, surely, is the strangest position of all for Mr. Schlesinger to take, and one even wonders if he is quite well. Since when is it no one's business to consult the views of Mr. Schlesinger? Presidents and princes have been beheaded for failing to consult Mr. Schlesinger's views on public matters. It boggles the imagination to suppose that the events of last week proceeded without at least one telephone call from General Dayan to Mr. Schlesinger. Let's just leave it that Mr. Schlesinger is overworked, and pledge together to restrain the impulse to ask him his views on public affairs until he is quite well again. Even if it takes years and years.

—*NR*, June 27, 1967, *pp. 674–676*

... the President even found time to mention his program for the redwood trees in California, at which point Mr. Arthur Schlesinger leaned over to me and whispered "better redwoods than deadwoods," whereupon I granted him a plenary indulgence for all his past sins ...

—On The Right, Jan. 23, 1968

... I would look kindly upon a national resolution specifying Mr. Schlesinger's disfavor as a minimal qualification for high office.

—ON THE RIGHT, Oct. 5, 1968

Arthur Schlesinger said that Nixon and Agnew would usher in the end of—I didn't quite catch the word, but it was something quite awful, like "America," or "the world," or something.

—*NR*, Nov. 19, 1968, *p. 1157*

Governor William Scranton, 1964

... he is so manifestly, at this point, the last hiccup of the Establishment's IBM machine. If at first you don't succeed, try Rockefeller. If secondly you don't succeed, try Nixon. If thirdly you don't succeed, try Henry Cabot Lodge. If fourthly you don't succeed, try Scranton. The effort at this point to escalate Mr. Scranton into a political *force majeure* would tax the talents even of a nation that devised the means of selling refrigerators to Eskimos.

—ON THE RIGHT, June 18, 1964

Security Risks

The new security risk in Washington is: the man who voted for Goldwater.

—ON THE RIGHT, Sept. 14, 1965

... it is not merely on account of the susceptibility to blackmail that homosexuals are kept out of critical government positions. It is because homosexuality is an unnatural condition. That, in any case, is the governing postulate, which has not been successfully undermined, not even by such skillful advocates of bisexuality as Paul Goodman and Gore Vidal. If the condition is unnatural, then the presumption is against the emotional balance of the addict, a good reason for declining to situate him in the clutch of the republic.

—On The Right, Jan. 6, 1968

Segregation

The day after the bombing a young and eloquent Birmingham lawyer gave an impassioned speech to his business club, the theme of which was that they, every one of them in that club, every white man in the South, were personally responsible for the tragedy at the Sunday School. He received a great ovation. It was thereupon suggested that as a gesture of amity, a Negro be there and then elected to membership in the organization. The motion was defeated.

—*NRB*, Oct. 1, 1963, *p. 1*

Self-Love

Over and over again there is the re-enactment of the Genesis; and the re-enactment of the causes of the downfall of so many of the illustrious gods of Greek and Roman mythology, for whom woman is merely the symbol, not so much of man's weakness against the cunning and wiles of the seductress, but of man profoundly and primarily in love with himself. André Malraux wrote a great novel about a man of affairs, brilliant, worldly, apparently omnipotent, who sought women because through them he found the ultimate means of making love to himself: when he embraced women he was actually embracing himself. The Protestant theologian Dean Fitch reminds us in his stunning book, *The Odyssey of the Self-Centered Self*, that our civilization has moved through several stages, and that we have recently entered upon the most acutely degenerate of them: the love of ourselves. For a period we loved God; then we loved rationalism; then we loved humanity; then science; then we loved ourselves, and in that concupiscent love all else has ceased to exist. We are become what the philosophers called solipsists—men who recognize reality only in themselves. And when this happens, our own private little worlds, sustained only by our self-love, are easily shattered, and as they shatter we advance the destruction of our entire civilization, and race towards the Apocalypse ever so much faster than thermonuclear bombs will take us there.

—NR, Aug. 27, 1963, p. 143

Sexual Revolution

The so-called sexual revolution, of which *Playboy* is the slickest harbinger, asks in effect that sanctions be removed against what used to be known as "illicit sexual behavior." The *Playboy* group correctly skewers the conflicting and vague laws that lie in the dusty statute books of the individual states; and a case could be made, let us say, for removing criminal sanctions against homosexuality between consenting adults. But the modernists want to go further and, in effect, remove the moral sanctions against such behavior: and that is something else again. All that is good is not embodied in the law; and all that is evil is not proscribed by the law. A well-disciplined society needs few laws; but it needs strong mores. And the kind of solipsism that is encouraged by the sexual revolution goes further by far than to encourage a loosening of the laws. It encourages the loosening of public attitudes.

—ON THE RIGHT, Oct. 1, 1966

Edgar Smith

Edgar Smith went to the Death House not far removed from the wasteful class of humanity, a young man clearly deracinated; bored and boring. He emerges as a profoundly interesting human being, brilliantly self-educated, balanced, witty, cool beyond the point a battery of psychoanalysts could have achieved working on the most plastic personality. The Death House is commonly thought of as a dehumanizing institution and it mostly is that. But it brought out in Edgar Smith a most extraordinary man who may not succeed in triumphing over the chair, but has clearly triumphed over himself.

—ON THE RIGHT, Nov. 9, 1965

Socialism

It is comforting to tell ourselves that in a free society no fraud can survive for very long after it is publicly discredited; but alas, that is not in fact the case—as witness, for instance, socialism, which is left without serious defenders, but whose forms encroach on us year after year.

—*Rumbles*, p. 129

Socialism has long since been discredited intellectually. But when did it get so creepy?

—*NR*, June 1, 1965, *p. 454*

Socialism—American Style

In effect, the government and the unions and the National Labor Relations Board are suggesting that every business is to some extent a public utility and that therefore the one most crucial decision regarding it, namely, whether it shall continue to operate or not, is under certain conditions the business of the government rather than that of its owners. The implications of that position shed light on the changing concept of socialism during the past generation. It used to be that socialism meant simply government ownership of the means of production. As far back as twenty years ago a leading theorist of socialism, Mr. G. D. H. Cole, lectured the Fabian Society on the necessity to recognize that outright ownership is merely a technicality. What, he asked, is the purpose of government ownership if, instead, the government can with far greater convenience control corporations by indirect means? What does it matter who owns the title to the business if wages are in effect determined by government (through monopoly rights given to labor unions and through minimum wage laws), if profits are controlled (through taxation), and if production quotas can be set (as during wartime and in periods of emergency)?

—On The Right, Dec. 17, 1964

Society

A society has the right to impose negative restraints; but positive acts of compliance it may exact only in extraordinary situations. One may not murder, steal, drive drunkenly, commit libel, undress publicly. But there is not, for each of these prohibitions, a corresponding injunction of an affirmative kind. To require participation in a social enterprise is a fatal habit for a free society to get into.

—Up from Liberalism, p. 204

Sociology

An incredible amount of mischief goes on under the general franchise of sociology, much of it terribly elusive, windy and amorphous. One has to struggle, among other things, with a strange and terrifying and tirelessly abundant jargon. (In sociology "social" is spelled "societal," and the antonym of "privilege" is "disprivilege.") But above all, the field of study seems to suffer from the inability of a number of brilliant men and women to impose on it any discipline, or scope. With the result that sociology is about everything; and, almost everywhere, it is a great favorite with students, who like to be led from a discussion of Tasmanian sex habits to discussions of mannerisms of Newport Upper-Upper-Class society, all in a single course.

—NR, March 28, 1956, *p. 22*

Softness on Communism

To be soft on Communism means to me to take measures against Communism less rigorous than those that the nature and threat of Communism demand. By that standard nothing seems to me more obvious than that this lack of rigor shoots through our policies at home and abroad.

—NR, Oct. 20, 1964, *p. 905*

Susan Sontag

Miss Sontag, whose sense of humor is about as well developed as King Kong's . . .

—ON THE RIGHT, March 18, 1967

Ted Sorensen

"We have seen too much success to have become obsessed with failure" —LBJ. Meaning? Ted Sorensen hasn't been fired. Absolutely nothing else.

—*NR*, Dec. 31, 1963, *p. 554*

South Africa

To some problems, a true conservative must always stipulate, there are no solutions. There is no solution to the problem of South Africa, that is to say no solution which simultaneously accommodates all the legitimate interests congested in the southern tip of Africa. It is not a "solution" to suggest that the Afrikaners and the Bantus integrate (in race relations Johannesburg is generations behind Biloxi, which is a generation behind Notting Hill, where integration has by no means proved feasible). It is not a solution to suggest to the Boers that they do to the southern tip of Africa what the Israelis did to a hunk of the Near East: march everyone out, and do their own labor (surely we do not want nine million Negro refugees driven north?). It is not a solution to assert that South Africa belongs to the blacks (who, as it happens, moved into the region *after* the whites), any more than it is proper to say that the American South "belongs" to the white man. . . . The whites are entitled, we believe, to historical pre-eminence in South Africa. But the present arrangement is increasingly proved to be unworkable. If they want to maintain a wholly white community, as the Israelis determined to maintain a wholly Jewish community, they would be entitled to more sympathy than they now are, attempting to maintain an all-white ruling class with a perpetual menial class which is all-black.

—*NR*, April 23, 1960, *pp. 254–255*

Some day, when you have nothing else to do, come up with a solution for South Africa, won't you? But remember the rules of the game. *All* the marbles have to end up each in a cavity—you can't just throw a few of them away, to make the game simpler. The people who picked apartheid are solidly committed to it; it is a radical solution in which they are investing their wit, their passion, and their means; they are men and women of urbanity and culture and understanding, and of courage, who are not fooling themselves, or trying to fool the world; men who, the more ignorant of them, feel the same contempt for the aimlessness of the American approach to race relations that Americans, the more ignorant of them, feel for the schematism of the South African approach. They may be wrong, as we may be: but we should try at least to understand what it is they are trying to do, and deny ourselves that unearned smugness that the bigot shows. I cannot say, "I approve of apartheid"—its ways are alien to my temperament. But I know now it is a sincere people's effort to fashion the land of peace they want so badly.

—*NR*, Jan. 15, 1963, *p. 23*

The South African courts have sentenced a batch of admitted terrorists to life in the penitentiary, and you would think the court had just finished barbecuing St. Joan, to hear the howls from the liberal press—which believes that the government of South Africa should confer medals upon, rather than jail, those of its citizens who, to express their discontent, set fire to factories and blow up bridges.

—*NR*, June 30, 1964, *p. 524*

Soviet Union

. . . the Soviet Union will behave exactly as she has behaved with respect to the last—was it fifty-five, at the last count?—treaties and agreements she has arrived at with the West. Whenever she is ready to do so, she simply breaks them, and to hell with public opinion. If we really wish to test whether there has been a change in the Russian attitude, why not send Ave over there to suggest fulfillment of the Potsdam agreements?

—*NRB*, Aug. 6, 1963, *p. 1*

Listening day in day out to Moscow Radio is one of the more tedious responsibilities of the unsung soldiers of the Cold War. But every now and then they are rewarded with a synaesthetic dialectical jewel, *e.g.*, last week's explanation of why Russians live longer than Westerners. Answer: they are not "exposed to the grave health hazards of baptism." Well, the Russians had better hang on to this world for dear life. They're going to have a hell of a time in the next.

—*NR*, Oct. 8, 1963, *pp. 264–265*

The Soviet Union does not "honor" treaties, it "observes" treaties, for so long as it finds it useful to do so. It honors only the imperatives of its own dynamic ideology, which laugh at the very concept of honor as applying to relations between socialist and imperialist countries: the sanctity of treaties is, for the Communist, merely one more bourgeois sentimentality that stands in the way of the conclusion of the world revolution.

—ON THE RIGHT, April 4, 1964

Soviet Union—the Intellectuals

Brezhnev scolded and ranted about the delinquencies of certain Russian artists and intellectuals. He was followed by Mikhail Sholokohov, who was awarded the Nobel Prize as recently as in 1965 and, unlike Boris Pasternak, was permitted to go to Oslo to receive it. Sholokohov proved that his first master is not his muse, but his warden. So the man with the Nobel Prize pounded away at "those who have betrayed the homeland and slung mud at everything most sacred to us." His reference was to the wretched Sinyavsky and Daniel, imprisoned a month or so ago for insufficient servility to the Communist system in their literature.

—ON THE RIGHT, April 9, 1966

The Space Race

What we have greatly to fear is our psychological reliance on Russian preoccupations and Russian timetables. Two or three years ago Khrushchev announced that he had no interest whatever in reaching the moon; whereupon the wind went right out of our sails, and many of us began to wonder whether there was any point in developing our fancy new water pistol if the other fellow wasn't going to challenge us with his. Now suddenly the Kremlin announces that they are, needless to say, going to the moon—and we sweat with apprehension about the lead they have over us.

My own inclination, considering the near absolute consistency of the Communists as bloody liars, was to assume that when they told us they weren't going to the moon, that they had every intention of doing so; and to assume that now that they say they are going there, that they have something quite other in mind, like maybe space platforms to circle our planet, loaded down with all those bombs they produced while we were sleeping off the Spirit of Camp David.

They do lead us about by the nose, the Communists, and all because of their superior political showmanship. And when you consider that *this* is the home of Barnum and Bailey, not Russia! Or does the Soviet encyclopedia reveal that Barnum and Bailey were really Russian after all? Maybe they were.

—On The Right, March 30, 1965

The very best explanation I ever heard for man's compulsive race to get to the moon was offered by a shrewd and attractive lady, wife of a law school don at the University of Indiana. "Don't you understand?" she asked, after the company had worn each other down with elaborate scientific explanations. They wheeled towards her: "Boys will be boys." The rhetoric, of course, can be escalated without difficulty, making the statement to read, "men will be men." That takes the hint of mischief out of it all; but it is much better with the mischief left in. Because there is a bit of mischief in adventure, and men who go off grandiloquently to meet their destiny often feel a trace of the excitement a boy feels when he goes out for the first time on an overnight hike.

—On The Right, Aug. 24, 1965

The Speculators

It may be that by the time these words are printed, de Gaulle will be repudiated by the only totally honest forces around, which are: The

Speculators. . . . The speculators. Whenever the word is used, the user visualizes sinful, greedy little men who profiteer from human distress. It is appropriate to explain that the speculators perform a vital economic function. It is they and they alone who signal to a society that it is engaging in pursuits whose strategic economic consequences are dangerous.

—ON THE RIGHT, Nov. 28, 1968

Dr. Benjamin Spock

Neither Dr. [William Sloane] Coffin nor Dr. Spock is a lawyer, indeed it is unlikely that either of them would recognize the Constitution of the United States if it crept into bed with them. Neither of them was ever heard to question the constitutionality of the Selective Service Act before that act was invoked to conscript soldiers to fight in this particular war.

—ON THE RIGHT, Jan. 11, 1968

Stalin: Destalinization

Soviet cartographers plagued with insomnia are sure these days to be counting Stalin place-names instead of sheep. The U.S.S.R. is studded with Stalingrads, Stalinos, Stalinsks, Stalinogorsks, Stalinskoyes, Stalinabads and even Stalin-mountains. A situation which, now that Stalin, Joseph is *non grata*, brings on the insomnia in the first place. In the interest of desperate Soviet mapmakers, the Formosa *China Post* is running a contest to find suitable replacements. Surely the soundest measure would be to change Khrushchev's name to Stalin, in which case the map of the Communist world could remain unchanged. We can think of other reasons why this is an appropriate suggestion.

—*NR*, May 23, 1956, *p. 4*

Harold Stassen

. . . his eccentric conceit and utter humorless narcissism put him beyond the line of vexatiousness—one merely feels sorry for him, as, say, for Senator Morse.

—ON THE RIGHT, Aug. 17, 1968

The State

The state is a divine institution. Without it we have anarchy, and the lawlessness of anarchy is counter to the natural law: so we abjure all political theories which view the state as inherently and necessarily evil. But it is the state which has been in history the principal instrument of abuse of the people, and so it is central to the conservatives' program to keep the state from accumulating any but the most necessary powers.

—The Catholic World, March, 1961, *p. 365*

State Department

Earlier this month the State Department gave the umpteenth performance of its popular play, *Please Tread On Me*, with Ceylon as guest star, and the usual cast.

—NR, May 23, 1956, *p. 3*

Three weeks ago, the State Department got around to releasing bound volumes of Yalta papers. . . . The evidence mounts that the State Department has edited this compilation in loving memory of Franklin Delano Roosevelt. Perhaps some day the Department will sponsor another collection of documents—in loving memory of millions of dead Poles and Chinese.

—NR, Feb. 1, 1956, *p. 6*

Reviewing a book for the *New York Times* recently, Professor Henry Steele Commager of Amherst observed: "We had been allied with the Soviet Union and China, and in one of the most remarkable shifts in history *we managed to maneuver ourselves into enmity with these. . . .*" The reference is presumably to the anti-Communists who penetrated our State Department.

—NR, Aug. 8, 1967, *p. 832*

States Rights

We believe that if there is such a thing as a mechanical safeguard to freedom, it is political decentralization. We welcome, then, the return of serious discussion of states rights; and we pray that those who today talk states rights, because of the proximate usefulness of the concept, will not toss it back to the wolves after it has served them—or failed to serve them —in a single battle. For the war is long.

—NR, April 18, 1956, p. 4

Statism

There is always a kind of self-fulfilling logic in the statist's approach to things. One has only to assure the relative impoverishment of the private sector, in order to be able to observe that only the public sector can afford to pay. So that one has to wrench oneself free of the governing superstitions in order to ask a question unsettlingly simple: how is it that as we grow richer and richer, we can apparently afford to do less and less for ourselves?

—ON THE RIGHT, Oct. 21, 1967

Adlai Stevenson

Everyone knows the formula for beginning a political address. But consider the baroque fulfillment of Adlai Stevenson. Listen ... You can actually hear the calls being given, as though the whole thing were a Virginia reel ...

Thank and compliment whoever introduced you. Thank you, my friends. And thank you, Senator Monroney, for that heartening introduction. *A note of levity.* Your references to my past contained a certain amount of exaggeration. I trust that your reference to my future was more precisely accurate. *Start in on the local politicians.* Your Senator makes it difficult, in a way, for me to say to you the things I had wanted to say about him. *Say it anyway.* I had wanted to say that the rest of us throughout this country have a great and warm affection for this man who carries with such gentleness of bearing his extraordinary wisdom and fortitude; and that we count—*Call him by his first name*—Mike Monroney one of the most distinguished, dedicated and effective fighters for responsible liberalism in America today. *Is he running for office?* But since he is here—and because he is also a man who likes to get right to the point—let me only say that I join you in thinking it is mighty important—*Stress national importance of local man*—not just to Oklahoma but to the United States—that Mike Monroney be returned to the Senate this fall. *Anybody else?* You seem to have a habit of picking good Senators here in Oklahoma. I know Bob Kerr isn't up for election this year but he is a long-time friend of mine, a man whose advice and counsel I have turned to on many occasions. *Everybody is crazy about the local man.* I do want to say here today how very much his leadership means not only to all of us in the Democratic Party, but to all of us, regardless of party, in the nation. *Any local boy out of office and still in the public mind?* And, finally, I have had the special pleasure of riding across country today on a highway named for one Oklahoma Governor—Roy Turner, whose friendship I have prized over the years, *Mustn't miss anybody, now*—and in company with your Governor Raymond Gary—who has already won the spurs of leadership in the rising generation of able, young Democratic statesmen. This is the kind of day—with these gentlemen— that makes me—*Say it in the vernacular*—mighty proud to be a Democrat—and I sure am proud. *The occasion. Whatever it is, it's a very special one. Your favorite.* It is a particular pleasure for me to join you here today at your state fair. I used to be a Governor myself; and of all the privileges of governorship, none pleased me more than my annual chance to take part in the great Illinois State Fair. *Things were better in the good old days.* And I am proud that during my administration of the state fair we reduced a Republican deficit of three quarters of a million dollars to barely a quarter. I'm told that under Republican management it's back up there again now. *Now wade in.*

And Adlai Stevenson did. The Republicans are against old age. And stuff and stuff. And dignity. And usefulness. And for big business.

"*Via capitum ovatorum dura est,*" Adlai Stevenson said, on opening a lecture series (on statesmanship) at Harvard, a couple of years ago. The road of the egghead *is* hard—so hard, he doesn't take it any more.

—*NR*, Oct. 6, 1956, *p. 5*

Adlai Stevenson, the *New York Times* reveals, has hired a speechwriter with a good common touch. How can he have done such a thing! Is there anything worse than the prospect of Stevenson's thoughts in *plain* language? So we didn't vote for him, does he have to do *that* to us?

—*NR*, March 26, 1960, *p. 188*

"Dr. Strangelove"

The movie, "Dr. Strangelove," is the talk of many Londoners, who though they know, most of them, that it is sick humor, relish it all the same. . . . Humor is a professional talent, whose only taboos are the listener's ultimate sanctuaries. There are not many of these left, and I have no doubt the producer, Mr. Kubrick, could do a very funny film on the battle of Verdun, or the Diary of Anne Frank.

—On The Right, March 26, 1964

Subversion

It is only in our time that the idea of the open society was transmuted into Holy Writ, put forward as the first loyalty of free men. Before, the first loyalty of free men was to freedom—and freedom is not served by extending to the enemies of freedom, freedom to mine the city, and whistle while they work.

—*NR*, Jan. 16, 1962, *p. 21*

Summit Conferences

Since Mr. Kennedy has chosen to meet with Khrushchev, he should take what advantages he can out of the meeting, and they are plenty. There is no metaphysical reason why such meetings need always improve the Communists' position. Mr. Kennedy must approach the encounter with a fierce desire to prevail. Let him close his eyes, and imagine standing there, opposite him, Richard Nixon. Then will he speak with the voice of avenging angels, and the glory of the world will lie about him.

—*NR*, Oct. 23, 1962, *p. 298*

A trunkload of promises from Khrushchev in return for substantive American concessions in nuclear testing is what we have most to fear.

If only Harriman could be persuaded to repeat to himself, before every meeting with Khrushchev—as dutifully and methodically as even the most experienced airplane pilot is required, before take-off, to go over, one by one, the list of checks (magnetos, OK; oil pressure, OK; right aileron, OK; left aileron, OK, etc. etc.), even if he has flown a thousand times before—K is a liar; K is a sneak; K is a ruthless dissimulator; K is head of a state committed at any cost short of its own survival to conquer the West; K is a master tactician. Only then might we hope to come back with anything at all from the Moscow Conference that means anything. Otherwise, it will be simply one more way station on the road to Western decline.

—NR, July 30, 1963, *p. 51*

Supreme Court

... there is about as much danger of the establishment of religion in this country as there is of the return of sanity to the Supreme Court.

—NR, July 2, 1963, *p. 521*

Mr. Anthony Lewis, the *New York Times'* principal claque for unconstitutional decisions rendered under the shogunate of Chief Justice Warren, and a tireless recipient of Pulitzer Prizes therefor, included the following straight-faced sentence in his article on the decision of the Warren Court wresting from the states their power to establish their own legislative structures: "*Today's decision does not affect the United States Senate.*" The Senate is no doubt relieved that, as of this writing, the Supreme Court has not abolished it.

—NR, June 30, 1964, *p. 518*

It is too bad that just because Mr. Robert Welch decided a few years ago that the time had come to impeach Earl Warren, effective criticism of Mr. Warren, presumably for fear of association with the John Birch Society, should have almost dried up. With a few honorable exceptions, about the only people making serious criticisms of the ideological fanaticism of Earl Warren and his quartet are, significantly enough, members themselves of the Supreme Court: Justices John Marshall Harlan, Potter Stewart, Tom Clark. . . . Congress has available to it the instruments necessary to curb what Professor Edward Corwin, the distinguished constitutional scholar, referred to as the "aggressions of the Warren Court." If it refuses to use them, the Warren Court may after all go down in history not as the agency that instigated the dissolution of the federal system, but as the agency that proved that it was thoroughly dead.

—NRB, July 7, 1964, *p. 1*

It is amusing, though perhaps sickly so, that the little house organ published by employees of the Supreme Court recently ran a feature on how to get back to your home at night from the Supreme Court building without being mugged.

—ON THE RIGHT, June 18, 1966

. . . the first Yogi who gets nominated—he'll have to get in even if he insists on standing on his head during the sessions of the court from which position, as a matter of fact, he could most reliably interpret the Constitution in the tradition of Earl Warren . . .

—NR, Sept. 19, 1967, *p. 998*

If one had to name the single greatest subversion of the Warren Court, it is this: that, typically, it has brought people around to where they approve of it, or disapprove of it, depending on whether they like or do not like, the policies it endorses. It has thus contributed to the decline of constitutional government.

—NR, July 16, 1968, *p. 685*

David Susskind

For three glorious weeks no one in New York had violated the community's bond of sophistication toward Khrushchev. Not a single television or radio program had offered a propaganda forum to the garrulous barbarian. . . . And then Mr. Susskind, with infinite, unique insensitivity, opened the door to Open End, sponsoring the dreary propaganda, the assault on the human mind and heart, of the principal slavemaster in history. And yes, at the one point when the desperate Mr. Susskind was trying to demonstrate his independence, Mr. Khrushchev drew him short: *Remember, you little squirt* (that was the unmistakable meaning of his words), *I am lord and master of the Soviet Union. Treat me with respect.* . . . And, of course, Mr. Susskind apologized. He might have said: But Mr. Khrushchev, I *have* no respect for you . . . but then what would he do *next* time he wants a Communist on his show?

—NR, Oct. 22, 1960, p. 232

Swiss Bank Accounts

Any Brazilian or Argentinian—or Indonesian—who took his money to Switzerland before Goulart or Perón or Sukarno took over the management of those countries contributed more to social well-being by investing his capital via Switzerland in productive enterprises, than by leaving it around to be squandered by the three left-wingers who in the name of human progress reduced the economic structure of their nations to ashes and set back by a generation any hope for improvement in the material condition of the people.

—On The Right, April 8, 1967

Switzerland

We were, indeed, in an a-political state, one of the wonders of the world. The reason the President of Switzerland is a relatively unknown figure is that politics, in Switzerland, does not wag the national dog, as politics does in virtually every other state in the world. No one much seems to care who is President—the President, whoever he is, will do what needs to be done, Switzerland will continue in its prescribed course, and get on with important matters, like making roads and watches, and rearing one's children. In the presidency of the Helvetic Confederation there simply isn't the glamour or the power of the kind that keeps so many men in so many lands awake at night thirsting, and busy during the day conspiring, and trafficking in demagogy; politics, in Switzerland, is under control.

—NR, Nov. 16, 1957, *p. 449*

Sybarites

Someone said a while ago that if Cleopatra were alive today, she would be living the life of Elizabeth Taylor. Well, if Quasimodo were alive today, he would be living the life of one of Elizabeth Taylor's husbands. Now it's Eddie Fisher's turn—and one hopes he will move aside gracefully, as gracefully as Debbie did when she was discarded. When one is married in Sybaris, one must do as the sybarites do. If only these people would play their musical beds without the benefit of reporters and photographers! Well, that will be for the next world. That will be the hell of it.

—NRB, April 17, 1962, *p. 2*

T

Tax Reform

The whole business is a mess, as is anything which decidedly appeals to different sets of rules. If we desire justice, it should be justice for all. Ideally there would be *no* exemptions, no, not even for colleges or churches or charities; no deductions, no not for business expenses or hospital bills; no subsidies, no not for farmers, or tenants, or small businesses: and lo, if all these deductions, all these business expenses, all these subsidies, were eliminated, the result would be, in effect, a subsidy for all—in the form of uniform, simplified, reduced taxation. . . . It occurs to us that any magazine capable of publishing these noble sentiments should be tax-exempt.

—NR, May 6, 1961, pp. 272-273

[From Chairman Bill's advice to the platform committees of the 1968 Republican and Democratic conventions:] Think big. Tax reform is urgently needed.The more intensively the subject is studied, the clearer it becomes that government is very poor at trying to make justice through discriminatory taxation. The heaviest burden is, relatively, on the shoulders of the lower middle class. Upward mobility becomes progressively difficult. Inflation heightens the graduated feature of the tax. The very rich have special privileges, loopholes. The very poor are strangled by bureaucracy, inflation . . . Proposal: Adopt the Friedman Plan. 1) Eliminate all personal deductions, 2) double the exemption rate from the existing $600 to $1200, an acknowledgment of inflationary reality, 3) set a uniform rate of around 20% on all income. The resulting revenue would equal existing revenue from incoming taxes.

—On The Right, May 18, 1968

It is almost impossible to say with certitude that any taxation arrangement is fair. The most that can be said about it is that it is efficient. And the closest one can get to fairness is impartiality. Yes, and that means impartiality to rich people too. Even to rich people we don't like.

—ON THE RIGHT, April 26, 1969

Technology and Freedom

Conservatism must insist that while the will of man is limited in what it can do, it can do enough to make over the face of the world; and that the question that must always be before us is, What shape should the world take, given modern realities? How can technology hope to invalidate conservatism? Freedom, individuality, the sense of community, the sanctity of the family, the supremacy of the conscience, the spiritual view of life—can these verities be transmuted by the advent of tractors and adding machines? These have had a smashing social effect upon us, to be sure. They have created a vortex into which we are being drawn as though irresistibly; but that, surely, is because the principles by which we might have made anchor have not been used, not because of their insufficiency or proven inadaptability.

—*Up from Liberalism*, pp. 223–224

The Telephone Company

... why does the telephone company have to charge us forever and ever for all those faculties that are quickly amortized? For instance, the little lightweight Princess receiver: okay, charge fifteen, or whatever, dollars per month extra, sufficient to pay the extra costs of production, and then some. But why do we have to be charged, forever and ever, extra dollars until our grandchildren's grandchildren grow so old that they cannot lift the receiver off the hook? Do you want the dial on your phone illuminated? A few cents extra per month. Forever. Why doesn't the telephone company settle, say, for 1,000 per cent profit on such installations and then, finally, send along the President of the Company to kiss you on both cheeks, and tell you that the little light is yours in perpetuity —all, unbelievably, all yours?

—*NR*, July 14, 1964, *p. 576*

Television

We cannot, after all, neglect to consider the challenge television has undertaken. It is more formidable by far than that of Scheherazade the slave girl, who, after all, was given a respite after her thousand and first tale. In undertaking to entertain us—indeed, to give us a choice of entertainment—every day and night of every week of every month of every year, television has undertaken a job it simply cannot do to everyone's satisfaction.

—NR, Jan. 2, 1960, *p. 9*

Television: And Free Speech

I would favor the passage of a law giving all broadcasters about whose loyalty to the United States there is no reasonable doubt (that would not be an innovation: loyalty risks aren't allowed to obtain licenses anyway) the right to broadcast anything they want, in any way they want, but only in those cities which have at least two television stations. I would expect abuses of this privilege to be controlled by community action. And to guard the interests of the minority, I would favor legislation directing the FCC to make available licenses in any community of over 50,000 people, for the construction of pay-TV stations, through which the pressures of the consumer are most keenly exercised, both positively and negatively. The government's role would then be limited primarily to antimonopoly action (there is nothing the government can do about a natural oligopoly).

—TV Guide, April 25, 1964, *pp. 17–18*

Television—the Half Smile

Always, when the camera first focused on the candidates, during the few seconds when they are being identified by the moderator, they would manage a warming half-smile. Perfectly proper, utterly professional—there isn't anyone in the business who doesn't do it, whether Elvis Presley, Eric Sevareid, Lyndon Johnson, or U Thant. Twelve years earlier I had signed up for what turned out to be a half-hundred consecutive weekly television episodes, and I noticed the other members of the panel regularly producing the half-smile—I remarked it not with contempt, but, increasingly, with envy—because I simply could not, and cannot to this day, manage it. At one point my wife, playfully, tried to make me practice, as if it were a calisthenic; but there is no practicing it, because, inevitably, you roar with laughter at yourself (try it). I have developed a sort of anti-tic at such moments—my lips will simply not part, unless I am moved by an elfin provocation, in which case I completely spoil the intended effect of a sort of half-smiled reserved benevolence by breaking out in a disconcerting sea of teeth.

—The Unmaking of a Mayor, p. 273

Tennessee Valley Authority

It is as difficult to talk to votaries of the TVA about their dreamchild, as it is to talk to the American Civil Liberties Union about the Bill of Rights. They don't want to discuss it, they want to burn incense to it.

—NR, Dec. 3, 1963, *p. 472*

I wonder why the idea of selling TVA is so sacrilegious. Senator Goldwater is made to sound as though it was his intention to send troops into Knoxville during the middle of the night with orders to pull out a few strategic plugs and flood the Tennessee Valley. What he in fact recommended was to sell to the highest bidder the steam-generating plants that are engaged in producing electricity—sell them to commercial users who would pay taxes, depreciation, and compete for business. The concept of the government regularly turning over to private business enterprises it has taken over in emergency situations—whether merchant marine ships after a war, or telestars after their development—is fundamental to the maintenance of a predominantly private sector.

—ON THE RIGHT, Nov. 10, 1964

Terrorism

Terrorism is abhorred. In Western moral textbooks, sure. But the successful terrorists don't have very much difficulty in making their way comfortably among the cosmopolitan elements of the Western world. It was only a matter of months between the time the Algerians swept a machine gun across the bodies of men, women and children bathing at a public beach, and their commander's arrival on an official visit to New York City where he was warmly embraced. Castro used to chop people up pretty much for the sake of it while at the Sierra Maestra, and when he first came to America a few months later he was treated like St. Francis of Assisi.

—*NR*, March 7, 1967, *p. 237*

Tolerance

It is an old saw that professional tolerance-teachers, almost all of them, harbor foxes in their bosoms that eat anyone who disagrees. Show me the most adamantly liberal professor at any university, and I will show you the likeliest candidate for dean of illiberal arts and letters. The critics of Lyndon Johnson who specialize in Johnson's inhumanity are beginning to display towards him what can only be described as attitudes such as are prerequisite to barbarism. . . . I do not like Mr. Johnson, but I do not believe him capable of any intentional cruelty in Vietnam. But the spirit of some of his critics is the spirit of the VC.

—ON THE RIGHT, April 2, 1968

Harry S. Truman

Many times in the past, Harry Truman has obstinately defended his record, whether against reason or taste; defended, in fact, everything he ever did, from lining up with Pendergast to dropping atom bombs over Japan, to threatening to emasculate music critics. He operates on the simple theory that what he does is correct; to which theory the corollary is that duty lies in constantly instructing a wayward public in the fact of his infallibility.

—*NR*, Sept. 15, 1956, *p. 4*

Truth

Conservatives do not deny the existence of undiscovered truths, but they make a critical assumption, which is that those truths that have *already* been apprehended are more important to cultivate than those undisclosed ones close to the liberal grasp only in the sense that the fruit was close to Tantalus, yet around whose existence virtually the whole of modern academic theory revolves. Conservatism is the tacit acknowledgement that all that is finally important in human experience is behind us; that the crucial explorations have been undertaken, and that it is given to man to know what are the great truths that emerged from them. Whatever is to come cannot outweigh the importance to man of what has gone before.

—Up from Liberalism, p. 182

The superstition that the hounds of truth will rout the vermin of error seems, like a fragment of Victorian lace, quaint, but too brittle to be lifted out of the showcase.

—NR, Jan. 16, 1962, *p. 21*

Truth is a demure lady, much too ladylike to knock you on the head and drag you to her cave. She is there, but the people must want her, and seek her out.

—ON THE RIGHT, Nov. 7, 1964

Mao Tse-tung

... the greatest genocidal maniac in the history of the world, the same Mao Tse-tung who killed four times as many Chinese as Hitler killed Jews.

—ON THE RIGHT, June 4, 1964

Moise Tshombe

After the kidnapping of Adolph Eichmann in 1960, lawyers the world 'round did their homework and agreed that the most venerable laws have it that a duly constituted tribunal can proceed to try someone against whom the state has lodged a complaint, irrespective of the means by which the defendant is captured and produced. . . . So that no matter the brazen illegality of the seizure of Tshombe's private plane, once delivered to Leopoldville, the former premier could be, and very likely would be, hanged by the neck until quite dead, with nobody around to read from any Congolese lawbooks, if there are any of them around uneaten.

—ON THE RIGHT, July 8, 1967

Turning the Clock Back

You cannot turn the clock back, they all say. To the extent that is true, it is an observation so overbearingly banal as to suggest idiocy on the part of the man who makes it. To the extent that it is intended metaphorically, i.e., to say that one cannot change the course of things, then it is, in the cautious words of Professor Hayek, "among the most fatuous statements in modern language—what it seems to be saying is that one cannot profit from one's mistakes." But of course one *can* profit from one's mistakes: a great body of learning—all of empirical knowledge—develops from that general rule, which is embedded in so many of the little apothegms of our society, like "Once burnt, twice shy," "Experience is the best teacher," etc., etc.

—ON THE RIGHT, May 28, 1964

Twit-Twit

. . . the garage attendant who dawdles over the telephone making twit-twit with his paramour while your radiator is boiling over. . . .

—*NR*, July 14, 1964, *p. 576*

can Ambassador to the Court of St. James. Mrs. Tynan, who apparently learned her social manners from our own Dwight Macdonald, is, to the vast relief of most Englishmen, an American. In any case, she accepted the Ambassador's invitation, and she buzzed about the residence sticking anti-Vietnam signs on the furniture, calling on us to bug-out. Only a few years ago, her husband was calling on the West to give over Berlin to the Communists, declaring manfully that he would sooner live on his knees than die on his knees. Mr. Bruce, asked by the press for comment, replied: "Stickers? What stickers? It wasn't drawn to our attention." It is no wonder he is a successful diplomat.

—ON THE RIGHT, March 5, 1968

Two-Party System

"The greatest difference," said Leonard Hall last week at San I
"between the Democratic convention and this convention i:
Democrats nominated a loser. We're here to nominate a win
Hall's statement is horribly accurate. The greatest difference be
two parties lies in the fact that they back different people, nc
ideas, for office.

—NR, Sept. 1

Traditionally, the nation's political business has been done t
ties, not three or more. We think this is as it should be. It has
quite apart from the obvious technical ones. Voluntary limit:
number of parties brings pressure to bear on minority politica
to accept reasonable compromises, abandon sectarianism, a
viable party nearest its position. By the same token, there is
the larger parties to make room for such groupings by giving s
attention to their demands. The two pressures militate to
consensus—and, therefore, to a more harmonious, less divi
On the other hand, the United States has traditionally
reasonably free to launch so-called "third parties," and this
should be. It enables groupings that do not find accommod
major parties to let off steam, for one thing, and to ascertain v
have the popular support they often claim. They are an ii
shotgun-behind-the-door, for possible use on the major pa
day, when, by failing to heed some sizable body of opinior
to perform well their traditional function. Obviously, 1
behind-the-door is useless if it is understood that nobody n
it.

—NR, Oct.

Mrs. Kenneth Tynan

On other fronts in London, there is Mrs. Kenneth Tynan, 1
Mrs. Tynan, who was a guest of the gentle Mr. David Bru

U

UNICEF

You are UNICEF's children, too, when you know that

1 of your pennies can provide five glasses of milk
5 cents' worth of penicillin can cure a case of yaws
10 cents can protect ten people from tuberculosis

And twenty million cents will permit UNICEF to occupy quarters on the sixth floor of the swank United Nations Plaza, instead of the unspeakable second floor. Yes, last week UNICEF was offered the second floor—identical in layout to the sixth, except for some additional space—at a saving over five years of $150,000 to $200,000, plus a large contribution from a New York company that wanted to rent the sixth floor. The executive director, touring in Africa, telegraphed to the real estate agents that under no circumstances would he accept second story space but insisted on the sixth; so, since ALCOA, the building's owner, had a "moral agreement" with the UN, that was that. A proposed new flier:

20,000,000 of your pennies can provide UNICEF with *6th* story space.

40,000,000 of your pennies can provide UNICEF with *12th* story space.

60,000,000 of your pennies can provide UNICEF with *18th* story space.

And so on. The building has 36 floors, so give-give-give.

—*NR*, June 14, 1966, *p. 561*

United Nations

In the scant ten years of its life, the UN has developed a more or less traditional attitude toward private property, whose existence, like that of God and Switzerland, it does not recognize. No enumeration of human rights that has got by any UN committee has listed the right to private property. (And not because such enumerations are abbreviated. One draft on human rights acknowledges some sixty-three rights, including the right to equal treatment for bastards.) In December of 1952, the right of nations to nationalize their natural resources, again with no mention of compensation, was upheld by a thumping majority—36-4. . . .

. . . the United Nations, true to form, continues to address itself to problems over which it has no jurisdiction and whose relationship to the preservation of peace is, at the least, tenuous. Such intrusions on the privacy of member states tend to strengthen the impression that so many Americans intuitively have of the United Nations as a meddlesome bureaucracy, dominated by statists who will settle only for the total colonization of the world.

—*NR*, Dec. 7, 1955, *pp. 6–7*

. . . a forum in which nations meet in order handily to exchange insults, bribes, intimidations, and cynicisms . . .

—*NR*, Nov. 16, 1957, *p. 449*

[Senator Goldwater] said that he backed ardently and enthusiastically the purpose of the United Nations. And indeed, who does not? Save, possibly, some of the most influential nations within the United Nations?

—On The Right, Aug. 18, 1964

WHOOPS! WHOA! LEAPING LIZARDS! IT CAN'T BE SO DEPT. But: we have it a) on the authority of *Nation Française*, that b) one Jacques Tems, of *l'Avenir du Tournaisis*, reports c) having seen in the magazine *Europe* that a Dag Hammarskjold Peace Prize has been awarded to—Generalissimo Francisco Franco! Imagine awarding a peace prize to a nation merely because it is peaceful. Something is beginning to shatter the order of reality established at the United Nations founding conference at San Francisco, where membership was denied to Sweden, Switzerland and Ireland on the official grounds that they were not "peace-loving nations"—as witness that they had not fought in the World War.

—NR, May 4, 1965, *p. 355*

The problem of Kashmir is now exactly eighteen years old, *i.e.*, as old as the independence of India. The United Nations is 20 years old. The United Nations has thus had eighteen years to solve one of the simpler problems in the world, and in a manner as simple as it is obvious—free elections. UN officials, however, have been too busy firing cannon into orderly ranks of Katangese, urging the recognition of Red China, railing against the Portuguese in Africa, against the South Africans in Southwest Africa, etc.

—NR, Sept. 21, 1965, *p. 802*

It isn't obvious what [Pope Paul] intends by coming to the United States. Some people have actually ventured the suggestion that he is coming in order to endow the United Nations with a little prestige, so to speak to perform a service for the American Association for the United Nations. Well, there is no priestly function higher than to go out among the sinners and preach, and the Holy Father will find probably the highest congestion of them in the United Nations since Jehovah closed down Gomorrah.

—ON THE RIGHT, Sept. 30, 1965

Apart from the inherent powerlessness of the UN, which issues from a mechanical dilemma (the UN is less powerful than its constituent members), and a spiritual dilemma (the UN seeks to serve goals some of its constituent members do not seek to serve), the UN becomes every day more ridiculous. Last year the Maldive Islands made it all the way to membership status with a population of 97,000, which is larger than Stamford, Connecticut, but considerably smaller than Peoria, Illinois, and in a year or two up will come the seven politically troublesome tinies carved out of old British sheikdoms along the Persian Gulf (combined pop. 86,000). And then after that, who knows? Every atoll with a post office will demand *its* vote (exactly equal, by the way, to that of France, Britain, the U.S., the USSR). Some are muttering that the UN will lose its political effectiveness. We are muttering that at least the UN has a problem its own size.

—NR, Aug. 23, 1966, *p. 819*

[From Chairman Bill's advice to the platform committees of the 1968 Republican and Democratic conventions:] Pledge cooperation with the Secretariat. But announce a policy henceforward of participating fully in all the debates of the General Assembly, but declining to vote. By so doing, we announce symbolically that we cannot pledge ourselves to abide by the decisions of the majority. We look upon them purely as advisory. Instruct our ambassador to the UN to raise the question of the East European countries whenever the subject of colonialism or neo-colonialism is raised.

—ON THE RIGHT, May 16, 1968

Marietta Tree, the queenly consort of Adlai Stevenson, said that over in the United Nations, everybody is praying that Humphrey will win. The last part was supererogatory. It was quite reassuring enough to learn that everyone over at the United Nations is praying. Shelley Winters was so overcome by this news that she volunteered the knowledge that she always knew that there was something terribly spiritual about India, and this confirmed it.

—NR, Nov. 19, 1968, *p. 1157*

Jesse Unruh

The canny and brilliant Jesse Unruh, lord of all he diminishingly surveys in the evenly-divided state Assembly ...

—*NR*, Nov. 28, 1967, *p. 1321*

Urban Renewal

The beauty of New York is threatened by the schematic designs upon it of the social abstractionists who do not look up from their drawing boards long enough to recognize what it is that makes for human attachments —to little buildings and shops, to areas of repose and excitement: to all those abstractions that so greatly inconvenience the big-think social planners. The obsession with urban renewal must, in due course, be tranquilized, before the City loses its hold on human sentiment.

—*NR*, July 13, 1965, *p. 588* (statement announcing his candidacy for Mayor of New York City)

The U.S.S.R.

Someone in the Soviet Central Ministry of Consumer Goods (Footwear Division) set, it seems, an impossibly high goal for children's summer shoe production this year. By late October, the first snow having fallen, Russian shoe factories were still churning out lightweight footwear, in a Stakhonovite passion to meet that quota. Result: Planner gets fired? More probably the weatherman, for letting that snow fall so early.

—*NR*, Nov. 10, 1956, *p. 4*

Gore Vidal

... Mr. Gore Vidal, the playwright and quipster who lost a Congressional race a few years ago but continues to seek out opportunities to advertise his ignorance of contemporary affairs.

—ON THE RIGHT, July, 1964

Vietcong

During Christmas week, the Walter Cronkite program gave us a documentary on the Vietcong, filmed by French photographers, with dulcet commentary by Mike Wallace. There were pictures of little children playing, and mothers darning clothes, and grandmothers kneading flour, and of course the soldiers fighting. *Mutatis mutandis*, the same sort of thing the inquiring photographer would find in any wartime situation.

Somehow, something is wrong with it all, is it not? In every situation there are children, and children almost by definition are appealing. Ditto mothers. Ditto grandmothers. And soldiers are brave, professionally so. Nobody ever said that the VC were not brave. Nor was it ever said about Genghis Khan or his followers. And then, too, it is of course the mark of enterprise to show pictures of the enemy at work and at play. Still . . . one wonders. How would Mr. Cronkite and Mr. Wallace have projected, let us say, scenes showing the off-duty lives of the Gestapo? Remember, there is no reason to suppose that the little children of the Nazi officers and men were unappealing, or that their wives were. Or, for that matter, that the Nazis were. Always assuming that they were not photographed killing or torturing unarmed civilians. Mr. Cronkite's general affability is

286

a part of his very general charm. But it is likely that in the hypothetical broadcast, he would have said something to the effect that we were looking at Nazis, against whom we were at war, because they constituted a threat to the survival of civilization. And, by the same token, one would expect that, viewing the VC at play, Mr. Cronkite or Mr. Wallace might have got around to saying that these were very possibly the same people who, the week before Christmas, descended on the town of Dak To, and cremated the villagers (using flamethrowers, a distinction without a difference, so far as the victims were concerned). It's the old problem. Some people just can't get worked up about the VC. And some people can't get worked up about the people who can't get worked up about the VC, which is worse.

—*NR*, Jan. 16, 1968, *p. 20*

Vietnam

A little hamlet in South Vietnam has a mayor, or the equivalent thereof, who does his level best to help the Vietnamese army—by cooperating with it, and reporting any manifest signs of infiltration. One morning shortly after dawn the villagers rise as usual to begin the day's work. And in the little square they find three stakes, to each of which is attached a human being, by means of a rope tied around the neck. Each corpse is neatly disembowelled. And propped up against the center stake is the legend: Thus Perish the Enemies of the Working People. Thus indeed perished His Honor the mayor, the mayor's wife, and the mayor's 12-year-old daughter. Now ladies and gentlemen, who will step forward and serve as the next mayor? Don't be bashful, step right up!

—ON THE RIGHT, Dec. 26, 1964

The terrible inconclusiveness of the struggle in South Vietnam works against the United States rather than for it. We are a people who like quick, neat solutions to our problems. The Communists, by contrast, are men of great patience, ever so much better at waiting for the results of the faraway future. . . . We are not only fighting Communists, but Orientals, who invented the peculiar form of torture known as the water-drip.

We are of a different temperament; and that fact is of significance at least as concrete as all the bridges and depots in North Vietnam which we are casually eliminating, as though we had all the time in the world at our disposal.

—ON THE RIGHT, May 1, 1965

. . . one supposes that General [Maxwell] Taylor was responsible for the notion that a bridge a day would keep the VC away.

—ON THE RIGHT, July 22, 1965

Do we really intend to have a team from Good Housekeeping attached to every military unit of the United States, to pass on whether the Marines are fighting the war according to the highest standards of American moral hygiene? American soldiers are being killed in South Vietnam every day. South Vietnamese are being killed there every day, and tortured beyond recognition by an enemy that cares nothing at all for the sanctity of the hamlet, or of the home, or of the ancestor, or of the spirit that is a part of the peasant's holding. The Vietcong's highly developed techniques for conscripting parts of the local population to cooperating in the conspiracy to deprive the whole of their freedom is one aspect of the military problem: to be met by techniques studied and developed at places like Parris Island; not at the executive suites of television offices.

—ON THE RIGHT, Aug. 14, 1965

. . . it is ever so modish, on the circuit, to disdain the government of South Vietnam. Inside Vietnam, Mr. [Norman] Thomas proclaimed, there isn't "a vestige of democracy." Well, to begin with, there *is* a vestige of democracy in South Vietnam, and rather more besides. It was a general democratic election that overthrew Bao Dai and elected Diem, and three national elections have since been held—rather more, in point of fact, than one might reasonably have expected in a war-torn area. There were no elections held in America during our revolutionary war, nor in England during the last and lengthy world war. Democracy is a luxury, for which all men reasonably seek. But it isn't the first order of business. The first order of business in South Vietnam is to repulse the enemy, as it is the first order of business here to reject the false and sophistical counsels of such as Mr. Thomas.

—NR, Dec. 28, 1965, *p. 1186*

The United States has played into the hands of the insurrectionists by the cant phrase, unfortunately used by President Johnson himself, that if the South Vietnamese in an election choose to go Communist, we will accept that as the will of the people, play taps, and recall the Marines. If we had adopted such relativist standards 25 years ago, we would never have liberated France, which settled down in 1941 quite comfortably to rule by the Nazis.

It is charged that the United States is being paternalistic towards South Vietnam. Indeed we are, and there is a place for paternalism in world affairs when the object of it is not only to effect hope for beleaguered peoples, but to contain the common enemy. And in due course the same Vichyssois who settled down comfortably to life everlasting with the Nazis cheered the American troops when they liberated their country.

—ON THE RIGHT, April 16, 1966

What the Senator [Richard Russell] then proposed was, of all things, a plebiscite, designed to ascertain the will of the people. The trouble with many plebiscites, particularly one conducted among a people only 10% literate, is that often they do not mean anything at all. In such cases as this, they are conducted not so much for the benefit of the people as for the benefit of the poll-conductors, so as to ease their Harvard-trained consciences. They ought not, in situations where moral and strategic considerations fuse, be thought of as binding, or even truly informative of the inner dispositions of a harassed people. It is unlikely that American liberals would pledge their troth to the majority if, say, it voted for a Nazi regime, complete with concentration camps and crematoria.

—ON THE RIGHT, April 30, 1966

If the war in Vietnam happens to have had the effect of stimulating competition for good grades among male American college students, that is probably the only good thing it has accidentally caused.

—ON THE RIGHT, May 19, 1966

The reason why Lyndon Johnson has not dealt with Vietnam via the United Nations is that a) Vietnam is too important a matter to consign to the babbling ministates of the UN to deal with, and b) the major presences in the UN are already committed: the Soviet Union is against us; England is, more or less neutrally, for us; France is, more or less neutrally, against us. So what is left for the UN to contribute? The views on the subject of Alex Quaison-Sackey?

—ON THE RIGHT, July 16, 1966

The word from Hanoi is that the government is so impressed by the performance of Harrison Salisbury, it is considering a change in policy to permit more foreign correspondents to come in to North Vietnam. What the Communists are so grateful for is Mr. Salisbury's eyewitness accounts of death to North Vietnamese civilians. That is being taken— not only by Hanoi but by many Americans—as triumphant ratification of the thesis that the U.S. has been fighting an (indefensible) war indefensibly.

... Only General Eisenhower, of all people, has spoken trenchantly. "Where," he asked on leaving the hospital, "*aren't* there any civilians?" Exactly the point. Where there are soldiers, where there are roads, railroads, bridges, railroad junctions, and supply depots, there are civilians; so that to discover, as Mr. Salisbury has done, that civilians have been killed in North Vietnam, is on the order of discovering that when you sprayed the weeds in your garden, you sprayed some grass, too. ...

It isn't news, of course, that civilians are the primary targets of the Vietcong, and have been for years. Mr. Salisbury, predictably, will not get around to asking his hosts why their agents in South Vietnam slice the throats of mayors and aldermen and farmers, and those of their wives and children, and moreover do so quite intentionally. That isn't news. It is generally accepted that the Communists will behave as they do. But let a drop of accidental American rain fall on the innocent cheek of a North Vietnamese, and Washington trembles.

—NR, Jan. 10, 1967, *p. 11*

Saigon. No one starves in Vietnam, except gourmets, which may be the reason why, finally, the French pulled out.

—ON THE RIGHT, Feb. 18, 1967

Well the Republicans are trudging the snows of New Hampshire. They are telling us that it is time for a change, but that they do not desire to make partisan politics out of the Vietnam War. What utter baloney. What other way is there to relieve ourselves of the current leadership?

—ON THE RIGHT, Feb. 8, 1968

It would seem clear that the failure of the U.S. Government to interdict the flow of material to North Vietnam from the Soviet Union is perhaps the major act of masochistic sentimentality in the postwar period. The estimates are never any lower than 60% and they go as high as 95% of the Soviet contribution to the material effort of the North Vietnamese and the Vietcong. If Lyndon Johnson's reasoning is correct that bombing the North is justified, then it is also correct to bomb the harbor of Haiphong and prevent the delivery there of the hundreds of thousands of tons of material being used against us, so effectively. . . .

—ON THE RIGHT, Feb. 8, 1968

What it comes down to, then, is this: Should the anti-Communist community endorse Westmoreland's proposal to increase by 50 per cent the American military in Vietnam? Or should the community insist that

President Johnson adopt instead measures calculated to reduce the will of the enemy to prosecute the war? Blockades; economic embargoes; a savaging of the overland supply routes; the unleashing of the Asian anti-Communist armies; the freezing of economic and agricultural credits. It needs to be repeated that our participation in the Vietnam War is justified only if Vietnam is the contemporary salient of a world enterprise, however loosely organized, that aims ultimately at the security of the United States. If that is what it is, we need to hit back with such weapons as we are in a position to use which spare us the most precious commodity we have, the American soldier. If that is not what Vietnam is all about, then we should get the hell out.

—ON THE RIGHT, March 19, 1968

General David M. Shoup of the Marines, who has opposed the war right along, makes a plain military statement of fact, that you can't win wars unless you resolve to destroy the armies of the enemy. We haven't even resolved to do that. Mr. Johnson's resolution is seen more and more visibly to be a resolution to lose the war very slowly, with dignity and restraint.

—ON THE RIGHT, April 28, 1968

There was a day, within living memory, when we were disposed to hang people who decided that the wisest course was to cooperate with the enemy, as we are asking the South Vietnamese to do.

—ON THE RIGHT, Nov. 7, 1968

... even if one rules that the United States should pull out of Vietnam it does not for that reason follow that Marshal Ky should coordinate his betrayal of his country with our betrayal of it. Marshal Ky is in Paris to defend the interests of his country, which are more gravely threatened at this moment by American indecision than by Vietcong determination.

—ON THE RIGHT, Dec. 24, 1968

Vietnam—Elections

Our concern for the purity of the democratic process in South Vietnam is abstractionist hypocrisy. We give money every year to governments in the world that do not even go through the motions of democracy—to all, for instance, of the African states, with the exception of the militantly anti-Communist states, which of course do not qualify. Our insistence that, half way through the bloodiest civil war in recent history, at a moment when it is not even clear whether the relatively humane side will even win the war, we are insisting on an election purer than you could get in a vote for chancellor of Oxford University. Underlying the insistence on that vote is the presumption that people of South Vietnam don't really want to fight for their freedom from North Vietnamese Communism. It just strikes a lot of American liberals as implausible that they should want to do so, hence they look for evidence to confirm that the South Vietnamese don't really want the war.

—ON THE RIGHT, Aug. 17, 1967

Vietnam Peace Talks

It isn't merely the usual call by U Thant to peace at any price, specifically the Communists'. The pressures are at their most intense. More professors, students, baby doctors, piccolo players are at us to cease fire. It could be that the conscience of the West is suddenly crystallizing. More likely it is evidence that the Communists and their sympathizers and their sympathizers' sympathizers have managed to muster all their forces to coordinate the drive to gull the influence-makers into a hyperthyroidal concern not for the South Vietnamese victims of cold-blooded death and torture by the Vietcong, but of concern for the civilians in North Vietnam who are accidentally victimized by our bombings of that area.

—ON THE RIGHT, Jan. 10, 1967

Vietnam and Popular Fronts

... the reasons against a popular front are roughly these, 1) the South Vietnam government would not consent to share power with the Communists; 2) if it were the kind of government that would consent, the

United States should never have sacrificed a life or a dollar to protect it; 3) the Vietcong, which is a division of the Communist movement of Vietnam, and under the direct control of the North Vietnamese, would not accept coalition government unless it was satisfied that the fiction of shared power would evolve as it did in Laos, merely as an interlude between their present position, and an improved position of power; 4) it is not desirable to share power with Communists because they don't believe in sharing power; because they act like barbarians; and because, in this instance, to give them power within the government is to break faith with those people of South Vietnam who put their trust in you to defend them precisely against the acquisition of power by the types who have been butchering them for ten years.

—On The Right, March 1, 1966

Vietniks

Certainly it is clear from the slogans of the Vietnamese peacemakers that they seem for the most part to be concerned about military action only when Communists are likely to be at the receiving end of it. I doubt, for instance, if one of the ten thousand souls who rallied in New York City to protest military action against South Vietnam, would appear at a rally to protest military action against, say, South Africa.

—On The Right, Oct. 23, 1965

Village Voice

The *Village Voice* is a little New York journal which energetically does its iconoclastic push-ups, once a week, and sort of looks about, whee! at its audience, as if to say, Have you *ever* seen anybody as irreverent as us-folks? The editors do it all with considerable panache, and although the readership is confined largely to adolescents who blush with the mischievous delight of seeing four-letter words in print, it also has a readership among bitter-end belletrists who enjoy the abandon of its criticisms, and Carthusian leftists who devour its dogmas even unto the fourth generation.

—On The Right, Feb. 17, 1968

Vocabulary

I am often accused of an inordinate reliance on unusual words, and desire —as would you in my shoes, I think—to defend myself against the insinuation that I write as I do simply to prove that I have returned recently from the bowels of a dictionary with a fish in my mouth, establishing my etymological dauntlessness. Surely one must distinguish between those who plunder old tomes to find words which, in someone's phrase, should never be let out, belonging strictly to the zoo sections of the dictionary; and such others as Russell Kirk who use words because a) the words signify just exactly what the user means, and because b) the user deems it right and proper to preserve in currency words which in the course of history were coined as the result of a felt need.

—NR, Feb. 11, 1964, *p. 100*

Voting Rights

The Amendment in question is an advance on the proposition that everyone should vote; and I do not believe that everyone should vote. I do not, even, believe that everyone should have the right to vote. Any such statement begets the responsibility to state an acceptable alternative and mine is this: that everyone should have the right to vote whose record or accomplishments more or less suggest that he attaches an importance to the vote that goes beyond his own immediate self-interests.

—ON THE RIGHT, Feb. 18, 1964

Voting Rights Legislation

True reform in the South would involve raising the standards for voting —and raising them impartially, for black and white alike. Perhaps more productive criteria could be found, but one that might be considered is a high school diploma or its equivalent. For the time being the imposition of such a test would undoubtedly mean the disqualification of more Negroes than whites, but that is merely a mechanical reflection of the existence of a disparity in training and accomplishment at the present moment which is precisely what the fuss is all about. What, after all, does the national association mean when it calls for the *advancement* of colored people?

—*NR*, March 9, 1965, *p. 183*

George Wallace

... he is no Richard Russell, or Donald Russell, or Harry Byrd. His reliance on the Federal Government in matters of material interest to his state, and his refusal to permit local school boards to make their own decisions on the matter of integration or segregation, weave together a kind of philosophical and opportunistic ambiguity from which statesmanship is seldom cut.

—NRB, Oct. 1, 1963, *p. 1*

For years George Wallace pretended that Negroes were enjoying the rights guaranteed under the Constitution, whereas of course they weren't. And then, having taken an oath to defend the Constitution of the State of Alabama which forbids re-election to its governor, Wallace thumbed his nose at it by the technicality of putting his pretty wife on his knee and running Mrs. Charlie McCarthy for Governor. By such an attitude towards the law, expressed at so many levels, Wallace has indirectly done a great deal not only to grant Negroes those rights they do have under the Constitution, which would be fine; but to grant them rights they didn't have, don't have, and shouldn't have, any more than white or yellow or pink people should have them.

—On The Right, May 10, 1966

The Wallace candidacy for North, South, East and West is, among other things, a great national reaction against the ravenous appetites of an overweening Federal Government to craft for us a great society, never

297

mind the disposition of those who are to benefit from it. Not inconceivably, we will be better off for the irruption. Wallace is to one position what Eugene McCarthy is to another. The country rejected (quite wisely) Eugene McCarthy, but the Democrats learned from him. The country will reject (quite wisely) George Wallace, but Democrats and Republicans alike stand to learn from the experience.

—*Look*, Oct. 29, 1968, *pp. 101–102*

War

War is the second worst activity of mankind, the worst being acquiescence in slavery.

—ON THE RIGHT, April 1, 1965

... wars require continual reaffirmation. It will no more do to state only once, at the beginning of a war, that it is justified, than to state only once, at the beginning of a marriage, that you love your wife.

—ON THE RIGHT, April 1, 1969

War on Poverty

Mr. Johnson has declared "unconditional war" against poverty, but manifestly there are any number of weapons he does not intend to use in order to prosecute that war. He is not, for instance, going to fire any guns, during the forthcoming campaign, on labor union monopolies, which aggravate poverty by extracting artificially high prices from employers, and so cause the price of living to rise. He is not going to drop any shells on his own Department of Agriculture, which pays bonuses to farmers to keep them from growing food, and so aggravates the problem of the poor by raising the cost of bread and butter. He is not going to torpedo the minimum wage laws, which do so much to keep the poor poor, by denying them work at the only price marginal producers are in a position to pay. And above all he is not going to do anything substantial —nothing beyond Mr. Kennedy's proposed reductions—to take government off the back of the people, to leave them freer to work for themselves, to cultivate and distribute the nation's wealth. It is, in short, going to be a sweetheart war. And, by the way, we are not going to win it with Mr. Johnson's choice of weapons.

—ON THE RIGHT, Jan. 18, 1964

Please note that by great strength of will I have avoided the ear-grating, melodramatic "war on poverty," When I first heard that President Johnson had called on us to declare a "war on poverty," so help me I thought he was calling out the troops to shoot poor people.

—ON THE RIGHT, May 18, 1967

Earl Warren

Anybody who showed as much respect for the Pope as the typical liberal now shows for Earl Warren, would be considered as a living violation of the separation of church and state.

—*Up from Liberalism*, p. 65

It occurs to us that Mr. Warren's remark that the people will not know in their lifetime the meaning of Kennedy's assassination, is consistent with Mr. Warren's position about the meaning of the United States Constitution. Certainly we shall not know during *his* lifetime what it means.

—*NR*, April 7, 1964, *p. 266*

One would have hoped that the surveys on Mr. Warren's performance would at least have acknowledged the view profoundly and passionately felt by men of great training and conscience, that he was a disaster to the

Constitution of the United States, to the highest standards of jurisprudence, and to the federal system: which is a lot for one Justice to be.

—NR, July 16, 1968, *p. 684*

Washington Post

[Senator William Jenner] was abused by the Establishment press, most persistently by the editors of the *Washington Post*, whose resolve never to coexist with anti-Communists has never wavered.

—NR, July 19, 1958, *p. 75*

. . . no one who is not a regular reader of the *Post* can hope to know what it is like to be catechized by the Cotton Mather of liberalism. The editors of the *Post* are men of such high moral standing that—"but what words of men, or tongue of man or angel, can one find adequate to this great theme?" as Randall Jarrell said about the liberalism of Benton College.

—NR, June 3, 1961, *pp. 341-342*

John Wayne

He is treated with barely disguised contempt [by the media at the 1968 Republican Convention]. *Nouvelle vague.* He is not merely a patriot, but an explicit patriot. Having committed *The Green Berets*, he is very much out in the Kulchur world. He takes the mike, says "I know this sounds corny but . . ." and proceeds to say the corniest imaginable things but, *mirabile dictu*, the delegates suddenly stop talking, and start applauding. The broadcasters explain that this is indeed a phenomenon, the sudden applause. They make you feel that the applause is not because there is a spontaneous enthusiasm for patriotic sentiment; but because the delegates are somehow afraid that the folks back home will be sore if they *don't* respond to the Duke paying tribute to our boys in Vietnam.

—On The Right, Aug. 6, 1968

James Wechsler

James Wechsler, editor of the *New York Post* and so relentlessly liberal he ought to be an Exhibit at the World's Fair . . .

—*NRB*, June 23, 1964, *p. 1*

Robert Welch

It is unlikely that Barry Goldwater, the political leader of the conservative and anti-Communist movement in America; that Walter Judd, one of anti-Communism's most eloquent and unyielding spokesmen; that Fulton Lewis Jr., among the most obdurate opponents of Communism abroad and statism at home; that Russell Kirk, whose books have done more to reanimate a full-bodied conservatism than anyone else's; or indeed that *National Review,* whose editors are lifetime students of Communism and liberalism, could be stampeded by the liberal juggernaut into unnecessary collisions with a man who is engaged in furthering conservative ends. These men have not bent under public pressure before, and are not likely to. Yet their opinion—our opinion—is that Robert Welch is damaging the cause of anti-Communism. Why? Because he persists in distorting reality and in refusing to make the crucial moral and political distinction. And unless that distinction is reckoned with, the mind freezes, and we become consumed in empty rages.

—*NR*, Feb. 13, 1962, *p. 84*

Welfare

Government welfare programs are justified only as a means of providing emergency relief for the needy that cannot be, or is not being, provided by nongovernmental sources. As a general rule, the more affluent the society, where the surpluses of private agencies and individuals grow, the less the theoretical need to depend on government welfare. Meanwhile a welfare program ceases to operate in the community interest when it:

    —encourages participation in it by persons who have no plausible claim to that community's care;

—encourages participation as a permanent condition, rather than as an expedient to be terminated as quickly as possible through gainful employment or other form of private support;

—encourages degenerate and socially disintegrating attitudes and practices;

—neglects to provide jobs for participants who are able to do work, thus denying them the opportunity, and the discipline, for self-help;

—is administered so as to create unnecessary bureaucratization and waste of public resources.

—The Unmaking of a Mayor, p. 176

Welfare State

... a commission should be appointed to examine unnecessary federal welfarist programs and to recommend their gradual elimination. For instance, the Rural Electrification Agency; the Interstate Commerce Commission; and much of the Agricultural Administration Agency, to name just a few. ... A commission should be established to program a gradual dissolution not only of the above agencies, but of the tissue of laws that grant such immunities to labor unions as distort economic life and impinge so gravely on individual freedom. And, ultimately a resolution by Congress should be passed to the effect that future welfare benefits, outside of social security, should be limited to those states of the union whose average income is below the national average.

—NR, May 17, 1966, *p. 455*

Theodore H. White

Surely he is the best political reporter in the language. Bias? He is loaded with it, but somehow it is inoffensive. It is easy to run fast over some of the preachier parts, or some of the most apodictical parts (I strongly suspect he knows literally, but absolutely, *nothing* about economics, in the best Democratic tradition). ... Although Mr. White is an Eagle Scout liberal, he does not feel it necessary, in refreshing contrast to such as Richard Rovere, to weep at the crossroads of public life over the existence of Barry Goldwater.

—Book Week, July 11, 1965

"Who's Who"

. . . Who's Who in America (from which the truly interesting people in this world are rigorously excluded).

—ON THE RIGHT, March 15, 1969

Roy Wilkins

Roy Wilkins, who judging from some of his past behavior is not naturally attracted to danger, is all the more heroic for having finally broken with the monolith on the dogma of Adam Clayton Powell Jr. He is the Tito among the Negro leadership which has been doing its demagogic best to translate the ouster of Adam Clayton Powell Jr. into an act of Congressional racism.

—ON THE RIGHT, March 9, 1967

Harold Wilson

Talk about a credibility gap, Harold Wilson is undoubtedly the world's most unbelievable politician. Indeed, one could have made a handsome living over the past three years betting on the opposite of everything Harold Wilson has averred, whether on Rhodesia, the common market, economic controls, or—most recently—the value of the pound.

—ON THE RIGHT, Nov. 25, 1967

Shelley Winters

Miss Shelley Winters . . . began by stating that she knew very little about politics and went on to overdemonstrate her point . . .

—NR, Aug. 25, 1964, *p. 715*

Shelley Winters volunteered that she felt a special sense of obligation to liberal politics because when she was a five-year-old girl, the New Deal "gave me a hot lunch, even though Herbert Hoover hated me." Really Mr. Hoover was a man of quite extraordinary vision.

—NR, Nov. 19, 1968, *p. 1157*

Wisdom

It is not safe to say: Knowledge is wisdom. In terms of sheer knowledge, sheer book learning, Lenin and Trotsky had few peers. Yet it would greatly have relieved the world had their teachers refrained from cultivating the minds, hence the powers, of these men.

—Rumbles, p. 132

World Council of Churches

It is a pity, the mess the gentlemen are promoting.

—On The Right, July 20, 1968

Y

Yalta

It is not surprising that Alger Hiss should defend Yalta. It is, though, surprising that he should defend Yalta in an American magazine. Had he applauded Yalta in *Izvestia*, he would have done so for the obvious reasons: Yalta did more toward Communizing the world than ever could be done by a lifetime of spying, which is all Alger Hiss could offer up for Communism.

—NR, Nov. 10, 1955, *p. 4*

Three weeks ago, the State Department got around to releasing bound volumes of Yalta papers. . . . The evidence mounts that the State Department has edited this compilation in loving memory of Franklin Delano Roosevelt. Perhaps some day the Department will sponsor another collection of documents—in loving memory of millions of dead Poles and Chinese.

—NR, Feb. 1, 1956, *p. 6*

Young Americans for Freedom

A new organization was born last week and just possibly it will influence the political future of this country, as why should it not, considering that its membership is young, intelligent, articulate and determined, its principles enduring, its aim to translate these principles into political action in a world which has lost its moorings and is looking about for them desperately? . . . The great [conservative] renewal of the last decade is reflected in the nuances in the Young Americans' statement of first principles. . . . Here is mention of the moral aspect of freedom; of transcendent values; of the nature of man. All this together with a tough-as-nails statement of political and economic convictions which Richard Nixon couldn't read aloud without fainting.

—*NR*, Sept. 24, 1960, *p. 172*

It *was* incredible [YAF's rally at Manhattan Center]. And looked at from one point of view, terribly funny. Here we are, well into the last half of the century, the overwhelming majority of our professors Stakhanovites in the cause of liberalism. Three decades of intensive indoctrination in state welfarism, anti-anti-Communism, moral libertinage, skepticism, anti-Americanism. And here was foregathered, at the Manhattan Center in New York City, possibly the largest student assembly of the year, certainly the most enthusiastic, to pay tribute, one after the other, to the most conspicuous symbols of everything they have studiously been taught by the intelligentsia to look down upon with contempt. It was as though the student body of the Lenin Institute took time off in the middle of the semester to pay tribute to the memory of the Czar.

—*NR*, March 25, 1961, *p. 187*

A most enterprising organization, by the way. At the University of Arizona, they countered a public fast waged by the local peaceniks, with an eat-in. I like that.

—On The Right, March 30, 1968